The Investor's Guide to
Coin Trading

Secrets for Profit in Coins and Precious Metals

Scott A. Travers

Foreword by
Ed Reiter

Introduction by
John Albanese
President, Numismatic Guaranty
Corporation of America, Inc.
and
David Hall
President, Professional Coin Grading Service

WILEY

JOHN WILEY & SONS
New York • Chichester • Brisbane • Toronto • Singapore

To my parents

Copyright © 1990 by Scott A. Travers.
Published by John Wiley & Sons, Inc.

Library of Congress Cataloging-in-Publication Data:

Travers, Scott A.
    The investor's guide to coin trading : secrets for profit in coins
and precious metals / by Scott A. Travers : foreword by Ed Reiter :
introduction by John Albanese and David Hall.
        p.   cm.
    Bibliography: p.
    Includes index.
    ISBN 0-471-60928-5
    1. Coins as an investment.   2. Precious metals—Handbooks,
manuals, etc.   I. Title.   II. Title: Secrets for profit in coins
and precious metals.
CJ81T734   1989
332.63—dc20   89-16415
                                                          CIP

Printed in the United States of America

10 9 8 7 6 5 4 3 2 1

FOREWORD

The notion of investing in rare coins is still a relatively new one. As a result, traditional investors with a Wall Street orientation sometimes view the coin market with a mixture of confusion and suspicion.

The Investor's Guide to Coin Trading will demystify this market for those who are confused and instill tremendous confidence in those who may be skeptical and suspicious.

It is, quite simply, the best book ever written on how rare coins are bought and sold and how to profit from that knowledge. In fact, it is the *only* book that ushers its readers behind the scenes and lets them see coin trading from an inner-circle dealer's point of view.

Scott A. Travers is eminently qualified to guide investor-readers on such a tour.

He is one of the most knowledgeable and influential coin dealers in the business.

He's a highly gifted author whose two previous books, *The Coin Collector's Survival Manual* and *Rare Coin Investment Strategy*, both earned the coveted Book of the Year Award from the Numismatic Literary Guild.

And, beyond all this, he has come to be regarded as the coin market's number-one consumer advocate—a recognized authority who shares his store of knowledge and fights for consumers' rights not only as an author, but also as a forceful public speaker. He's a frequent guest expert on TV and radio programs and a regular participant in other public forums as well.

Scott Travers deals with many traditional investors. Over the years he has worked closely with individuals, companies, partnerships, and funds whose roots are planted firmly in the world of stocks and bonds. He has shown them clear evidence of rare coins' potential for profit appreciation, and as a bonus he has helped them to appreciate the coins' intangible assets as hand-held, historic works of art.

Travers has close ties with pure collectors too. And he strives to indoctrinate *them* on the positive aspects of treating rare coins as an investment. He preaches that pleasure and profit—for collectors and investors—need not be mutually exclusive and can in fact coexist in a way that is mutually beneficial. Indeed, this combination of psychic and physical income, this dividend double-header, is one of the attractions that make rare coins so appealing.

The Investor's Guide to Coin Trading continues Travers' quest to broaden the coin market's base and expand the knowledge of every individual buyer and seller of coins. Like rare coins, the book is multidimensional.

On one level, it's the finest book ever written on coin trading, and the only book to deal with that subject comprehensively.

On another level, it's part of Travers' ongoing efforts to safeguard the interests of coin consumers.

On a third level, it serves to break down the barriers that separate investors and collectors, and in the process it enhances the entire coin industry's strength and unity.

The Investor's Guide to Coin Trading gives investors a perspective they've never enjoyed before.

It covers the panorama of this fascinating field—from ancient Greece to present-day America, from bullion coins to numismatic rarities, from technical analysis of marketplace performance to aesthetic evaluation of rare coins as objects of art.

Above all, it gives "outsiders" the necessary tools to buy and sell coins as they've never done before, on the very same level as marketplace insiders.

Using the information in this book, they too will be able to trade coins sight-unseen, just as they trade commodities. And they'll know how to handle coin transactions face to face (sight-seen) when that approach is more advantageous.

The Investor's Guide to Coin Trading is quite possibly the most significant book ever to focus on a collectible—*any* kind of collectible—as a vehicle for investment.

Anyone even considering an investment in rare coins should invest in this book first and read it from cover to cover.

It's informative, insightful, and indispensable.

ED REITER
Senior editor, *COINage* magazine and
former numismatics columnist, the *New York Times*

ACKNOWLEDGMENTS

The author extends credit to the following individuals who lent their expertise, knowledge and ability in the preparation of the text:

John Albanese; Leonard Albrecht; Ann Marie Aldrich; David T. Alexander; Gary Alexander; Bruce Amspacher; Michael Q. Anderson; Dennis Baker; James E. Bandler; James U. Blanchard III; Q. David Bowers; Walter Breen; Peter Carrigan; Pedro Collazo-Oliver; William L. Corsa Sr.; D. Larry Crumbley; John Dannreuther; Beth Deisher; Thomas K. DeLorey; Silvano DiGenova; James DiGeorgia; Al Doyle; William Fivaz; Joe Flynn; Harry J. Forman; Leo Frese; Michael Fuljenz; Betty Furness; William G. Gay; Klaus W. Geipel; William T. Gibbs; Richard Giedroyc; Philip Gottesman; Paul M. Green; David Hall; Kenneth Hallenbeck Jr.; James L. Halperin; David C. Harper; George D. Hatie; Michael R. Haynes; Leonard H. Hecht; Leon Hendrickson; Ed Hipps; Charles Hoskins; Ron Howard; Jeff Isaac; Steve Ivy; Sheldon Jacobs; Eliot Janeway; James J. Jelinski; Donald H. Kagin; Chester L. Krause; Julian Leidman; Robert J. Leuver; Kevin Lipton; Andrew P. Lustig; Steve Mayer; Bruce McNall; Raymond N. Merena; Bob Merrill; James L. Miller; Warren Mills; Lee S. Minshull; Phoebe D. Morse; Bernard Nagengast; William J. Nagle; Gary North; John Pasciuti Sr.; Martin Paul; William P. Paul; Donn Pearlman; Robert Rachlin; Arnold I. Rady; Ed Reiter; Robert S. Riemer; Bernard Rome; Bob Rose; Joseph H. Rose; Maurice Rosen; Michael Keith Ruben; Steve Rubinger; Howard Ruff; Margo Russell; John Sack; Mark Salzberg; Howard Segermark; Michael W. Sherman; James C. Sherwood; Leslie Jacques Simone; John Slack; Michael J. Standish; Rick Sundman; Fred Sweeney; Anthony J. Swiatek; Paul F. Taglione; Sol Taylor; Michael J. Toledo; Julius Turoff; Karl Weber; Bob Wilhite; Diane Wolf; Gordon Wrubel; Stanley Yulish; and Keith M. Zaner.

Credit is also due the following companies and institutions:

American Numismatic Association; American Numismatic Association Certification Service (ANACS); Amos Press Inc.; Auctions by Bowers and Merena Inc.; Coin Dealer Newsletter and Certified Coin Dealer Newsletter; Habsburg Feldman, S.A.; Heritage Capital Corporation; Krause Publications Inc.; Miller Magazines Inc.; Numismatic Certification Institute (NCI); Numismatic Guaranty Corporation of America (NGC); Numismatic Literary Guild Ltd.; Professional Coin Grading Service (PCGS); and Salomon Brothers Inc.

The following individuals are accorded special recognition and thanks for their contributions of time, advice, support, photographs and other materials:

John Albanese, founder and president of NGC, for his countless hours of support and guidance, his generosity in providing photographs and text, his assistance in reviewing photographs and the manuscript and his words of wisdom throughout this project, which helped to make it worthwhile.

Leonard Albrecht, director of ANACS, for his supervision of the outstanding photographs used to illustrate the grading chapters and other areas of the book.

William L. Corsa Sr., who continues to serve as a never-ending source of inspiration and spontaneity, and who takes a clear and forceful interest in the outcome of the projects in which I am involved.

David Hall, founder and president of PCGS, for allowing the use of PCGS memos to dealers, as well as excerpts from his book, *A Mercenary's Guide to the Rare Coin Market.*

Ed Reiter, my numismatic editor, who refined the organizational structure of the manuscript and provided invaluable research assistance and support, as well as photographs and other materials.

Robert S. Riemer, who served as my assistant in selecting grading photographs.

Maurice Rosen, editor-publisher of the *Rosen Numismatic Advisory,* who permitted reprinting of the outstanding public service interview he conducted, "More Confessions of a Ripoff Coin Salesman," as well as other excerpts from his newsletter, and who reviewed many of the trading strategies suggested in this book.

Mark Salzberg, for his diligent and scholarly review of past and current grading standards.

Howard Segermark, president of the Industry Council for Tangible Assets, for his invaluable research assistance concerning cash requirements, his permission to reprint ICTA's interpretation of reporting requirements for coin dealers, his concise explanation of the Coin and

Bullion Dealer Accreditation Program and his overall support throughout the project.

Michael W. Sherman, former director of operations for Heritage Capital Corporation, for assistance in obtaining the necessary permission forms for use of Heritage's material, for providing beautiful color photographs for the cover and for his astute advice.

John Slack, CBS Radio, Boston, who continues to allow me to use his radio programs as a soapbox to inform consumers of the perils and pitfalls of coin buying, as well as the incredible profit potential and marketplace expansion which has allowed investors to trade coins like commodities.

Anthony J. Swiatek, editor-publisher of the *Swiatek Numismatic Report*, who authored a superb section on the 10 best commemorative coins and who reviewed the manuscript for clarity and depth of focus.

Karl Weber, my editor at Wiley, who served as an inspiration in helping to translate the idea for this book into a viable, working reality.

SCOTT A. TRAVERS

New York, New York
January, 1990

CONTENTS

INTRODUCTION

John Albanese and David Hall

What makes a coin rare? For that matter, what is a coin? Essentially, a coin is a piece of metal, usually—but not necessarily—round, issued by a government, stamped with distinguishing designs and inscriptions, and meant for use as money. In most cases it bears a statement of value and can be spent for that amount; put another way, it has legal-tender status for its face value. This is what distinguishes a coin from a medal: A medal is not legal tender.

Some coins with high precious-metal content—those made of gold or silver, for example—are priced in accordance with the current market value of that metal. These are known as "bullion coins." Coins whose prices are based on supply and demand—the number of pieces available and the number of people who want them—are said to be "numismatic" or "collector" coins. Rare coins belong to this group.

In the past, collectors normally used mintage figures to determine the rarity of a coin. These are numbers showing how many examples of any particular coin were manufactured. The rarest issues were those of which the fewest examples were made. Today there is far more emphasis on pristine condition; most investors favor coins that never have entered circulation—coins that never have been passed from hand to hand. And experience has shown that many coins with relatively high mintages are quite scarce—even truly rare—in uncirculated or "mint-state" condition. That's because few pieces were preserved at the time they were produced. Such coins are said to possess "condition rarity."

The quest for high quality is so pervasive today that buyers will often pay far more—5, 10, or 20 times as much—for one mint-state coin than they will for another that is only marginally less desirable. This emphasis on perfection led to the adoption of a codified "grading

1

system" in the late 1970s to determine the condition of each coin. The system assigns numerical values to coins to designate their level of preservation. Numerical values range from 1 for a coin that is barely identifiable to 70 for a coin without any flaws, one that essentially is perfect.

The system identifies 11 different grades in the mint-state or uncirculated range. They start at Mint State-60 (or MS-60), which denotes the minimum uncirculated level, and progress up to Mint State-70, which represents absolute perfection and is almost never awarded.

Initially, the system provided just one intermediate grade between 60 and 70: It used MS-65 to denote a coin in "gem" mint condition. (One leading nonprofit grading organization used MS-65 to refer to a coin in "choice" mint condition, a level of quality somewhat below "gem," but almost everyone else equated 65 with "gem" quality.) In response to marketplace demand, grades of 63 and 67 soon were adopted as well, and later the remaining numbers between 60 and 70 were filled in.

To qualify as even MS-60, the lowest uncirculated grade, a coin can have no wear; higher mint-state grades are awarded on the basis of factors such as sharpness of strike (the amount of detail the coin had at the time of manufacture), luster, eye appeal, and absence of cuts, nicks, and scratches. A similar numerical range is used in grading proofs, which are specimen-quality coins produced each year for sale to collectors; these are designated as Proof-63 or Proof-67, for example, rather than Mint State.

The use of numerical grades created a need for independent coin grading services—companies that assign grades to coins submitted for their review by dealers, collectors, and investors. Within a few years, however, a "grading problem" arose because the existing services were perceived to be applying the standards inconsistently. Essentially, the grading standards tightened. Coins to which one grade was assigned in 1980, for instance, were viewed as being several points lower—and therefore less valuable—in 1984. This caused many investors to lose confidence in the coin market.

By the mid-1980s this problem was seriously restricting the industry's growth. Then, in 1986, a group of leading dealers joined forces to bring into being a new kind of coin grading service—a service owned and operated by professional numismatists, people with many years of hands-on experience in gauging coins' condition and market value.

We were among the principals involved in this new enterprise, which we named the Professional Coin Grading Service (PCGS). David Hall was the founder and president; John Albanese served as one of the finalizers, or final graders, before leaving to form a new grading service called the Numismatic Guaranty Corporation of America (NGC).

PCGS introduced a series of innovations that almost overnight revamped and revitalized the industry. One was its use of a sonically sealed plastic holder, or "slab," to house a coin after grading; an encoded tab specifies the grade. This protects the coin against damage and helps safeguard the certification process. Another innovation was a pledge that dealer members would purchase any PCGS-graded coin at their current "buy" price for that coin in that condition, provided that the coin was a type that they handled in the course of normal business.

PCGS and NGC both determine grades through a process of consensus. At each service, all coins are reviewed by at least three expert graders before a final grade is assigned. When there is significant disagreement, even more experts may be consulted. At both services, grading is done by experienced coin dealers on a contract basis. The graders at both are among the finest in the world.

Marketplace acceptance of PCGS was immediate and enthusiastic. Before long, coins in the company's hard plastic slabs were changing hands sight-unseen, almost like commodities, at price levels recognized throughout the industry. NGC enjoyed similar acceptance when its somewhat thicker holders made their market debut in 1987.

Today the trading of PCGS- and NGC-certified coins (coins that have been graded and encapsulated by these two grading services) is a healthy, thriving business. Virtually all the major coin dealers hold membership in PCGS, NGC, or both, and trading of these coins is facilitated by computer systems such as the American Numismatic Exchange (ANE), the coin market's equivalent of the New York Stock Exchange.

The industry has solved its grading problem, and many investors who departed because of that problem have now returned, along with thousands of newcomers drawn by the allure of rare coins and the new sense of confidence that permeates the marketplace today.

Many investors have trouble understanding why changing market conditions brought about changes in coin grading standards in the early 1980s. Because of this, some have chosen not to invest in coins. Yet if they gave more thought to the subject, they'd realize that similar patterns also occur routinely in other investment arenas.

During the 1970s, when the real estate market was calm and stable, many people thought of prime real estate as a beautiful brick building on a choice corner lot on a main street. Investment real estate was something with exceptional eye appeal. In the real estate boom of the 1980s, people's perceptions changed. Today far less desirable property is being touted as investment real estate—two-family houses that need extensive work, and even places that look like glorified shacks. When the market is bullish, real estate standards tend to relax.

Likewise, when Wall Street was calm, conservative stock analysts would stick to certain rules of thumb in choosing what to buy and recommend. To meet their criteria, a stock would have to have a certain dividend yield and a very low price/earning (p/e) ratio—usually less than 10. But when the market turned bullish, many stock analysts changed their strategy. They started to recommend more over-the-counter stocks; they bought stocks with higher p/e ratios or lower dividend yields. They felt that in order to participate in the market, they had to ease their standards.

The same kind of pattern occurs with bonds. As yields go down, the people who recommend bonds tend to stretch. Many well-known bond funds are now putting junk bonds into their portfolios and talking of taking Third World debts and turning those into bonds. They're all out there chasing higher yields—and to do that successfully, they have to lower their standards.

In bull markets, people are tempted to purchase things they normally wouldn't buy. With so much money floating around, they lose their sense of value.

This is what happened in the bull coin market of 1979 and 1980. Grading standards loosened, and many people purchased overgraded coins (coins represented to be in a higher level of preservation than they actually were) at inflated prices. Those people are suffering even now.

Today's coin buyers face no such problem. The rare coin industry has undergone a total revolution, and the cause of that revolution is certified grading.

For the first time in history, buyers can be absolutely assured that they are receiving properly graded coins. What's more, rare coins enjoy unprecedented liquidity. The marketplace has never been more efficient. Standardized grading has heightened its efficiency to a level undreamed of in years gone by.

Simply stated, it's much easier to buy and sell coins today. You can literally pick up the telephone and make an important purchase or sale of coins with the same efficiency and assurance you'd expect if you were buying or selling stocks or bonds. Just a few years ago this would not have been remotely possible.

As word of this "coin revolution" spreads throughout the financial world, we look for still more investors to add rare coins to their portfolios. And as participation increases, prices are bound to rise dramatically. During the next decade, we anticipate greatly expanded involvement in the rare coin market by financial institutions. We also foresee computer grading; within the next few years, there will be a machine that grades coins—and that, of course, will further enhance the standardization of certified coins.

Other major developments will be in the financing and storage of rare coin purchases. Several banks have experimented already with financing of such acquisitions, and we look for this trend to accelerate. In years to come, you will be able to go to many banks and brokerage firms and borrow 60 to 90 percent of the current market value of your rare coin holdings.

Coin storage is a natural offshoot of this concept. Without a doubt, the coming decade will witness the establishment of several large depositories specializing in the storage of precious metals and rare coins. The day is not far off when an investor will be able to call such a depository and say, "Transfer $50,000 worth of MS-64 double eagles ($20 gold pieces) from my storage account to Merrill Lynch."

The combined features of computer grading, bank financing, and coin storage will lead to daily trading of huge blocks of the more generic rare coin issues. This is starting to happen even now: Nearly weekly we see trades involving 100-coin blocks of certified U.S. silver dollars.

A further benefit of the market revolution is the fact that certification has brought out some truly spectacular coins. Once it became clear that PCGS and NGC had the right solution to the grading problem, an unbelievable flood of tremendous rarities started pouring in to both services. Apparently there is something very appealing about having your coins graded by an expert third-party service and sealed in attractive plastic holders. We are seeing more truly rare coins today than at any time in history; the availability of stunning rarities has probably never been greater. And since coin prices are relatively low compared to prices of other collectibles such as paintings and antiques, investors can make some marvelous buys today. Again, this will attract more people to the marketplace.

Keep in mind, too, that with certified coins, dealers now can get by with much lower markups than in the past; in fact, they *must* control markup if they are to stay competitive. It used to be common for coins to be marked up 50 to 100 percent over their wholesale value, but with certified coins the markups average 10 to 30 percent. Dealers can live with these levels because the market acceptance of the coins is now so high, stimulating faster turnover and higher volume. And lower markups in turn help create greater consumer confidence and make it far more likely that coin investors will end up with handsome profits.

Rare coins have outperformed not only unrelated investment vehicles, but also those within their own family of tangible assets. Even during times of low inflation and declining bullion prices, when gold and silver were plummeting in value, rare coins have more than held their own. In part that's because many people who started out strictly as investors, people who bought coins simply as an inflation hedge, have been transformed into active, involved collectors. Over the years we've seen thousands of investors turn into hard-core collectors—and this is yet another market fundamental that adds to rare coins' allure.

We're confident that after reading *The Investor's Guide to Coin Trading* you will feel the same kind of affinity for this fascinating field. Scott Travers is not only an authoritative chronicler of the coin market and an expert coin grader, but also a leading coin investment analyst and enthusiastic advocate of rare coins' attendant joys and pleasures. True, this book is meant primarily as a guide on how to make money from coins—but it's also filled with pointers on how to derive pleasure in the process.

This book may irritate certain coin professionals; it's honest and frank—more so than some coin dealers would like. But the public needs to know what's really going on within the inner circle of this market; that's the only way we'll win people's confidence and gain the credibility to fuel continued growth.

Rare coins have been a sensational investment—but until now, insiders have had a distinct edge. *The Investor's Guide to Coin Trading* will enable every reader to become an insider, and that's crucial to making a profit in this market.

Scott Travers is uniquely qualified to conduct this guided tour. He's a highly respected member of the market's inner circle, yet he enjoys a well-earned reputation for helping outsiders.

But the best protection for consumers is insistence on third-party, independent grading.

Chapter

1

COIN TRADING COMES OF AGE

I firmly believe rare coins will be traded daily on Wall Street soon.

John Sack, Shearson Lehman Hutton, on
page 1 of *The Wall Street Journal*,
October 20, 1988

Bill Thomas took out his quote sheet one warm summer afternoon. Based on the quotes in the sheet, he decided to enter bids on 17 items. He called up his broker, bought these 17 highly recommended investment items and wired the broker the necessary funds—$10,500. His transaction was then confirmed on magnetic media.

Three months later, while checking his computerized teletype, Bill was surprised and delighted to see that his investment had appreciated to $38,211. He placed another quick call to his broker, sold his position, and made himself a tidy profit of $27,711, less the broker's commission.

Was Bill Thomas trading stocks? No. Was he trading a conventional security? No. Not unless you consider rare coins a traditional investment—for that's what Bill was trading.

Rare coins!

At the time of this writing, rare coins are *not* considered a traditional investment. They are—and should be—viewed only as a supplement to traditional modes of investment and not as the primary vehicle.

But rare coins—coins that command a premium based on rarity, quality, or both—are turning up increasingly not only in hobbyists' collections, but also in the portfolios of many savvy investors. And the coin market is gaining great sophistication and using trading methods that strongly resemble those employed on Wall Street.

CERTIFIED COINS

Bill Thomas turned his handsome profit by buying and selling certified coins, rare coins that had been authenticated and graded by the Professional Coin Grading Service (PCGS) and the Numismatic Guaranty Corporation of America (NGC). These two organizations have revolutionized the coin industry by virtually commoditizing rare coins—transforming them into highly liquid trading units that change hands sight-unseen very much like commodities.

At PCGS and NGC, coins are submitted to a panel of independent graders who render arm's-length decisions and offer consensus opinions as to the coins' level of preservation. The coins are then sonically sealed in tamper-resistant plastic holders, commonly referred to as "slabs," and sent to their owners for sale through an extensive trading network that includes a number of computerized exchanges.

The independent grading services and the trading networks those services have spawned now allow investors like Bill Thomas to buy and sell rare coins with ease and confidence. No longer is misrepresentation a source of constant concern, as it was for coin buyers just a few years ago. PCGS and NGC offer professional and consistent grading, and both companies back their certification with meaningful guarantees.

Rare coin transactions for half a million dollars or more are taking place today over the telephone and among leading experts. Such transactions never would have occurred in the past without examination of the coins (see Figure 1-1). The grading services have created a medium that permits rare coins to be traded safely, sight-unseen.

As time goes by, PCGS and NGC will be recognized and trusted even more, and sight-unseen trades will become even more routine. All this will enable rare coins to achieve still greater popularity with investors.

Population Reports

Besides the role they play in standardizing the grading of rare coins, PCGS and NGC perform another important service by issuing periodic population reports. These reports tell how many coins of each date in each U.S. series they have certified in each of the major grades (see Figure 1-2).

The population reports furnish valuable insights into the relative rarity of different coins, from series to series and from grade to grade.

Figure 1-1. Iraj "Roger" Sayah, an Iranian-born California investor, changed the way we perceive ourselves as an industry. In 1988 he apparently began to buy millions of dollars of certified coins. Levels of these coins skyrocketed, and some coins could be found increasing by the minute. (Photo by Ed Reiter)

This type of information can play a significant part in determining the value of any given coin.

WHY BUY COINS?

There are numerous reasons for including rare coins in your portfolio. The portability of coins and their liquidity are important considerations. But the most important consideration is that *rare coins perform*.

In recent years coins have outperformed traditional forms of investment such as stocks and bonds and real estate. And coins are predicted to do even better in years to come. Wall Street has begun to recognize their potential, and major brokerage firms are starting to place substantial sums of money in rare-coin limited partnerships. Kidder, Peabody & Co., for example, has assembled a $40-million rare-coin limited partnership that can be expanded to as much as $50 million. Shearson Lehman Hutton, too, has jumped on the certified rare-coin bandwagon and is selling PCGS- and NGC-certified coins to its investors.

Over the coming years, this infusion of new funds seems likely

Page No.   89
12/01/88

PCGS Population Report, Copyright 1988

PCGS No	Date	Denom	Variety	DSIG	60	61	62	63	64	65	66	67	68	69	70
7037	1875	T$1		MS	1	0	1	1	1	0	0	0	1	0	0
7038	1875-CC	T$1		MS	1	3	7	3	4	1	0	0	0	0	0
7039	1875-S	T$1		MS	5	11	31	42	11	4	0	0	0	0	0
7040	1875-S/CC	T$1		MS	0	0	1	1	0	0	0	0	0	0	0
7041	1876	T$1		MS	2	2	8	17	3	2	1	0	0	0	0
7043	1876-S	T$1		MS	6	8	13	17	9	1	0	0	0	0	0
7044	1877	T$1		MS	1	5	6	8	4	0	0	0	0	0	0
7045	1877-CC	T$1		MS	0	0	3	2	1	0	0	0	0	0	0
7046	1877-S	T$1		MS	12	22	19	16	10	1	0	1	0	0	0
7047	1878-CC	T$1		MS	0	0	0	1	4	1	0	0	0	0	0
7048	1878-S	T$1		MS	3	9	10	17	11	6	1	0	0	0	0
TRADE S$1 Proof					36	40	85	199	245	87	18	0	0	0	0
7053	1873	T$1		PR	1	3	6	12	3	2	0	0	0	0	0
7054	1874	T$1		PR	3	3	2	11	11	2	0	0	0	0	0
7055	1875	T$1		PR	2	3	3	16	16	4	1	0	0	0	0
7056	1876	T$1		PR	7	3	7	10	12	4	0	0	0	0	0
7057	1877	T$1		PR	0	1	11	13	12	4	0	0	0	0	0
7058	1878	T$1		PR	1	1	5	19	19	3	3	0	0	0	0
7059	1879	T$1		PR	5	8	11	29	25	21	2	0	0	0	0
7060	1880	T$1		PR	7	8	13	32	39	23	6	0	0	0	0
7061	1881	T$1		PR	3	2	7	18	46	7	2	0	0	0	0
7062	1882	T$1		PR	6	3	8	27	33	7	2	0	0	0	0
7063	1883	T$1		PR	1	4	11	12	29	10	2	0	0	0	0
7064	1884	T$1		PR	0	1	1	0	0	0	0	0	0	0	0
MORGAN S$1 Mint State					2100	4753	22652	84549	87500	33378	3233	263	15	3	0
MORGAN S$1 Mint State,Proof Like					272	579	2161	6349	6559	2515	251	22	0	0	0
MORGAN S$1 Mint State,Deep Mirror					87	142	480	1055	1002	422	56	4	0	0	0
7070	1878 7/8TF	S$1	WEAK	MS	2	6	31	89	37	5	0	0	0	0	0
7071	1878 7/8TF	S$1	WEAK	MSPL	1	1	3	10	3	0	0	0	0	0	0
97071	1878 7/8TF	S$1	WEAK	MSDM	0	0	1	2	1	0	0	0	0	0	0
7072	1878 8TF	S$1		MS	30	50	141	350	179	28	0	0	0	0	0
7073	1878 8TF	S$1		MSPL	12	10	13	47	25	3	0	0	0	0	0
97073	1878 8TF	S$1		MSDM	2	1	5	9	3	2	0	0	0	0	0
7074	1878 7TF	S$1	REV 1878	MS	9	28	129	404	218	28	0	0	0	0	0
7075	1878 7TF	S$1	REV 1878	MSPL	3	10	28	52	22	7	0	0	0	0	0
97075	1878 7TF	S$1	REV 1878	MSDM	0	2	8	5	5	0	0	0	0	0	0
7076	1878 7TF	S$1	REV 1879	MS	16	17	68	155	110	14	0	0	0	0	0
7077	1878 7TF	S$1	REV 1879	MSPL	0	1	6	18	4	2	0	0	0	0	0

Figure 1-2. Page from the PCGS population report. (Courtesy PCGS)

Page No. 90
12/01/88

PCGS Population Report, Copyright 1988

PCGS No	Date	Denom	Variety	DSIG	60	61	62	63	64	65	66	67	68	69	70
97077	1878 7TF	S$1	REV 1879	MSDM	0	0	1	6	2	0	0	0	0	0	0
7078	1878 7/8TF	S$1	STRONG	MS	16	37	95	212	104	14	0	0	0	0	0
7079	1878 7/8TF	S$1	STRONG	MSPL	3	0	12	17	15	1	0	0	0	0	0
97079	1878 7/8TF	S$1	STRONG	MSDM	1	2	1	6	1	0	0	0	0	0	0
7080	1878-CC	S$1		MS	42	93	306	625	362	77	13	1	0	0	0
7081	1878-CC	S$1		MSPL	10	14	60	87	39	9	0	0	0	0	0
97081	1878-CC	S$1		MSDM	1	5	7	8	6	4	0	0	0	0	0
7082	1878-S	S$1		MS	26	59	354	1242	1193	297	13	1	0	0	0
7083	1878-S	S$1		MSPL	2	13	48	132	81	24	0	0	0	0	0
97083	1878-S	S$1		MSDM	1	1	3	4	4	1	0	0	0	0	0
7084	1879	S$1		MS	14	18	140	382	288	42	2	0	0	0	0
7085	1879	S$1		MSPL	0	4	6	24	10	2	0	0	0	0	0
97085	1879	S$1		MSDM	2	3	5	7	3	1	0	0	0	0	0
7086	1879-CC	S$1		MS	15	15	48	81	32	6	0	0	0	0	0
7087	1879-CC	S$1		MSPL	4	8	14	13	1	0	0	0	0	0	0
97087	1879-CC	S$1		MSDM	0	0	0	2	3	0	0	0	0	0	0
7088	1879-CC	S$1	CAPPED DIE	MS	21	8	13	17	4	0	0	0	0	0	0
7089	1879-CC	S$1	CAPPED DIE	MSPL	3	1	2	6	0	0	0	0	0	0	0
7090	1879-O	S$1		MS	38	49	140	241	118	15	1	0	0	0	0
7091	1879-O	S$1		MSPL	10	8	8	12	4	0	0	0	0	0	0
97091	1879-O	S$1		MSDM	1	0	3	1	2	0	0	0	0	0	0
7092	1879-S	S$1		MS	14	61	459	2576	4610	2952	406	50	3	0	0
7093	1879-S	S$1		MSPL	7	19	119	447	678	269	32	3	0	0	0
97093	1879-S	S$1		MSDM	1	1	5	19	40	20	3	0	0	0	0
7094	1879-S	S$1	REV 1878	MS	45	57	63	61	19	2	0	0	0	0	0
7095	1879-S	S$1	REV 1878	MSPL	2	2	5	6	1	0	0	0	0	0	0
7096	1880	S$1		MS	6	23	130	459	212	29	1	0	0	0	0
7097	1880	S$1		MSPL	0	1	10	14	17	1	0	0	0	0	0
97097	1880	S$1		MSDM	0	0	2	2	8	1	0	0	0	0	0
7100	1880-CC	S$1		MS	19	56	213	571	413	111	9	3	0	0	0
7101	1880-CC	S$1		MSPL	1	10	36	49	38	7	0	0	0	0	0
97101	1880-CC	S$1		MSDM	0	1	4	5	3	0	0	0	0	0	0
7108	1880-CC	S$1	REV 1878	MS	9	11	49	80	74	17	1	0	0	0	0
7109	1880-CC	S$1	REV 1878	MSPL	1	1	3	2	0	0	0	0	0	0	0
97109	1880-CC	S$1	REV 1878	MSDM	0	1	1	2	0	0	0	0	0	0	0
7114	1880-O	S$1		MS	24	78	140	163	57	0	0	0	0	0	0
7115	1880-O	S$1		MSPL	7	6	8	10	2	0	0	0	0	0	0
97115	1880-O	S$1		MSDM	5	2	2	4	3	0	0	0	0	0	0
7118	1880-S	S$1		MS	50	139	825	4125	6982	4727	667	52	3	2	0
7119	1880-S	S$1		MSPL	8	53	260	1115	1655	850	101	8	0	0	0
97119	1880-S	S$1		MSDM	2	3	23	74	113	77	15	1	0	0	0

Figure 1-2. (Continued)

to continue and to accelerate, stimulating even greater enthusiasm in the coin market and pushing coin prices even higher.

A FORMULA FOR INVESTING IN COINS

Rare coins and bullion should be a part of every investor's port-folio. However, there are definite limits to the role they should be assigned.

Coins and bullion combined should account for no more than 25 percent of an individual's total net worth, excluding the value of his or her primary residence (house, co-op, or condo). No more than 15 percent of an individual's total net worth, again excluding the value of the primary residence, should be invested in rare coins alone. And no more than 10 percent of the total net worth should be invested in bullion.

COIN TRADING NETWORKS

The use of dealer networks to buy, sell, and trade rare coins is not a new development. Teletype networks first linked both major dealers and smaller firms several decades ago.

What's new is computerization. Computer networks have intro-duced unprecedented speed and sophistication to the long-distance buying and selling of coins. A third "s"—security—is added to the process when the networks base their trading on the use of certified coins.

What's more, some trading networks make membership available on at least a limited basis not only to full-time dealers, but also to qualified individuals—collectors and investors in particular.

Trading in Privacy

Unlike trading networks in the securities field, the coin computer networks are not now subject to government regulation. Thus their operations aren't monitored as closely as securities, and trading infor-mation provided to outside parties isn't as complete. This arrangement appeals to those who favor a free-market approach.

Trading on the Exchange

For sight-unseen trading of certified coins, the most important net-work, as this is written, is the American Numismatic Exchange (ANE).

(Important developments now under way could fundamentally alter the situation.)

ANE (the industry calls it "Annie") was founded as an adjunct of the Professional Coin Grading Service, and was originally known as the American Numismatic Information Exchange (ANIE). Its purpose is to provide a means of electronic trading for PCGS-graded coins.

PCGS and ANE both came into being in 1986. The following year, the Numismatic Guaranty Corporation was founded, and since then NGC has become the most important competitor for PCGS. ANE has always accepted only PCGS-graded coins for trading on its network.

NGC is currently involved in negotiations that may result in trading of its coins on the ANE network. But a number of NGC dealer-members are urging the establishment of a new computer network to handle NGC coins. Either way, it seems likely that within the near future NGC coins will enjoy the same kind of computer trading advantages currently provided for PCGS by ANE.

Member firms of ANE use the computer network to trade PCGS-certified coins—sight-unseen—on a dealer-to-dealer basis at wholesale bid and ask prices. The member firms include many of the biggest and most influential dealerships in the industry.

Current prices are listed in the Numismatic QUOTE System (NQS), a computerized price-information exchange that ANE maintains for PCGS coins. ANE members use personal computers to access this system.

Market-maker members of ANE are permitted to post bid and ask quotations on NQS. A market-maker who posts a bid price on NQS is required to purchase at least $1,500 worth or ten coins at the NQS price if contacted by another market-maker. Each market-maker posting an ask price on NQS is required to sell at least one such coin at the quoted price when contacted by another market-maker. All bid and ask quotations pertain to PCGS-graded coins and are effective on a sight-unseen basis.

Under ANE's rules, a market-maker is obligated to buy or sell at his or her listed quote, without prior inspection, any PCGS coin that may be tendered by any other market-maker if the description and grade shown on the coin holder are the same as the description and grade associated with the listed quote on NQS.

Market-Makers

An ANE market-maker is required to give sight-unseen bids on PCGS coins and must have an authorized trader available every weekday for six hours, according to the time belt in which the PCGS outlet is located. The hours are 11 A.M. to 5 P.M. Eastern time, 10 A.M. to 4 P.M. Central time, 9 A.M. to 3 P.M. Mountain time, and 8 A.M. to 2 P.M. Pacific time. If a given coin is listed in the Numismatic QUOTE System, the market-makers are required to make bids on any examples that are offered to them, assuming that they make a market in that coin. ANE is open on days when the commodities exchanges are open and the New York Stock Exchange is open. If either is closed, so is ANE.

All bid and ask prices posted on NQS by ANE market-makers are determined and quoted by each dealer independently. Accordingly, any given market-maker may or may not be willing to purchase or sell PCGS coins at the prices quoted by other market-makers on NQS. The market-maker members of ANE make markets individually.

Dealers who subscribe to the ANE system are able to display on their computer screens the seven highest bid prices and the seven lowest ask prices for about 1,200 different PCGS-graded rare coins. The system permits participants to trade simply by touching a key to signify an intention to buy or sell.

Associate Memberships

In 1988, ANE began offering associate memberships to private collector-investors. For a membership fee of $97 per year, associate members receive a subscription to a newsletter and population report and can purchase coins from ANE member firms at the NQS listed wholesale prices plus a transaction fee.

ANE is based in Atlanta, Georgia, with offices in Newport Beach, California. The network's technical services are provided by the American Teleprocessing Corporation (ATC) of Houston, Texas, the same company that operates the FACTS coin and bullion trading network.

The FACTS Network

Whereas ANE handles formal sight-unseen transactions, the FACTS computer network provides an efficient way for dealers to trade coins on a more informal—and sometimes "sight-seen"—basis. FACTS is a much less formal network, serving in effect as an electronic bulletin board that brings together interested buyers and sellers. Members can use it to buy and sell the spectrum of rare and bullion coins, not just those certified by any particular grading service.

American Teleprocessing describes FACTS as a "real-time" network offering "instantaneous access" to more than 300 full-time coin and bullion dealers. According to ATC, participating dealers transmit more than 3,500 trading and market information messages every day.

The FACTS network also provides up-to-the-minute "spot" prices on gold, silver, platinum, palladium, and copper; Dow Jones stock market updates; and market quotes from Handy & Harman as well as from companies in London, Zurich, and Hong Kong.

To access the FACTS network, a member needs an IBM or IBM-compatible personal computer. ATC provides all the required software.

The CoinNet System

CoinNet is a network similar to FACTS but somewhat less comprehensive in its services and less expensive in its fee structure. Robert Sloat, of Westport, Connecticut, operates this network under the name Information Networks, Inc.

CoinNet furnishes coin-market information to the Reuters teletype network, which incorporates some of the highlights in the data it transmits to stockbrokers, bankers, and investment advisors.

The Teletrade Auctions

In 1987, New York City businessman Bernard Rome introduced Teletrade auctions network as a means for individuals—coin dealers, collectors, investors and other interested parties—to buy and sell coins automatically, simply by calling a toll-free telephone number.

Teletrade is totally electronic and doesn't require the use of a personal computer. All a subscriber needs is a touch-tone phone. Teletrade subscribers can buy or sell coins by telephone just by giving instructions directly to the system's computer. They also can position their coins for future sale.

Initially, trading on this exchange was limited to coins with grading certificates from the American Numismatic Association Certification Service (ANACS). Now Rome has expanded the system to accommodate certified coins from PCGS and NGC, as well.

Subscribers can gain access to the system 24 hours a day, 365 days a year, by calling one of several 800 telephone numbers and giving the computer a secret code. Then, by pushing a series of telephone buttons, they can designate the coin that they want to buy or sell.

A synthesized voice gives them the current bid on file with the system. At that point they can increase the bid or proceed to another lot. This listing will remain in the computer until the price reaches that level, at which point the coin will be sold.

Teletrade is a national electronic marketplace for certified coins.

Its auctions are designed to allow persons to bid on coins which have been consigned to Teletrade.

Nutrex

The Numismatic Trading Exchange (Nutrex), a division of the National Numismatic Network, has developed a trading network similar to ANE. All major grading services are expected to be represented on this system, which itself is expected to be on-line in 1990. A number of leading market participants, including the *Coin Dealer Newsletter* principals formed Nutrex.

SELLING COINS BY TELEPHONE

Telemarketing—soliciting orders by telephone—thus far has proven to be an inefficient way to sell coins. In fact, it has given rise to a long list of abuses related to overgrading and overpricing, some of which are detailed elsewhere in this book. However, we have witnessed a significant reduction in the abuses—and I foresee a time when a new, improved form of telemarketing will serve coin buyers well. And I see it as an outlet for large numbers of coins and therefore a major factor in the coin market's future growth.

There's nothing inherently wrong with selling coins by phone; the ethical problems stem not from the method of sale, but rather from the greed of certain sellers. Nonetheless, the high prices charged for telemarketed coins do derive to some extent from costs connected with the medium. Today's coin telemarketers face telephone bills in the millions of dollars a year. And that makes it difficult for them to offer clients good value on the coins they buy by phone.

The FTC Steps In

High telephone bills aside, the prices charged for coins by some telemarketers have been little short of outrageous. This was one of the problems that caught the attention of Phoebe Morse, Boston regional director of the Federal Trade Commission, and prompted the FTC to take steps to halt the abuses. The FTC has brought suit against a number of coin dealers, accusing them of false and misleading practices in trade and in commerce; in so doing it has obtained a number of liquidation orders and consent decrees. This, in turn, has frightened other offenders into cleaning up their act.

Dealers who previously bought coins for one price (1X) and sold them for 12 times that amount (12*X*) are now buying coins for 1*X* and selling them for 3*X*. In some cases they're even buying for 1*X* and selling for 2*X*. It's still unconscionable for someone to make a systematic 100 or 200 percent profit on coin sales to the public. But it isn't nearly as unconscionable as a 1,000 or 2,000 percent markup.

According to Phoebe Morse, the FTC has no intention of regulating the entire coin industry. But she says it will continue to litigate against telemarketers and other coin dealers it believes are deceiving consumers on a systematic basis.

SELF-REGULATION

The overwhelming majority of the nation's coin dealers are fair and honest business people, who have lent both moral and financial support to efforts aimed at weeding out abuses and abusers. They recognize the damage inflicted on the industry by the problem dealers and their attendant bad publicity.

The best self-regulatory mechanism of all has been the emergence and widespread acceptance of independent, arm's-length grading of rare coins. As news of this phenomenon spreads and more consumers learn that they can rely on such grading, the industry will move even closer to full acceptance by investors of a more traditional bent.

Whether or not we want to admit it, we in the coin business really should be thanking the FTC. By taking the initiative against the bad apples in our barrel, the FCC has helped create the activist type of environment needed to spur our industry into taking positive steps on its own.

The Future of Telemarketing

Telemarketing is still a bad way to sell coins and an even worse way to buy them. The state of the art hasn't reached the point where telemarketer-dealers can target likely buyers with a high enough rate of success to avoid enormous phone bills. Telemarketing coins today is literally like throwing darts at a dart board while wearing a blindfold.

For their part, consumers should *not* buy coins from telemarketers; even at today's lower levels, the prices being charged remain too high. For now, at least, my advice to a consumer who gets a call from a coin telemarketer would be very short and simple: Just hang up the phone—no questions asked.

In time, I'm convinced, this will change. Already, Wall Street firms are expressing keen interest in rare coins. Merrill Lynch has even jumped into the market, putting together two multimillion-dollar limited partnerships built around ancient coins. As we see this trend continue, other reputable firms will turn to selling coins by telephone. They'll offer better deals than today's coin telemarketers and, drawing upon their years of marketing expertise and their long association with investors, they'll target their clients more accurately.

This kind of sales approach isn't cost-effective with ancient coins because those coins are not commoditized. But once Merrill Lynch or another brokerage house comes out with a U.S. rare coin limited partnership, it will be a different story. Brokerage houses will be able to target people who already know about coins, people who really don't need to be *sold* on coins but want to *buy* coins. And there's a world of difference between being sold coins and wanting to buy them.

By the way, I agree with John Sack's statement, which was quoted at the outset of this chapter: Rare coins *will* be traded on Wall Street soon.

Reaching Out and Touching Coin Investors

As rare-coin limited partnerships thrive and word of their success gets around, as people learn that not every coin dealer is a boiler-room operator with huge phone bills and overpriced coins, as people discover that they can buy a coin graded by NGC or PCGS at a certain price and get good value—as all these things happen, the sale of coins by telephone is bound to grow substantially in volume as well as in respectability.

The telephone really is a great way to get in touch with clients, and cost-effective telemarketing will greatly increase the demand for rare coins.

As telecommunications are refined in the next several years, growing numbers of people will buy coins through this mechanism. The industry may even reach a point where collectors will be able to hold up a coin to a special camera on or next to their telephone and show that coin to another collector in another part of the country.

Like all coin dealers, telemarketers will have to be content with lower profit margins. In fact, as I have noted, those margins have already dropped sharply.

There's a positive side however, not only for the buyers who end up with better deals, but also for the dealers who realize lower profits on those deals. While their profit margins decrease on a deal-by-deal basis, their overall volume of sales will grow tremendously. And that will make for a much more efficient marketplace.

Chapter

2

CHARTING THE INVESTMENT PERFORMANCE OF RARE COINS

Dishonest dealers often mislead buyers by quoting appreciation rates for rare coins from an index compiled each year by Salomon Brothers, a New York investment bank. These quotes show appreciation of 12 percent to 25 percent a year. However, the Salomon index is based on a list of twenty very rare coins while the coins sold by dishonest dealers are more common coins that are not likely to appreciate at the same rate, if at all.

Consumer Alert: Investing in Rare Coins, issued jointly by the Federal Trade Commission and the American Numismatic Association

TRADING VERSUS INVESTING

There's an enormous difference between coin trading and coin investing. People who buy coins must make a distinction between the two and decide which it is they're trying to do.

A coin trader is someone who buys and sells coins—often the very same coins—on a constant basis. An investor, by contrast, is someone who purchases coins with an eye to holding on to them for a longer period of time.

Traders will accept occasional short-term losses in order to maintain a continuous cash flow. If they're astute, they'll come out ahead in the long run. Turnover is the key to their game plan: They don't want to tie up their money for any length of time in any specific area of the market.

Investors stay the course and ride out the smaller storms in quest of a bigger payoff at the end. They're more interested in higher long-term gains on a smaller number of coins.

Traders *can* make large short-term profits. But investors who are not traders rarely do. Furthermore, if you're a trader, you can buy certified coins at their lowest sight-unseen price; if these coins increase in value in the short term, you can sell them at the sight-unseen price. *Beware of dealers who guarantee short-term profits to investors who are not familiar with the marketplace. Usually, only traders profit in the short term. And any guarantee of a profit is probably not legal.*

With this warning in mind, let's examine the evidence bearing on the crucial questions: What kinds of profits can you expect if you become an active investor in rare coins? How do rare coins stack up against other investment vehicles?

THE SALOMON SURVEY

An annual survey by Salomon Brothers Inc. tracks the performance of more than a dozen different investment vehicles, showing how they have done over the prior year and also over the past 5, 10, and 20 years. In addition to rare coins, the survey also encompasses such alternative investments as stocks, bonds, oil, diamonds, farmland, housing, gold, silver, stamps, and Old Masters' paintings.

Rare coins have been part of the survey since 1978. At that time the coin market was nearing the peak of its greatest-ever boom—a boom that was being fueled by an influx of investors into the field. Through the use of historical data, the price study has been stretched to cover the 10 years before that.

Then, as now, the coin information was gathered for the survey by Stack's, a coin dealer. The firm concealed its involvement with the project, acknowledging it in 1986 only after the link was publicized in the numismatic press.

To gauge the performance of the coin market as a whole, Stack's tracks the prices of 20 individual U.S. coins that in its opinion constitute a representative cross-section of the market. This "market basket" includes collector-type coins in denominations ranging from the half cent through the silver dollar. A principal of the firm describes these as "choice uncirculated" specimens, but not "gems." This is thought to be the equivalent of Mint State-63, although Stack's has staunchly resisted the use of numerical grading. The company determines the values of the coins from auction results, reports of important private sales, dealers' quotations, and the prices shown in fixed-price lists.

Pros and Cons of Salomon Brothers' Statistics

This portfolio appears to have serious deficiencies. For one thing, it is neither large nor diverse. For another, it doesn't reflect the changes that have taken place in coin grading standards over the past 10 years. And apparently, no gold coins have ever been factored into the calculations.

No group of only 20 coins can accurately mirror the marketplace as a whole. And this group isn't representative anyway, consisting as it does primarily of "choice uncirculated" 19th-century silver coins.

Stack's responds by likening its basket to the Dow-Jones 30 Industrials. The 20-coin list is the same kind of microcosm and has the same kind of validity, it insists.

Grading standards are far stricter now than they were in the early days of the Salomon survey. In view of this, the "apples" of bygone years really may be lesser-grade "oranges" by today's more stringent yardstick.

Defenders of the survey maintain that the grading changes haven't had the same dramatic impact on mid-level mint-state coins—the kind in the Salomon portfolio—as they have had on high-end pieces. These, they say, haven't been downgraded significantly, if at all, and certainly haven't suffered substantial loss of value because of reduction in grade.

According to a Salomon Brothers official, gold coins were excluded from the rare-coin survey at the outset, primarily because the investment banking firm was tracking gold in bullion form with a separate index. Bullion value, however, has no bearing at all on the prices of rare gold coins such as high-relief Saint-Gaudens double eagles, which typically sell for many thousands of dollars.

The accuracy of any survey should be questioned when it excludes a major component of the marketplace.

Uses and Abuses of the Salomon Survey

In adding rare coins to its survey, Salomon Brothers had good intentions. In fact, an argument can be made that the Salomon statistics actually may be too conservative. Their results would be more impressive if the market basket included at least a few wonder or super-grade coins, which have experienced (and continue to enjoy) the most spectacular rise in market value.

What is of supreme concern is that flaws in the Salomon survey have played into the hands of unethical coin dealers, including those engaged in boiler-room telemarketing operations.

The Salomon survey has generated a tremendous amount of favorable publicity for rare coins and attracted enormous sums of new investment money into the coin market. Unfortunately, however, the survey has been a highly useful marketing tool for unscrupulous dealers. They have been able to manipulate it easily because of the shroud of secrecy that surrounded its compilation for so long and the seemingly unscientific methodology on which it is based.

It is, without a doubt, the single most important price performance study involving rare coins—and the single most misused.

THE *COIN WORLD* SURVEY

Another ongoing survey of coins' price performance—and a far more comprehensive one—is conducted by *Coin World*, the weekly newspaper widely regarded as the journal of record in the numismatic field.

Coin World tracks the performance of U.S. coins in 52 different series, and does so in all grades that are widely collected. It publishes its findings in "Trends index" charts at regular intervals.

Using December 1983 as a base month and assigning a value of 100 to each separate measurement for that month, the survey shows how prices have moved up or down since that time. It gauges the marketplace as a whole and details the movements of each individual series. In all, it constantly updates more than 16,000 different valuations—quite a contrast with the Salomon survey's list of just 20 different prices.

The study is conducted, supervised, and compiled by Keith M. Zaner, the highly respected editor of the influential "Trends" section that appears each week in *Coin World*. Zaner monitors major auction sales, important private transactions, dealers' price lists, and other key market indicators.

It's clear from the Trends index values that high-level mint-state coins have substantially outperformed the rest of the market. As of December 1988, coins graded MS-65 were indexed as a group at 191.79. In other words, their value had nearly doubled in the five-year period since the survey's base month. The market as a whole had an index of 112.46, but the other two major components of the study—coins graded MS-60 and AU-50—were barely above the break-even point. Those were indexed at 101.83 and 103.19, respectively.

Coin World's MS-65 value index consists of the average of 1,325 different prices from each individual series that Coin World provides values for. Coin types that traditionally have turned in a lackluster price performance, such as copper and nickel coins, are averaged in too.

The *Coin World* Guide

Trends index values are featured in a brilliant guidebook written by Coin World's editors and introduced in January 1989. The book is Coin World Guide to U.S. Coins, Prices and Value Trends (published yearly by Signet/New American Library; value trends by Keith M. Zaner, text by William T. Gibbs, edited by Beth Deisher). It is a tool of inestimable value to anyone engaged in buying and selling U.S. coins. I recommend it enthusiastically and extend to it my very highest endorsement.

Concisely yet comprehensively, the pocket-size, soft-cover 320-page book covers the gamut of U.S. numismatics. It provides mintage figures and current market values for every U.S. coin since the nation's first issues in 1793. It also contains a wealth of historical information regarding U.S. coinage. Most important of all, it puts current prices in longer-term perspective by charting each coin's performance over a period of 4½ years, from December 1983 to June 1988.

At the start of the price list for each different series of coins, a "Coin World index" chart is displayed (see Figure 2-1). This shows how the series has performed on three different levels: as a whole (in all available conditions) and in two specific grades.

For obsolete series such as Barber half dollars, the two grades charted are AU-50 and MS-65—the highest commonly available circulated and uncirculated grades. For currently issued series such as Kennedy half dollars, the two listings are MS-65 and Proof-65. All of the prices are based on the Trends listings. They show how prices have moved up or down at six-month intervals.

THE "RED BOOK" AND "BLUE BOOK"

Prior to publication of the Coin World guide, the leading annual price guide in the numismatic field was without question A Guide Book of United States Coins—better known as the "Red Book" because of the color of its cover.

$2.50 quarter eagle
Indian Head quarter eagle chart

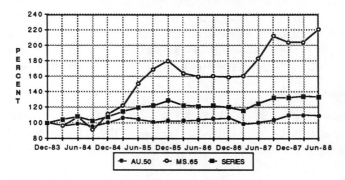

Indian Head

Date of authorization: Jan. 18, 1837
Dates of issue: 1908-1929
Designer
  Obverse: Bela Lyon Pratt
  Reverse: Pratt
Engraver
  Obverse: Charles Barber
  Reverse: Barber
Diameter (Millimeters/inches):
  17.78mm/0.70 inc
Weight (Grams/ounces):
  4.180 grams/0.13439 ounce
Metallic content:
  90% gold, 10% copper
Weight of pure gold:
  3.762 grams/0.12095 ounce
Edge:
  Reeded

	F-12	VF-20	EF-40	AU-50	MS-60	MS-63	MS-64	MS-65
1908	170.	190.	205.	240.	420.	1375.	3500.	8250.
1909	170.	190.	205.	240.	420.	1375.	3500.	8350.
1910	170.	190.	205.	240.	435.	1400.	3550.	8600.
1911	170.	190.	205.	240.	420.	1375.	3500.	8450.

— Insufficient pricing data	* None issued

Values of U.S. coins — 177

Figure 2-1. A page from *The 1989 Coin World Guide to U.S. Coins, Prices and Value Trends.* (Courtesy Amos Press, Inc.)

First published in 1947, the Red Book is among the all-time non-fiction best-sellers. Exact sales figures have never been released, but many millions of copies have been sold.

Like the *Coin World Guide*, the Red Book provides mintage figures and retail price values for all U.S. coins, past and present, and does so in a wide range of preservation levels. It also contains historical information. However, it lacks the price performance charts that serve as a sort of signature for the *Coin World Guide*. It also has fewer details on current market issues such as grading.

The Red Book prices are based on information furnished by several dozen marketplace participants. In effect they represent informal composites of the prices submitted, although some contributors have argued that their suggestions have not been taken into consideration.

The Red Book was written and revised for many years by the late R.S. Yeoman, who died in November 1988 at the age of 84. Yeoman also authored a companion volume known as the *Handbook of United States Coins*, or, more familiarly, the "Blue Book"—again because of its cover.

Published yearly since 1941, the Blue Book furnishes wholesale values for U.S. coins—those that collectors might expect to receive from dealers if they chose to sell their coins.

Both the Red Book and the Blue Book are handy reference works and certainly belong in every coin library. However, they no longer have day-to-day market relevance as they did several decades ago. Up until the early 1960s, Red Book prices, in particular, were used as points of reference in many coin transactions.

As the market became more active and prices began to move more quickly, dealers and collectors turned to more timely price guides—notably the weekly *Coin Dealer Newsletter* (or "Grey Sheet"), which made its first appearance in 1963. More recently, the Grey Sheet has been joined by the *Certified Coin Dealer Newsletter* (or "Blue Sheet"), which furnishes weekly values for coins that have been certified by the various grading services.

THE NGC MARKET INDEX

In March 1988, the Numismatic Guaranty Corporation introduced an innovative index of rare coin prices based on the performance of a broadly diversified basket of investor-quality coins.

The NGC Numismatic Index measures the long-term performance of the U.S. coin market by tracking the average annual gain in the overall market value of the coins in its basket since January 1, 1978.

Unlike other surveys, the NGC study takes into full account the changes that have occurred in coin grading standards during the period of the study. This makes it more valid than surveys that give too little weight—or no weight at all—to the changes.

To simplify mathematical calculations, NGC's president, John Albanese, selected a portfolio of coins that would have been worth an even $100,000 on January 1, 1978. After analyzing them thoroughly, he determined that on January 1, 1988, the same coins were worth $471,325.

That means the portfolio increased in value by an average of 16.77 percent a year during the 10-year period. And that number—16.77—becomes the first numerical expression of the index.

Albanese chose a portfolio with well over 100 coins, including components from all the U.S. series that are purchased most extensively by investors. The basket stresses gold and silver coins because those are the biggest sellers within the investment arena. At the same time, it includes a representative group of copper, nickel, and copper-nickel coins to provide comprehensiveness and balance. Silver and gold commemorative coins are part of the mix, as well.

By 1978 standards, all the coins in the NGC portfolio would have been graded Mint State-65. By today's standards some remain MS-65, but others are viewed as MS-64. At this point NGC is not disclosing the contents of the basket. Albanese believes that doing so might encourage attempts to manipulate the market in these coins.

MODERN PORTFOLIO THEORY

A prudent portfolio of "blue-chip" rare coins would have been a fine investment 10 or 20 years ago. Coins of extremely high quality would have been good values five years ago or even a year ago. Many coins continue to increase in value handsomely. In fact, some financial experts have argued that rare coins' risks and rewards can be measured and defined numerically.

But is there any way to use this information today, right now, in choosing an overall investment portfolio (stocks, mutual funds, etc.) that would include rare coins in a suitable percentage?

One potential tool is modern portfolio theory or MPT.

MPT is a mathematical procedure that seeks to obtain an optimum combination of high yield and low risk from a given portfolio of investment instruments. First expounded in 1952 by Harry Markowitz, the theory has gained wide acceptance and usage in the intervening years.

MPT counsels that returns can be maximized and risk minimized by diversifying the contents of a portfolio. Diversification eliminates the risk of an unsystematic approach through which the portfolio's contents are selected just at random.

The idea is to choose a mix of investment instruments that reasonably can be expected to rise or fall in value at different rates, rather than in tandem. Ideally, some would be likely to rise in value during a period when others were declining—thereby keeping the overall portfolio on a relatively steady course.

One use of MPT would be to identify the broad trends of rare coins and the best kind of coins (MS-65, if the *Coin World* statistics are used) to be included in the overall portfolio mix. The risk and reward factors associated with rare coins would be taken into consideration mathematically, and diversified financial portfolios could be constructed at levels where the risks are balanced with the rewards: the higher the potential profit, the higher the potential risk.

A Graphic Look at Rare Coins in MPT

The following statistics represent *Coin World*'s Trends index values (retail prices) for MS-65 coins. These numbers are monthly averages from December 1983 through December 1988.

Trends index values

	Market	AU-50	MS-60	MS-65		Market	AU-50	MS-60	MS-65
Dec. 83	100.00	100.00	100.00	100.00	July 86	105.64	102.71	104.33	139.51
Jan. 84	98.10	98.50	98.14	97.35	Aug. 86	104.82	101.50	103.08	138.50
Feb. 84	98.75	99.89	98.59	97.23	Sept. 86	104.07	101.99	102.03	134.66
Mar. 84	100.72	101.55	100.70	100.20	Oct. 86	104.31	102.14	102.76	133.57
Apr. 84	101.12	101.45	100.91	103.30	Nov. 86	103.91	101.74	102.26	133.85
May 84	101.52	101.17	102.70	107.36	Dec. 86	104.30	102.78	102.75	133.61
June 84	101.93	101.89	103.27	106.20	Jan. 87	103.89	101.78	101.64	133.24
July 84	99.96	99.22	100.30	103.97	Feb. 87	103.15	100.51	100.94	131.95
Aug. 84	99.57	99.36	100.16	101.23	Mar. 87	103.20	100.30	100.45	131.87
Sept. 84	99.31	99.54	99.78	101.64	Apr. 87	103.36	100.12	100.06	132.83
Oct. 84	98.96	99.08	99.80	102.43	May 87	103.48	100.36	98.54	133.11
Nov. 84	98.58	98.63	99.75	102.47	June 87	103.88	100.66	98.56	135.80
Dec. 84	98.83	98.44	99.76	106.13	July 87	104.45	100.73	98.70	139.96
Jan. 85	99.91	99.50	100.57	110.59	Aug. 87	105.01	101.09	98.74	143.67

Trends index values (continued)

	Market	AU-50	MS-60	MS-65		Market	AU-50	MS-60	MS-65
Feb. 85	100.08	99.79	101.00	110.68	Sept. 87	105.81	101.55	99.37	149.66
Mar. 85	101.43	102.16	102.40	111.98	Oct. 87	105.99	101.88	99.38	149.36
Apr. 85	103.70	103.94	105.72	118.49	Nov. 87	106.30	102.19	99.19	151.12
May 85	104.95	105.21	106.83	121.69	Dec. 87	106.60	102.50	99.51	151.31
June 85	105.77	105.65	107.34	125.44	Jan. 88	107.13	103.18	100.49	151.53
July 85	106.47	105.68	107.58	129.58	Feb. 88	106.96	102.85	100.10	151.24
Aug. 85	106.35	105.21	107.19	131.00	Mar. 88	106.79	102.39	100.44	150.05
Sept. 85	106.56	104.78	106.76	134.40	Apr. 88	106.56	101.66	99.85	152.23
Oct. 85	106.95	104.92	106.77	137.32	May 88	107.19	101.95	100.77	153.91
Nov. 85	107.29	105.08	107.60	139.10	June 88	108.69	102.09	101.02	167.65
Dec. 85	107.52	104.91	108.32	140.42	July 88	111.43	103.61	102.45	181.66
Jan. 86	107.18	104.56	107.92	139.68	Aug. 88	112.32	103.41	102.61	189.13
Feb. 86	107.07	104.83	108.12	138.18	Sept. 88	112.17	103.58	102.02	191.57
Mar. 86	106.47	104.63	106.50	136.55	Oct. 88	112.25	103.51	101.14	196.07
Apr. 86	106.11	104.31	106.42	136.91	Nov. 88	112.40	102.98	102.23	190.72
May 86	106.03	103.95	105.88	138.17	Dec. 88	112.46	103.19	101.83	191.79
June 86	105.96	103.00	105.27	139.04	*16,576 values in market*				

These *Coin World* statistics can be expressed graphically too. In Figure 2-2, a graph charting an initial investment of $1,000 is used to illustrate the price performance of MS-65 coins from January 1984 through December 1988.

In Figure 2-3, the Standard & Poor's 500 stock index is introduced for much of this same time frame. A graphic illustration is made of a comparison between rare coins in MS-65 and the S&P 500 (with dividends and splits reinvested).

Another useful type of financial analysis can be expressed visually, as shown in Figure 2-4. Here we see a financial "pie" split among various investments. MS-65 coins constitute 41.8 percent (15 percent average; 9.2 percent risk). Other components of this portfolio allocation include 20 percent invested in Fidelity U.S. Government Reserves, a money-market fund (average: 7.4 percent; 0.4 percent risk), and 18.6 percent invested in Merrill Lynch Pacific Fund, a foreign stock fund (32.3 percent average; 36.1 percent risk). Smaller components are 13.8 percent allocated to Fidelity High Income Fund, a high-yield corporate bond fund (14.3 percent average; 8.3 percent risk), and 5.8 percent invested in the Fidelity Magellan Fund, the much ballyhooed aggressive stock fund (20.6 percent average; 26.6 percent risk).

The graphic performance of Portfolio Allocation A compared with the S&P 500 is illustrated in Figure 2-5. Again, the same time is used

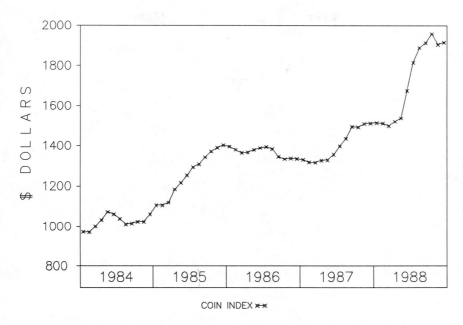

Figure 2-2. Value of a $1,000 investment using *Coin World*'s monthly statistics for MS-65 coins. (Courtesy *Coin World*)

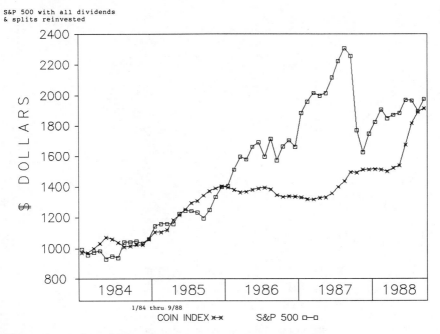

Figure 2-3. Value of $1,000: MS-65 coins versus S&P 500.

29

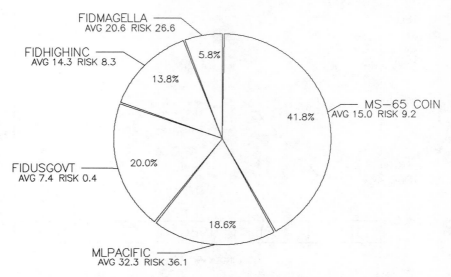

Figure 2-4. Portfolio allocation A; 41.8 percent has been invested in MS-65 coins.

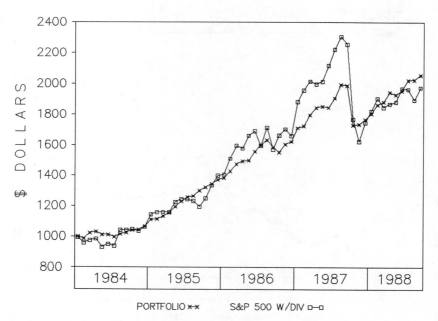

Figure 2-5. A comparison of portfolio allocation A to the S&P 500.

here and throughout this section: January 1984 through September 1988.

In Portfolio Allocation B (Figure 2-6), we see that 38.4 percent is invested in MS-65 coins; 32.1 percent is allocated to Merrill Lynch Pacific Fund; 20 percent is placed in Fidelity U.S. Government Reserves; and 9.5 percent is placed with Fidelity Magellan Fund. This portfolio's expected average is 19.56 percent, while its expected risk is 12.85 percent.

This "expected risk" number is what mathematicians refer to as the "standard deviation." In other words, this portfolio can either increase or decrease by the expected risk number, in this case 12.85 percent. The "expected average" is a random sampling of 12 of the nearly 60 months of accumulated data. This number does *not* represent any one 12-month period.

Figure 2-7 is the graphic illustration of Portfolio Allocation B compared with the S&P 500.

These types of graphic analyses are used by brokerage houses in assessing overall portfolio risks and in selecting suitable investments based on balanced risk and reward ratios. The graphs and explanations

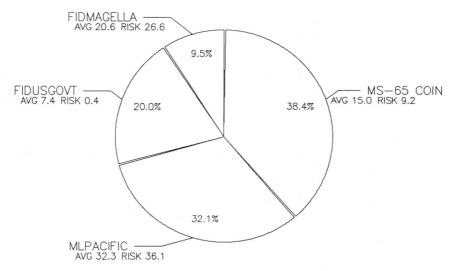

Figure 2-6. Portfolio allocation B; 38.4 percent of this portfolio has been invested in MS-65 coins.

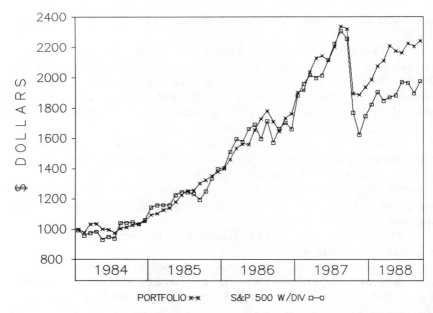

Figure 2-7. This graphic depiction contrasts portfolio allocation B with the S&P 500.

presented here are an oversimplification but a sound presentation of the fundamental concept.

WHAT PERFORMANCE CHARTS TELL US

The Salomon report and other market surveys show that rare coins have an excellent track record, particularly over the past two decades. During that period they have outperformed all other forms of investment. However, such reports must be kept in proper perspective. Used out of context by unscrupulous purveyors of overgraded, over-priced coins, they can lead the unwary into making costly mistakes.

With coins as with stocks, bonds, real estate, and any other form of investment, good judgment is the key to getting good value—and that, in turn, is the key to getting a good return. Market reports can help point the way, but they're only road maps.

Chapter

3

PRICING OF RARE COIN INVESTMENTS: THE FAIR AND THE UNFAIR

Our percentage of gross profit is approximately 52 percent on the average, and this is not an unexpected profit, in light of the fact that we pay an average of 17 percent to our telemarketing personnel (who you'll recall provide over 80 percent of our business to us), plus an additional 10 percent to 12 percent to companies who provide us with the names of their customers to call.

Thus, with a cost of 48 percent of the product itself, and on top of that an additional 27 percent or more, our prices are usually marked up from a $1 base to a $2.10 retail price.

. . . Our MS-65 coin might be found to be an MS-64 on the average. It is not that some of our MS-65 coins are not found to be MS-65, but that some of them are found to be MS-63 or MS-64.

. . . we cannot live with the "average" markup that some of these dealers claim to operate under, a matter of 30 percent or so. All of the above stated facts clearly demonstrate that we simply can't accommodate such a low markup.

Stanley Apfelbaum, President
First Coinvestors, Inc.
(in his report to shareholders
for the three months ended
December 31, 1987)

Artie was a commodity salesman. For five years he made a healthy six-figure income selling commodity contracts to unsuspecting clients who eventually lost most of the money they invested. After a while the Commodity Futures Trading Commission (CFTC) revoked Artie's license. Accustomed to making very substantial commissions, Artie sought to maintain his standard of living. And where did he turn? To the rare coin investment market.

The year was 1980. The coin market was booming. He was offered a commission of 25 percent of the gross sales. And in no time at all, Artie was making $300,000 a year as a rare coin salesman—even though his commodity license had been revoked. Rare coins are not securities. The coin field is an unregulated industry. There are convicted felons in the business; now that they're out of prison, they're selling coins.

In recent years important strides have been made. Programs are in place—among them the Coin and Bullion Dealer Accreditation Program (CABDAP)—to keep convicted felons out of the field (see Figure 3-1). This is an important self-regulatory process. But back in 1980 such safeguards did not exist. The consumer didn't have CABDAP to turn to, and people like Artie—people who were guilty of offenses or even outright crimes in other investment fields—could move from selling commodities to selling rare coins.

Artie's is neither a hypothetical nor an isolated case. There are documented cases of real Arties who were making tremendous sums in commodities, lost their commodity licenses, moved into selling rare coins, and continued to do tremendously well. But for Artie to have been earning a six-figure income selling rare coins in the early 1980s, there had to be many investors who were very unsuccessful.

Figure 3-1. Accredited dealers may display this logo. (Courtesy Coin and Bullion Dealer Accreditation Program)

Artie was making a 25 percent commission; certainly there were others above him making commissions, as well. And in many cases, the types of coin dealers employing people like Artie were actually giving their investors a value of only five or ten cents on the dollar. Those coin dealers aren't in business any more.

COIN INVESTING 1980 STYLE COMPARED WITH TODAY

In the early 1980s, investing in rare coins was a shot in the dark; people didn't know what they were getting. In fact, a lot of those telemarketing salespeople didn't know what they were selling—and that made them even better at plying their trade. In the late 1980s and early 1990s, we're seeing a tremendous difference in the structure of this industry. The commoditization of rare coins has made it far easier for dealers to sell coins, and for consumers to buy them, at fair levels; but it also has greatly reduced the profit margin on each individual transaction. Where rare coin investment firms previously provided their clientele with "value" of five or ten cents on the dollar, today most dealers—in order to stay in business—must provide value of 85 or 90 cents on the dollar. That's a massive difference. But in the long run the difference is actually very beneficial to the coin field, because it will help attract an enormous influx of funds.

Tens of millions of dollars will be poured into rare coins now because of commoditization and the scaling down of commissions. The Arties of this world have been exposed. Consumers have heard about such abuses. Media coverage has been extensive. In some cases, the Federal Trade Commission (FTC) has spotlighted the problems by alleging that certain coin dealers and their telemarketing personnel have engaged in false and deceptive practices in trade and in commerce.

The FTC has steadfastly refused to regulate this industry. However, it has brought suit against a number of coin dealers, and this has spurred the industry to clean up its act. This in turn, along with the reduction of dealers' profit margins, is what has attracted such tremendous sums of money to the field.

THE COMMISSION STRUCTURE FOR TRADITIONAL INVESTMENT PRODUCTS

Certainly the coin field hasn't been alone in furnishing big commissions to its sales force. Stockbrokers, too, frequently receive very substantial fees—and these are often higher percentagewise for less stable securities such as over-the-counter stocks than for rock-solid blue chips. This, of course, is meant as an incentive to "push" these kinds of instruments, which are riskier for the client but generate more profit for the firm.

At one time, brokers' commissions were uniform at all firms. That changed, however, in May 1975, when the fee structure was deregulated. Since then, intense competition has led to wide variations in what different firms charge for their services and how much of a cut they give their brokers. It also has led to de-emphasis on the word "commission." Nowadays, firms often camouflage commissions by using such terms as "markup," "markdown," "add-on," "levy," and "sales charge." Any way you say it or slice it up, it's money the clients pay and the sellers pocket. The only difference is, it's more difficult to label, trace, and quantify.

On large, uncomplicated transactions, the commissions may be very small percentagewise; in the bond markets, for example, markups may be fractions of 1 percent. By contrast, companies have been known to reap a windfall of 40 percent or more on deals involving over-the-counter stocks.

How much of this money goes to the individual brokers who actually handle the transactions? The average payout to brokers in 1983 was 41.9 percent of the commission dollar, according to the Securities Industry Association (SIA), which represents roughly 95 percent of all securities firms. That figure was up from 37.6 percent in 1978. In his book, *Mugged on Wall Street*, E.F. Hutton vice-president C. David Chase says that today, "because of increased costs and many firms' lower profits, payouts are moving toward 1978 levels." Chase estimates that "middle-tier" producers are getting an average payout of 37 percent of the revenue they generate. "Big producers"—those bringing in revenue of $1 million or more a year—are taking home upwards of 40 percent of this money, he says. And "lower-end" producers are receiving about a 25 percent payout and are, in many instances, "quickly fired or weeded out over 12 to 18 months."

PROFITS TO THE COIN DEALERS: THEN AND NOW

Prior to 1986 it was commonplace to see a rare coin marked up several hundred—and in some cases several thousand—percent. In one case documented by the FTC, the Boston-based Rare Coin Galleries of America (RCGA) sold a $250,000 rare coin portfolio to the parents of a retarded child, who had received the money in settlement of a lawsuit against a hospital and a doctor. The money was supposed to have provided lifetime income to care for the child. The FTC alleged that in return for that $250,000, RCGA gave the parents coins that were later appraised at approximately $5,000. They never got their money back.

In some cases, pension and profit-sharing money was placed in Keogh plans tied to rare coins, and the coins turned out to be virtually worthless. Too often we saw flagrant misrepresentation before the coin industry took the necessary steps to self-regulate. Now we see a highly structured marketplace in which coin dealers operate with a 15 or 20 percent profit spread when selling coins at retail.

To earn a living selling investment coins at such a margin, dealers must sell a lot of coins. No longer can they make a "killing" by giving their customers five or ten cents' value on the dollar. They have to go out and generate much more business. The good news is that with the introduction of fairness and stability, and with the elimination of abuses, there's much more business available. The commission structure in coins has never been tighter than it is today—but as a result of that, the coin field is able to attract many more serious investors.

LOWER COMMISSIONS AS A RESULT OF GRADING SERVICES

Much of the credit for the coin market's cleanup belongs to the independent grading services or "slab" services, such as Numismatic Guaranty Corporation of America (NGC) and Professional Coin Grading Service (PCGS). Since these slab services emerged, we've seen a steady decline in the profit percentage to coin dealers—and a corresponding increase in buyer confidence. Today the only way that dealers can fudge on the grade of a coin is by indicating that the coin has been adjudged of premium quality (PQ) by a slab service when in reality it hasn't. One example of that occurred in mid-1988, when a number of coins turned up in counterfeit PCGS slabs on which one large and purportedly reputable coin dealer had placed its special signature PQ stickers. These were coins in counterfeit slabs, and the company was selling them at its PQ profit margin. This shows that although there are many premium quality coins, a PQ label can be abused.

But how low is low? Maurice Rosen, writing in his April/May 1987 *Rosen Numismatic Advisory*, answers the question:

Until recent months, for many years coin investors had been conditioned to accept a dealer markup of about 20–33 percent, let's say $100 "buy" and $125 "sell," or "cost + 25 percent." I say "conditioned" because actual markups may have been higher, but that's another story. The "cost or bid +25 percent" markup, if honestly, properly and skillfully used is a major plus for many investors because markups of 50 percent–100 percent–200 percent–even 500 percent were (and still are) quite common. Coins are physical property requiring expertise to buy and an inventory can be expensive to maintain. Dealers are not trading paper via book entries, [as securities dealers do].

Along come the slabs and the contention by some people that since now all coins of the same issue and grade are "equals," you need only be concerned with a price. In other words, the price is the thing, forget the individual characteristics of the coin. Consequently, some people add, a "cost + 25 percent" markup is a hosing, 10 percent is even too much, 2–4 percent is more like it. They are making it seem as if J. Fred Muggs (remember him?)—the chimpanzee—is as capable of picking coins to buy as are skilled, veteran dealers. In essence, all you have to do is read the label. "Turn them upside down, they're all alike," some people assert.

Let me say here and now that this is dangerous, potentially ruinous advice. Their claims have a basis if the current structure is eternal, etched in stone never to be changed, altered or amended in any way. But think for a moment. During the last couple years, coin consumers have been told that precision grading is necessary. That it is an exercise which is now "do-able," whereas in the past, it couldn't. That because of great price differences between neighboring grades, such as 63 & 65, a 64 grade was needed. That between the grades 60 & 63 we need 61 & 62. Between 65 & 67 we need 66.

I ask you: Who can prove that we have reached the limit of the grading evolution process? Who is ready to say that the price gulfs between most 63 & 64 coins, and between most 64 & 65 coins are perfectly swell? That we don't need any more precision? Or identification? Or classification? That the resulting price differences of 200%–300%–400% are noooo problem?

Don't get me wrong. I'm not advocating (for now, anyway) micro-precision grading, with new grades such as: 63.5, 64¼, etc. But, in reality these "grades" do exist. They exist simply because grades can not be pre-cisely compartmentalized. Coins trade at wholesale on a continuum of prices between published quotes because of the many variables which, collec-tively, form a grading opinion. Let's call some of these variables: eye-appeal, personal tastes or whatever you wish. It is because of this, plus the not to be overlooked possibility that some of the coins passed on by any grading service will be overgraded as well as undergraded (none claim, so far, perfection) in the opinion of various market participants, that to view certified coins as being produced identically from a cookie mold can be a serious mistake.

Do the opponents of my opinion want to see all professional market players (dealers) literally replaced by robots? By computer key operatives? By chimpanzees? If so, old George Orwell (of "1984" fame) will be spinning in his grave as will the thousands of collectors who over the years have endowed their coins with life, identity and affection so that future generations can do likewise. COINS ARE DIFFERENT. Each possesses a combination of factors which appeal more to some people, less to others THOUGH THEY MAY ALL HAVE THE SAME NUMERICAL GRADE. What's more, until micro-precision grading is here, if ever, most market players in their "mind's eye" at least, view grades such as "64.5" or "65 minus." I ask you: With which similarly priced "64" certified coin would you be happier—a 64.0 or a 65 − ?

TELEMARKETERS' MISREPRESENTATIONS

Overgrading is much less of a problem today because most knowl-edgeable consumers are insisting on coins that have been certified independently by NGC or PCGS. What we do see today in some cases, however, is a serious overpricing problem. Telemarketers dealing with clients who don't refer to the *Certified Coin Dealer Newsletter* (CCDN) are taking coins that might be worth $2,000–$3,000—coins that have been certified by legitimate grading services—and selling these coins for $12,000, $15,000, or $20,000. They simply call people on the phone, tell them they have "independently certified coins, coins of very special premium quality and rarity," and sell them for tremendously inflated sums. The buyers either don't have access to price lists or don't bother trying to get them. Then again, back in the early 1980s some people didn't even bother using their eyes and common sense when they were sold coins that were called MS-67, MS-68, or MS-69, and the coins looked as if someone had taped them to the bottom of a pair of shoes and done a tap dance.

The profits were tremendous in the old days of no regulation. Consumers had no idea what they were buying and no idea how to get their coins appraised. In fact, they were as likely to get ripped off when selling coins as when buying them. In far too many scenarios a person with valuable coins would walk into a coin shop, offer them for sale, and be told that they were worth a fraction of their actual market value. The slab services have fully exposed such abuses. Today you would be highly suspicious if you bought a coin that was certified by NGC as MS-65 and a dealer offered you $100 for the coin at the same time 50 dealers around the nation were willing to pay $3,000 for it sight-unseen. You would know at once that something was wrong— that the dealer was being dishonest. No longer can disreputable dealers get away with saying, "This is a worthless coin; listen to us, we'll give you $50 for it," knowing full well that they can turn around and sell it for thousands of dollars.

The following material is reprinted with permission from an interview published in *The Rosen Numismatic Advisory*. It chronicles a typical rip-off telemarketing sales pitch and should underscore the buyer-beware caveat. Investors who place blind faith in a telemarketing salesperson could find themselves a victim of one of the types of scams outlined by Ed.

More Confessions of a Rip-Off Coin Salesman

(Copyright © 1988 by Maurice Rosen Rare Coin Confidential)

Who is Ed? He's an intelligent, young family man who for two years worked at five telemarketing firms ("rooms," as he calls them), making a living by "jamming" prospects on the telephone to buy rare coins, usually at ridiculously high prices. Due to the highly delicate nature of Ed's confessions, I did not use real names.

MAURICE ROSEN: How many firms did you work for, selling coins?

ED: Five—all on Long Island, probably within 20 miles of each other.

M.R.: Tell me about the first firm. What did you do there, and how did they operate?

ED: The first I'll call Alpha. They were the worst offender of the five. I worked from a script until I developed my own presentation. This was not a one-call-close operation. You would "cue" them for a dollar amount, get "yes" answers to questions, such as, "Are you an investor? Do you want to see a 20–40 percent annual return?"

M.R.: Is this firm still in operation?

ED: No. I left after a few months because I found out that they were selling horrendously overgraded coins. They were buying things such as Walking Liberty halves at some $40 each and selling them at $450—at best AU coins sold as MS-65 at over Grey Sheet prices. This was during the spring months of 1986, when these coins were at their peak and the rare coin telemarketers were racking up big sales.

M.R.: How much business did they do when they were going strong?

ED: At the peak, they were averaging between $90,000 and $150,000 per month. One of the things which brought them to the ground was their buyback guarantee. It was in writing that they would buy back at the grade sold at current Grey Sheet bid. So as people got more and more unsettled, they started to have to eat a lot of these coins. That killed them.

M.R.: How were the coins marketed and presented? What prices were charged?

ED: They'd send out a copy of the Grey Sheet to substantiate their prices, which were usually "ask" plus 5 percent. To the customer, it looked like a close spread.

M.R.: How would you handle customers' objections about the coins not being MS-65?

ED: They would quadruple-dip everything to give the coins phenomenal luster, all heavily dipped in a cleaning solution to make the coins appear near-flawless.

M.R.: Did the salespeople ever chuckle about selling these coins, ripping off people?

ED: No. To keep the morale of the room alive, they'd never sit around and discuss their 400–500 percent markups with us. Never. The owner claimed even to us that these were very nice coins, that the client was getting a good deal. It was all for the salesmen's benefit.

M.R.: Tell me about the second firm you worked for.

ED: Beta was also selling uncertified coins. The pitch was always to knock certified coins. They would sell high-end MS-63s as 65s, so the clients were at least getting decent coins. Commemorative halves were big sellers. They're not Morgan dollars, where it takes 100-odd pieces to complete a set, every coin looking the same. Each coin had a story to tell.

M.R.: What were your commissions at Alpha and at Beta?

ED: At Alpha, it was high because they were charging a lot. It was 20 percent on low monthly production, 25 percent on high production. The breaking point was $20,000 a month. If you sold over that, you got 25 percent on all your monthly sales. At Beta, it was a flat 15 percent.

M.R.: Were you displeased that the commission at Beta was lower?

ED: No. There are very few firms paying 20–25 percent anymore. Most of those that do are hiding behind NCI* certified coins, selling them at full Grey Sheet prices; on those, they'll pay 20 percent. At Beta, the leads were investor card decks—people who responded to a generic coin investment lead card. Again, we'd send out a package, not too elaborate, but the client got a nicer coin. I was at Beta for about four–five months. Those card decks are a tough row to hoe; a lot of those people are 18-year-old students and old people with nothing else to do. So I went to another operation.

M.R.: Okay, tell me about Charley.

ED: I'll stay with the name Charley, because the owner is someone I actually fear. They sell in a completely different manner. It's not just an outbound telephone operation. They advertise in a lot of coin publications—lowball items just to get the phone to ring. Occasionally, they can sneak into stock market-oriented daily newspapers. It's a bait-and-switch operation. Nobody sells Silver Eagles at spot; you'd say, "That was based on closing date pricing; now, it's three weeks later at a different price." It made a lot of sense, because you had people calling in. You'd switch them from bullion to rare coins, where there was a good markup. But the owner made a huge amount of false claims to his staff. Again, a good deal of what they sold was NCI-certified coins. They'd sell NCI Walkers, Morgans and gold at just under Grey Sheet bid to make it look like a bargain—which, in fact, it's not. There are certain gold pieces with NCI papers that can be massively marked up. I point to a Liberty Head half eagle in MS-63. You can pick it up for about $500 [Blue Sheet NCI bid is $455, whereas a PCGS MS-63 is $1,450 bid]. In the Grey Sheet, it's $1,425. So that was a favored coin of most sellers. Same with the Indian quarter eagle, Indian half eagle and Liberty Head eagle. Telemarketing heaven!

M.R.: Let's move on to your next telemarketing operation, Delta.

ED: Delta is a pure outbound operation, selling raw coins—not half as sleazy as Alpha, but selling probably MS-60s as "borderline MS-65," as

*The Numismatic Certification Institute (NCI) of Dallas, Texas, admits that its grading standards can be nearly two points less conservative than those of some other services. Thus, NCI's grading can be decidedly less conservative than that which is used by NGC and PCGS—services whose standards are generally in line with quotes as reported by the Coin Dealer Newsletter [CDN]. Among various disclosures on an NCI certificate is that it may not be proper to equate coins it certifies with CDN quotes of equal numerical grade. Nonetheless, some coin firms market NCI coins based on a direct link to CDN quotes. In actuality, NCI coins which grade MS-65, as an example, generally wholesale for about 30–45 percent of CDN bid quotes. This implies that someone who pays CDN "ask" plus 5 percent may be paying over three times wholesale bid!

they'd call them. Again, you'd sell around certification. It's a very high-pressure operation, a one-call close: Get them on the phone; don't let them off without a sale.

M.R.: How were some of these sales conducted?

ED: They were very profitable, again making at least a 400–500 percent markup, as well as auto-charging on credit cards—just charging up people's credit cards without authorization, which I think is a federal crime. So they were graduate salespeople from there. To this day, I still speak to people on the phone who got [bilked] by them. They sold any garbage they had around. The owner was a bit deranged; I met him a couple times. He opened a firm after that and got arrested there, too. So my opinion is that [the owner] will be doing some serious time. They were a small operation with a real barracuda pit. Every guy there was writing at least $20,000–$30,000 a month. They were early in the business. Since there weren't many rooms then, they cleaned up.

M.R.: Let's go back to your fourth firm, Delta, with their "borderline" grading.

ED: Sure. Their game is unique. How they still thrive amazes me. They never try to give a coin a straight numerical grade. They'd call it a borderline 63, or a 63 + /65, or a borderline 65 and so on. They would never put on their invoice something you can pin down, which was a unique twist. Without question, it was deliberately evasive. They usually sell a Mint State coin, or close to it. Their favorite is the Liberty half eagle because there's so much room in the coin. They'd sell a borderline 63 for $695. The Grey Sheet bid is $1,425. The coin would be a commercial Unc worth $200–$250. I saw a lot of what went out; I'm surprised they'd show the stuff to their salesmen.

M.R.: Weren't there people who wanted a full-graded coin, as the Grey Sheet reports them?

ED: No. Most of these coins stuck with the customers. Look, people like a bargain. They thought they were cheating us! None of the coins were certified. We'd easily sell 10 a week.

M.R.: What [made Delta's key salesman] so successful?

ED: The whole pitch was, we want to show you a profit in the short term; we want the coins back so we can sell them again; we want to show you that 30–40 percent profit. The room worked their pitches around his because he was amazing. On a 15 percent commission, he can make an easy $5,000 a week. A franchise player! He's been in coins for only three years.

M.R.: Epsilon, your present firm.

ED: I've been there for two months. Epsilon is still a different operation. They are constantly flooding the coin periodicals with full-page ads. They call coins "Gem BU," but they barely make AU—but the coins are priced in line with AU prices or close to them. The clients are very low-end people. It's an old firm with thousands of names, so it makes my job easier when I outbound calls to rekindle the fires of coin buying. They sell things like rolls of gem BU Morgan dollars at $475, but they're probably AU/Unc worth $300 or so—not too bad a deal, compared to other places. They never use numerical grading.

M.R.: Was auto-charging ever done with the approval of the owners of the telemarketing firms?

ED: Almost always, the salespeople did it on their own, though I suspect one firm which recently shut down because of auto-charging had the owner's tacit approval, because he was desperate. There are a number of salespeople I've heard of who go to a room with their book intact, with credit card numbers, and just auto-charge up a storm, get commissions and then vanish before the owner becomes wise. But I've yet to hear of overgrading shutting down a firm.

M.R.: When a client called to find out the progress of his portfolio, what did you tell him?

ED: It was always a sticky situation. For sure, you painted the rosiest possible scenario to not have him send the coins back. One firm I worked for would send the client a "profit check" and hold the coins eight weeks. Say a client bought $2,000 worth of coins. A year later, he insists upon sending his coins in. We'd send out a check for $500–$600 and keep the coins for eight weeks. We were "actively trying to broker the coins," we'd tell him, then send the coins back with a note that "we tried." They'd keep the $500–$600—which would usually work! So, he might think that he "got us" and won't contact us again. Now, if the client wants to trade up, we would certainly credit him the full amount, because there would be a ton of profit on the new sale. The whole trick was keeping the coins with the client.

M.R.: Why did badgering a prospect on the phone sometimes work?

ED: When a credit card can be used, you say, "It's on approval. Just look at the coin; it's a beauty. When you see it, you'll want it; you have nothing to lose."

M.R.: What was the return rate—the percentage of sales which came back and didn't stick?

ED: Shockingly low, all across the board. If 5 percent came back, I'd be surprised. Most people keep the coins for the long term. It's amazing; as much flagrantly overgraded material as I've seen go out the doors, the return rate is very low. Again, the people are not knowledgeable. They don't know grading, pricing or the market at all.

M.R.: Tell me about the abusive selling of NCI-certified coins. Their MS-65s seem to be wholesaling at some 30 to 45 cents on the Grey Sheet dollar. Tell me how they are sold.

ED: I'm amazed at this. Most of the TM [telemarketing] people I know are trying to stay with certified coins now, only because if the stuff hits the fan and you go to court, you can say, "I'm not a numismatic expert. They [NCI] are. They said that it's MS-65." So it gives them credibility and seems to take them off the hook. I know for a fact that a certain dealer is one of the biggest NCI customers. He sends more coins to NCI than almost anyone else in the country. He's supplying literally 50-60 TMs around the country. He's selling at least $10 million a year, most of it NCI coins. He sells NCI MS-65 silver dollars at about 55 percent of Grey Sheet MS-65 bid to TMs. They'd easily double up. Pick [another] industry with that markup!

M.R.: How many TM firms have been active here on Long Island? Which is the biggest?

ED: Well over 100. From one- and two-man operations to the largest I know, which currently has over 50 salespeople on the phone at three separate room locations. They write about $1 million a month. About 90 percent of what they sell are NCI coins. I know, because I interviewed there.

M.R.: Despite everything we spoke about, how do you feel about coins as an investment?

ED: I personally have more affection for rare coins—type coins and so on—than I ever had. If I had the funds, the only thing I'd buy would be coins graded by NGC, from what I know. The fact that some dealers boycotted [NGC] is a testament to its tough grading standards. They felt they couldn't make money with [NGC]. They may have gone back to NCI material, where they can make a lot more than 10–20 percent on a coin. Once again, it's the coin, not the plastic around the coin.

M.R.: How do the various salespeople justify what they are doing?

ED: Truly, many don't know. That [Delta] salesman I told you about has no idea that a Blue Sheet exists and no idea that there are two levels of certified coins. All he knows how to do is sell—and sell darn well. The owners of these operations would tell him and all the other salespeople, "We're selling good deals. We're not hurting anybody."

This interview has been provided courtesy of The Rosen Numismatic Advisory. *The name of the interview subject, as well as the firms he worked for, has been changed.*

PROMISES OF LIQUIDITY

In my book *Rare Coin Investment Strategy*, I profiled coin dealer Michael G. DeFalco, of Claremont, California. I said that he was a reputable dealer—that he had a buyback guarantee and would honor it. At the time, DeFalco was viewed as a pioneer in offering to buy back coins at fair market prices and at the same grade at which he sold them. He maintained what is known as a two-way market: He guaranteed not only to buy coins at one given price, but also to sell them to somebody else at another given price. I quoted Michael J. Standish, who was then director of numismatic investment services for DeFalco's firm, as saying: "If I'm a coin dealer and I offer a buyback today and one year from now I decide to get out of this business, what's my guarantee worth? So as far as guarantees go, I'd throw them out the window."

I portrayed DeFalco as an honest and reputable dealer, indicating that he was one of the dealers on whom you could rely when he gave you a buyback guarantee. Thereafter, DeFalco fell under an ethical shadow. According to an article in the August 31, 1988, issue of *Coin World*, he was ordered to stand trial in Pomona, California, on five of six felony counts of grand theft stemming from the sale of coins. One count was dismissed because the alleged victim did not appear. Authorities accused DeFalco of selling customers' coins without their permission and without forwarding the proceeds to the customers. However, DeFalco was later cleared of the charges.

As DeFalco's case indicates, buyback guarantees are only as good as the people who issue them. "Guaranteed" markets have a number of disadvantages. For example, suppose a dealer (and this is quite common) has a certain coin or medallion and guarantees to buy it from people she previously sold it to for, let's say, $1,000—and she's selling it for $1,150. Now anybody looking at this transaction might say, "Oh, she's making a $150 profit. Well, it's a little excessive, but I guess it's fair." In actuality, that dealer may buy very few of those coins back from previous customers; she may be buying them on the open market for $100, $200, or $300 per coin or per medallion—and selling them for $1,150. So while it looks to the public as though the dealer is making a $150 profit, the dealer in fact may be making a $1,000 profit because very few people sell those coins or medallions back. Two-way markets created by dealers should not be relied on. Some reputable dealers try to make a conscientious effort to sell coins like this in a reputable way, but these dealers are more the exception than the rule. As a general rule, stay away from a guarantee of a two-way market. Buy a coin on its own merits. Buy it for what it is.

Legitimate Two-Way Markets

Two-way markets offered by PCGS and NGC are valid and legitimate. Hundreds of dealers offer to buy and sell coins sight-unseen based on what PCGS and NGC assign as a grade. If someone wants to trade coins, it's perfectly acceptable to buy coins based on the NGC and PCGS grade sight-unseen, so long as the buyer really expects to trade those coins rather than hold them for an extended period. An example of where it *wouldn't* be advisable to hold for the long term when you're buying sight-unseen would be PCGS common-date S-mint silver dollars. The trading range on these is anywhere from $285 to $540; so when they're at the bottom of their trading range ($285) it's advisable to buy these coins in quantity. Many such sight-unseen coins are not nearly as attractive as their on-sight counterparts—the premium-quality coins you can pick from. And when they get toward the top of their trading range (above $500) it's time to sell those coins and make a tidy profit. But in many cases, PCGS S-mint dollars turn out to be less than the glistening jewels you expect them to be.

SELF-PROMOTION AND OTHER GROWTH TRICKS

This industry is more talented than any other in promoting itself and advertising itself and billing itself and in systematizing the process through which coins are graded. Coins are, in fact, a product; the manner in which we market our product will make the difference between our being a $3 billion industry or a $20 billion industry—or being an industry even larger than that.

The more things change, the more they stay the same. NGC and PCGS have changed the reality of the marketplace, making it more liquid and more honest. But, except for the individuals becoming involved in institutional transactions, the types of people trading in our $3 billion coin industry are much the same as before. If we have a potential for $200 million to be traded by reputable Wall Street brokerage houses, their presence can create a tremendous difference in the climate of the marketplace.

Chapter
4

THE DEVELOPMENT OF GRADING STANDARDS

Coin-grading services are a fairly new phenomenon. We feel confident that independent grading services will remain an important component of the industry on a permanent basis, but we also feel obliged to ask: What if they don't? What if the day were to come when the coin holder's value was no more than that of the plastic from which it's made? If that day ever does come, and collectors and investors have to crack their coins out of the holders, strict grading is what will protect them.

John Albanese, Founder and President,
Numismatic Guaranty Corporation of
America, in an article in *Barron's*

THE ROOTS OF GRADING INCONSISTENCIES

It's March 1980. At the offices of one large metropolitan coin company, the salespeople (or "investment counselors") are scurrying around with copies of the Grey Sheet in their hands. Prices are up again, excitement is in the air, and the company's clients are just as enthusiastic as its staff. A man walks in the door, plunks down $25,000, says that he wants to invest in rare coins, and is given a group of coins chosen for him personally by the principal of the firm.

Let's return to the present and reexamine this scene with the benefit of hindsight. The six coins this man purchased were graded MS-65. And the grading was legitimate by the standards of the day. The firm had acquired them from other dealers as MS-65, and they would have been accepted as such by most leading companies of the day. As time progressed, however, perceptions changed. A mere two years later the coins had come to be viewed as MS-64. By 1985 they were looked on as MS-63. And by 1989 all were widely considered to be no better than 63; in fact some of them were graded 62.

What happened? The coins didn't change, but the grading standards did. At the height of the market boom in 1979 and early 1980, prices were rising so rapidly that strict grading didn't seem essential; even if a coin was somewhat overgraded, the relentless market surge would soon push its resale value well past its purchase price—even in the somewhat lower grade. By mid-1980, though, the price binge was over and coin buyers and sellers were forced to look at grading in a much more sober light. No longer could they forgive minor imperfections by borrowing against a coin's future gains; those gains were no longer assured, and the grade had to be justified then and there.

As time went by, the surge not only stopped but gave way to a deep, protracted slump, and grading standards tightened even more. The written standards, notably those of the American Numismatic Association, remained as they had been before the slump. But major changes occurred in the way those written standards were interpreted and applied, even by the ANA Certification Service, then the leading arbiter in the coin grading field.

THE ANA'S EMERGENCE—AND SUBSEQUENT DECLINE—AS A LEADING GRADING SERVICE

The ANA Certification Service (ANACS) started grading coins in March 1979, right around the peak of the coin market's greatest boom. Almost at once its grading certificates became important marketing tools for many dealers and a huge bone of contention for many others. Critics complained that ANA grading was often inconsistent and even downright inaccurate. But ANA certification was helping to feed the frenzy in the marketplace, so dealers continued to deluge the service with coins to be graded. At one point these coins were arriving at the ANA headquarters in Colorado Springs at the rate of 12,000 per month.

As prices fell and many dealers' grading tastes grew more finicky, ANACS faced a dilemma: If it adhered to the liberal standards set in its early months of operation, its grading would be out of step with the new reality; but if it tightened its standards, the earlier ANACS certificates would be cheapened and the service would suffer a loss of credibility. In the end, it seemed to straddle the two approaches and, in the process, really satisfied no one.

By February 1982, ANA President Adna G. Wilde, Jr., felt compelled to appoint a committee to review the many complaints and formulate guidelines for improving the situation. The committee chairman, scholar-researcher-dealer Q. David Bowers, reported a few months later that the panel had uncovered a number of inconsistencies in ANACS grading and that these were "embarrassing to the ANA." He said there was ample evidence "that a coin graded one way on Tuesday may be graded another way Friday, or that a coin graded at 10 A.M. may be different at 4 P.M." ANACS remained the dominant grading service for several years thereafter, but its reign was an uneasy one.

Perceptive dealer and market analyst Maurice Rosen pinpointed ANACS's problem—and accurately predicted its subsequent decline—in a 1982 interview published in *COINage* magazine.

"I strongly approve of the concept of an independent grading service," Rosen told *COINage*'s Ed Reiter, "but only if it is competent. In the case of ANACS, the level of competence and experience simply isn't great enough now. I believe it can be improved to the point where it will gain broad acceptance—but in order for that to happen, the ANA will have to spend some money and get the right people to run it. In other words, the grading service itself must be upgraded." Unless that happened, Rosen said, ANACS might wither and die, and a new grading service beyond the ANA's control might take its place.

Nearly four years passed before Rosen's prediction came true. But when it did, ANACS fell from favor faster than you could say the word "slab."

ANACS had been providing split grades on authoritative-looking photocertificates that stated that the grade was ANACS's opinion. If a coin was assigned the grade MS-63/65, that meant ANACS believed the coin to grade MS-63 on the obverse and MS-65 on the reverse. In an attempt to recapture what it considered to be market share, however, ANACS began to encapsulate its graded coins in holders similar to those provided by NGC and PCGS. The ANACS slab provides an overall grade—one number, such as MS-63—to make the certified product more marketable.

In Figure 4-1, an ANACS holder is displayed. The final grade is verified by both ANACS and a member of the Professional Numismatists Guild, Inc., a dealer organization. A hologram is displayed on the reverse. ANACS refers to this as an "ANACS cache."

PCGS AND THE REVOLUTION IN GRADING AND PRICING

Those who were dissatisfied with ANACS organized a number of competing grading services during the early and middle 1980s. Most

Figure 4-1. ANACS cache. This is the encapsulated product of the American Numismatic Association Certification Service (Photo courtesy ANACS)

had one thing in common: They were formed by coin dealers. And this was no coincidence. Influential dealers were among the most vociferous critics of ANACS, primarily because they didn't believe it was giving proper weight to commercial considerations in its grading. Essentially, they viewed ANACS as too academic and out of touch with reality as reflected in the marketplace.

The search for an alternative ended successfully in 1986 when David Hall of Newport Beach, California, one of the nation's most talented coin traders, announced the formation of the Professional Coin Grading Service (PCGS). It was clearly an idea whose time had come —and come in a big, big way. PCGS scored the equivalent of a first-round knockout, quickly dethroning ANACS as king of the coin-grading hill. In a very real sense, 1986 meant as much to the grading "revolution" as 1789 did to the French Revolution and 1917 to the Russian Revolution. That was the year certified coins came into their own, the year the coin market witnessed and accepted a new order in grading.

The PCGS Formula

Several key ingredients made up the revolutionary PCGS formula. First, it engaged leading dealers—including Hall himself—to do the grading.

And they graded by consensus: Three different experts would view a given coin and assign it a grade; then the coin would be examined by a "finalizer," who would weigh the consensus and assign it a final grade. I often explain the PCGS consensus approach at seminars by having volunteers come to the front of the room and hold up numerical grades (Figure 4-2), pointing out that if, say, six graders assign a grade of 69 and two graders assign a grade of 70, the final grade probably will be 69. PCGS applies this concept using a minimum of four graders.

Second, PCGS introduced the use of a sonically sealed, hard plastic holder to encase both the coin and a PCGS tab stating the coin's date, denomination, variety, and grade (Figure 4-3). This holder (soon dubbed the "slab") made it possible to buy and sell coins sight-unseen, almost like commodities. And that process was further eased by a third major feature of PCGS's program: its guarantee to purchasers. PCGS dealer members agreed that they would accept the grade assigned to any coin by the service and buy it, sight-unseen, at their current bid price for that level.

"From day one," Hall declared in a 1986 interview, "I've been a big supporter of ANACS. I've supported the ANA and ANACS financially, and I've been a consultant to ANACS—one of the experts they go to when they need help. But ANACS merely renders an opinion on coins. At PCGS, we not only grade coins, but also offer cash for them. When we grade a coin, it's not just an opinion; it's money on the table."

Figure 4-2. Seminar attendees learn consensus grading. (Photo courtesy Harvey C. Travers)

Figure 4-3. PCGS-graded coin. PCGS revolutionized the coin business with the introduction of its tamper-resistant, sonically sealed coin holder and its concept of rare coin market-makers. (Photo courtesy PCGS)

"I don't see us being a competitor to ANACS," Hall continued, "because we do something entirely different. The public will decide how they want their coins graded. The marketplace will decide. And I'm sure that whoever provides the most beneficial service will be the one that does the lion's share of the business."

FORMATION OF ANOTHER LEADING GRADING SERVICE

It soon became clear that PCGS was the lion and ANACS was the lamb. But the new leader's dominance didn't go unchallenged for long. Soon after PCGS began operations in Newport Beach in February 1986, one of its organizers, highly respected coin dealer John Albanese, withdrew and began drafting plans for a new grading service of his own. Albanese felt that PCGS had an Achilles' heel: the possible conflict posed by the fact that its principals were dealing in coins. He set out to form a service that would offer the best of both worlds—the professionalism of PCGS and the independence of ANACS. In the process he stopped buying and selling coins himself.

Figure 4-4. NGC-graded coin. This is NGC's publicity photograph. The real encapsulated product is similar to that of PCGS, incorporating a hologram security device to prevent tampering. (Photograph courtesy NGC)

NGC's Philosophy

Albanese's grading service opened for business in August 1987 as the Numismatic Guaranty Corporation of America. It is based in Parsippany, New Jersey, some 35 miles west of New York City. NGC policy prohibits full-time employees from dealing in coins. Coin dealers do work part-time grading coins for NGC, but finalizers must be full-time employees and therefore nonparticipants in buying and selling coins. At present the two finalizers are Albanese and Mark Salzberg, who had been a prominent coin trader before joining the company. (PCGS now has about half a dozen finalizers, all of them major dealers.)

Like PCGS, NGC encases each coin in a hard plastic holder along with an ID label (Figure 4-4). A flexible white plastic insert grips the coin securely, preventing it from rattling around and possibly being damaged.

To enhance the security of their holders, NGC and PCGS both incorporate holograms into their packaging. These make it much more difficult to produce effective counterfeit holders. Both services' holders have raised edges, making them easy to stack.

FEES AT PCGS AND NGC

The companies' fee structures differ only slightly. Both offer a range of services, and both charge according to the speed with which a coin is certified and returned. Basic certification at PCGS costs $22 plus postage, but this may entail a wait of 45 days or more. "While-you-wait" grading costs $125 per coin. At NGC the basic charge is $23 plus postage, with a present turnaround time of about five weeks. Overnight service offered by NGC costs $75; same-day walk-through is priced at $125.

GRADING SERVICES AND THEIR STANDARDS

To some extent, the companies reflect their leaders' personalities. David Hall is more aggressive and maintains a higher profile; Albanese, by contrast, tends to be cautious and low-key. So perhaps it's not just a coincidence that NGC grading is viewed as being somewhat more conservative. Although NGC-graded coins sometimes bring moderately higher premiums than those graded by PCGS, coins from both services are readily accepted at prevailing market levels—even in sight-unseen transactions.

"We are consumer-oriented, and this is very crucial," NGC's Albanese maintains. "We strive to protect the consumer by grading coins so strictly that the grades we assign will hold up under even the most adverse market conditions. We assume that the consumer is going to have to liquidate his coins in a bear market, and therefore we're very conservative. Everything we do is aimed at giving consumers a heightened sense of security."

NGC and PCGS both provide their customers with written guarantees that offer protection against overgrading. They pledge that in the event the purchaser believes a coin to be overgraded, it can be resubmitted for a small fee; if it is then assigned a lower grade, the company will compensate the customer for the difference in fair market value between the two grades. NGC's guarantee (see Figure 4-5) does not apply to copper coins because they are susceptible to oxidation after being sealed in their plastic holders. To date, PCGS has not made a similar exception—an inconsistency that could prove troublesome and expensive after the passage of years. It's likely that PCGS will have to deal with this difficulty in the future.

IMPORTANT GRADING DIFFERENCES

When PCGS and NGC first began competing head to head, their grading standards were markedly different in certain areas. PCGS seemed

Guarantee

NGC guarantees that all coins submitted to it shall be graded by a minimum of three (3) NGC grading experts in accordance with NGC grading standards and procedures.

In the event the purchaser of an NGC coin believes that the coin has been overgraded with respect to such standards and procedures, the purchaser may submit any such coin to NGC for regrading under a procedure which assures that graders are unaware of the grade originally assigned. The fee for such regrading shall be $20. If the grade determined under such regrading procedure is lower than that originally assigned to the coin, NGC shall pay the difference between the fair market value of the coin, as determined by arm's-length current bids of NGC dealers, at the newly established grade and the grade originally assigned to such coin.

WARNING: EXCEPTION TO NGC GUARANTEE COPPER COINS CAN OXIDIZE AFTER SEALING. IN SUCH AN EVENT, THE COIN GRADE MAY DIMINISH. THEREFORE, THE NGC GUARANTEE SHALL NOT BE APPLICABLE TO COPPER COINS.

Clerical error with respect to the description or grade of the coin which would be readily noticed on inspection shall not be subject to the NGC guarantee herein stated.

Figure 4-5. NGC guarantee. Copper coins are not covered under NGC's guarantee. PCGS has a similar guarantee which includes coverage for copper coins. (Courtesy NGC)

to apply looser standards than NGC for grading gold coins in particular, as well as for grading Morgan dollars. As time went by (although it denies any change) PCGS may have tightened its standards for gold coins, especially Saint-Gaudens double eagles. It may have tightened its standards a bit for silver dollars too, but the apparent change seems to have been more dramatic with the gold. Current price lists, notably the *Certified Coin Dealer Newsletter*, reflect this apparent market shift. If you look at them today, you'll see that the prices for NGC and PCGS gold are about the same.

It may not be clear, but this signals a hidden risk for people buying certified coins today. Based on current prices, an investor may conclude that PCGS and NGC gold coins are equally good deals. But that may not be the case. The investor who buys a PCGS gold coin and gets one that was slabbed in the earlier period, when PCGS grading standards were apparently looser, may acquire a coin that's not the equivalent of today's more stringent standards. During that earlier period, NGC gold coins commanded a premium over their PCGS counterparts.

PCGS persistently denies any change in its standards. In fact, PCGS issued its dealers the following statement and survey findings:

. . . PCGS GRADING STANDARDS WILL *NOT* CHANGE!!! The whole PCGS concept and the major reason for our success has been the creation of a grading standard which is accepted in the market place and which will not change. We recognize the importance of a permanent grading standard, and we intend to do everything possible to keep our standards permanent.

The major factor in maintaining a permanent grading standard is building a permanent grader reference set. We now have $215,000 (our cost) in coins in our grader reference set. We will continue to expand this set. We intend to have at least $500,000 worth of coins in the set by the end of the year. The coins in the set never change. Graders may mentally waffle because of hot or cold market conditions, but if they refer to the grading set they have a permanent, unchanging standard. By the way, we have never changed the coins in the set. The coins that are in the set today will be in the set ten years from now.

. . . Some of you have expressed concerns that we intend to change our standards because of the results of the grading survey. This will *not* be the case. We will use the grading standard to remind the graders which coins to be more careful on, which areas to refer to the grading set on. The problem is not with the PCGS standards (as represented by the grading set). The problem is with the application of these standards. For example, the area which you feel PCGS is most brutal on is MS67 coins (a score of 6.18% on the 1 to 10 scale). Will PCGS loosen its standards for MS67? No! PCGS will remind graders that they should occasionally be grading a coin "7". PCGS will remind graders that the grading scale does not stop at MS65. PCGS will put some MS67 coins into the grader reference set (any volunteers?).

I hope you understand the PCGS position on grading standards. If you have any questions or comments please call or write me personally.

Let's take a look at the results of the grading survey. First, here's how your responses averaged on the 1 to 10 scale (1 = too loose, 10 = too tight):

Overall	5.29	Walkers	4.82
Silver Dollars	4.59	Copper	5.87
BU Type	5.80	Circulated Coins	5.13
Proof Type	5.68	MS60	5.07
$20 Saints	4.51	MS61	5.13
$20 Libs	5.08	MS62	5.06
Small Gold	5.89	MS63	5.21
Gold Commems	5.94	MS64	5.03
Proof Gold	5.96	MS65	5.24
Silver Commems	5.07	MS66	5.75
Buffalos	5.60	MS67	6.18
Mercs	5.31	No grades	6.76

Speaking of no grades, here's your specific response on each of the no grade areas:

PVC	6.37	Planchet Flaws	5.68
Questionable Toning	6.81	Rim Nicks	5.80
Altered Surfaces	6.15	Scratches	5.46
Environmental Damage	5.67	Cleaning	6.03

The no grades represent a policy, not a grading standard. The PCGS no grade policy will be changed. When PCGS first started, the no grade policy was instituted to protect PCGS market-makers. The concept was that coins with *major* problems shouldn't be placed in PCGS holders. Unfortunately, grader interpretation of that policy gradually became tougher and tougher. The result was that coins with *minor* problems were getting the "no grade" designation. This was not the original intention of the no grade policy. As our survey clearly shows, PCGS authorized dealers don't like the current no grade policy. Frankly, we don't like it either. It will therefore be changed effective immediately. PCGS will continue to "no grade" coins with *major* problems. However, coins with *minor* problems will no longer be rejected by PCGS. I feel you should see a 50 percent to 75 percent decrease in the rejection rate. I welcome your comments and suggestions.

IDENTIFYING ILLICIT PCGS COIN HOLDERS

Step #1 From the insert

Determine if the insert is genuine.

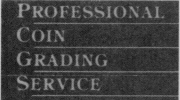 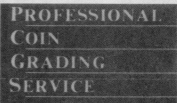

GOOD INSERT

The serifs on the good insert slant from the letters at a 45° angle. Note the S and the E in SERVICE. The serif on the G is longer.

BAD INSERT

The serifs on the bad inserts are vertical. They cut off squarely and do not angle out. Also there is no serif on the G.

Step #2 From The Plastic Cases

It is important to check the plastic holder even if the insert is o.k.

Area to examine on case

Bad case has a more obvious raised area which is approximately 3/16" long.

Good case has small raised area along the edge where the holder was cut from the injection molded sprue. About 1/16" long.

Figure 4-6. How to identify counterfeit PCGS holders. (Courtesy Heritage Capital Corporation)

For most coins, PCGS and NGC have maintained comparable grading standards right from the start of their operations. Consistency, in fact, has been among the most important assets of both companies. However, the exceptions—notably gold coins and silver dollars—may represent a potential long-term problem for PCGS. By apparently tightening its standards for those coins in order to meet NGC's competition, PCGS may have opened the door for abuses if indeed these fluctuations in standards did occur. Many savvy market traders are confused about PCGS's standards. These professionals remain uncertain whether PCGS loosened its standards or was merely the victim of an onslaught of counterfeit holders.

Figure 4-6 provides illustrations and instructions for identifying counterfeit PCGS holders. This identification sheet was distributed to clients by Heritage Rare Coin Galleries after discovery of the illicit holders.

OTHER GRADING SERVICES

Although PCGS and NGC are the biggest and most influential coin grading services, several other services do merit consideration.

American Numismatic Association Certification Service

If you want your coins certified but not encapsulated, ANACS offers an optional grading service that furnishes certification only.

Numismatic Certification Institute

The Numismatic Certification Institute is an affiliate of Heritage Capital Corporation of Dallas, a multifaceted company that also operates Heritage Rare Coin Galleries, the highest-volume coin dealership in the nation. By its own admission, NCI uses less conservative grading standards than PCGS and NGC. James L. Halperin, cochairman of the board and a principal grader for NCI, says they are ¾ to 1½ points less conservative. The problem with this is that less scrupulous coin sellers (including telemarketers) can use NCI-graded coins to mislead unwary customers into thinking they are getting good value. Typically, such sellers will quote current prices for PCGS or NGC coins and then provide NCI coins of the same grade instead. By PCGS or NGC standards, the NCI coins would be of a lower grade and therefore worth substantially less money.

Hallmark Grading Service

Hallmark Grading Service Inc., hadn't started operations as of August 1989. Billing itself as "The Connoisseur's Grading Service," Hallmark identified its sponsors as Lee J. Bellisario, Bowers and Merena Galleries, "and other leading professional numismatists." Hallmark holders are expected to carry "Premium Quality" grade designations when appropriate, as well as mintage figures and other relevant research data.

GRADING SERVICES AS A STABILIZING FORCE

The emergence of widely accepted third-party grading services has stabilized the coin market. It has blunted the bitter dispute over grading that previously threatened to undercut coins' potential for price appreciation. At the same time, it has given coins liquidity akin to that of commodities and helped create a climate in which they can thrive as investments.

As the pioneer in this movement, PCGS deserves a great deal of the credit for its success. NGC has made a major contribution, as well, by providing an authoritative "second opinion." And while PCGS may not appreciate the competition from its own business viewpoint, that competition is obviously healthy for the coin market as a whole. It keeps both services on their toes and forces them to hold their fees down and their standards up.

Population Reports

Both services have been issuing periodic "population reports" showing how many coins of each date in each U.S. series they have certified in each of the 11 proof or mint-state grades. These have become valuable tools for coin buyers, sellers, and researchers, for they offer a good picture of relative rarity within each series.

How to Submit Coins

PCGS and NGC both process only coins submitted by dealer members. A list of these members can be obtained by writing to the service in question.

Before buying coins, collectors and investors should be absolutely certain of the grading standards used in determining the grade and, of course, the price. Just because a coin is called a 65, that's not necessarily a guarantee of anything. It can be a dealer's good-faith opinion (or bad-faith opinion), which means nothing. The most important things to know are whose grading was used and how much the coin is worth in the given grade for the given grading service.

The addresses of the various grading services are as follows:

American Numismatic Association Certification Service
818 North Cascade Avenue
Colorado Springs, CO 80903

Hallmark Grading Service Inc.
10 Wheeling Avenue
Woburn, MA 01888

Numismatic Certification Institute
Division of Heritage Capital Corporation
Heritage Plaza
Highland Park Village
Dallas, TX 75205

Numismatic Guaranty Corporation of America, Inc.
P.O. Box 1776
Parsippany, NJ 07054

Professional Coin Grading Service
P.O. Box 9458
Newport Beach, CA 92658

GRADING BY LASER: A GLIMPSE OF THE FUTURE

The year is 2025; the place is a coin grading laboratory. A technician in a white coat places a coin in a laser machine, which scans it. The information is stored in a satellite, where it can be retrieved as desired. The clinician then transfers the coin to a conveyor belt, which whisks it to a second work station. There a second scientist positions a laser that scans the coin. The process is repeated a third time. If all three lasers agree on the coin's grade, it is sent to the encapsulation room and sealed in a permanent plastic holder. If there is disagreement, a fourth laser is used to "finalize" the grade.

This may sound highly futuristic, but it's altogether possible that this kind of grading lab may be a basic part of the rare coin marketplace a generation from now. In fact, the technology for laser grading of coins is already in place today. But laser grading has its limitations. Most of all it is limited by the shortcomings of the people who program computer equipment to guide the lasers. A computer is only as good as the information it's given. A computer cannot make intelligent or rational decisions; only the human mind can do that.

One of laser grading's principal advantages is consistency. In a sense it is a way of "fingerprinting" a coin so that each time a given coin is laser scanned, the computer will be able to identify the coin and call up its previous grading history. This will enhance the stability of grading in the future and reinforce coin buyers' confidence in the process. In the absence of such a safeguard it has been a common practice for dealers to resubmit a single coin to one or more grading services, sometimes dozens of times, until it receives a higher grade than the one assigned originally. This is not as frivolous as it may seem: In some cases, the difference of a single point—say, from MS-65 to MS-66—can mean a difference of thousands of dollars in price.

With laser grading, there won't be the incentive for repeated submissions. Once a coin has been graded, its "fingerprint" will be on permanent file, easily retrievable from the computer's vast memory. Suppose a dealer sends a coin to a twenty-first-century grading service and it's laser graded MS-64. If later that coin is resubmitted, the laser will read the fingerprint; the computer will search its memory and identify the coin; and the grading service will know that the coin was graded once before. It also will know the grade that was assigned, and it won't change that grade.

This doesn't mean that every grading service will grade every coin the same. There will be variations from one grading service to another, just as there are today. But within each service the grading will be consistent for all coins of a given series—all Morgan dollars, for example, or all Saint-Gaudens double eagles. The variations will result from the differing attitudes and standards of the people who operate the services. If John Albanese of the Numismatic Guaranty Corporation were to input his personal grading criteria into a computer guiding a laser grading machine, a certain set of standards would be fixed in its memory. If David Hall of the Professional Coin Grading Service were to input *his* criteria into a computer, the resultant laser grading would be different. And if Jim Halperin of the Numismatic Certification Institute input *his* criteria, a third set of grading standards would result.

Perhaps someday (a day that may be a lot closer than many believe, according to one reliable source), Albanese, Hall, Halperin, and other highly knowledgeable graders will program a computer (or series of computers) with everything they know about grading: their life's experience. Grading then could become a timeless process. If these individuals decided to take a hiatus from the coin field or even to retire permanently, their knowledge would still be available to benefit and guide future generations of collectors and investors.

The time is fast approaching when laser technology and computer grading will be not just the stuff of speculation but everyday facts of life. I can foresee a time in the *very* near future, in fact, when grading services will use laser technology on at least a limited basis to confirm their consistency. So keep an open mind when you hear people say that grading is an art, not a science. Today's art may be tomorrow's science.

Chapter
5

HOW TO GRADE
RARE COINS

From your perspective as a buyer or seller, the most important part of the grading spectrum is the grading of Mint-State coins—coins that have not passed from hand to hand to hand, have not circulated, and have no wear on their very highest points. The difference in price in these "upper-end" coins is tremendous; you literally *can't afford not to know how to grade these coins.*

The following grading descriptions appear in the second edition of my book, *The Coin Collector's Survival Manual* (Prentice-Hall Press/ Simon & Schuster, Inc., 1988). The accompanying photographs, shown here for the first time, should demystify the grade assignation process.

The definitions here refer strictly to business-strike coins, although the use of the numbers has been extended to Proofs, also. The fact that a coin in the Mint-State category should possess no wear has not been reiterated, so please remember *always* to carefully inspect a coin's highest points, no matter how high a grade it's purported to be in.

Mint State-70. An MS-70 coin must be absolutely perfect in every respect.

An MS-70 must have full, radiant, dynamic luster; dramatic, breathtaking, and universally beautiful eye-appeal; and no imperfections or flaws whatsoever (that includes the entire coin: obverse, reverse, edge, and rims).

Coins in the perfect classification must be fully struck, for anything less than a full strike would cause the coin to possess less-than-perfect aesthetic appeal.

Coins classified as MS-70 cannot possess any mint-made imperfections. This, too, would cause the coin to possess less-than-perfect aesthetic appeal.

Mint State-69. The MS-69 designation is reserved for perfection's threshold examples of the first magnitude.

Coins graded MS-69 must have no visible imperfections on either obverse or reverse under a 10-power glass.* However, under higher-power magnification, some flaws might become obvious. Under 10-power magnification, one or two nearly imperceptible rim flaws might be visible.

The MS-69 designation can be used only if the coin has full and vibrant luster and, in general, if it has all the characteristics of the MS-70, with the exception mentioned.

Mint State-68. A coin graded MS-68 must appear perfect under 10-power magnification, with the exception of a nearly imperceptible scratch, nick, or flaw which appears in a non-grade-sensitive area (e.g., the hair).

Upon first glance, an MS-68 will appear to be perfect; and even some experts might have trouble finding the imperfection.

The MS-68, like the MS-69, may show some nearly imperceptible rim flaws under a 10-power glass.

The overall eye-appeal must be dramatic and awe-inspiring.

Dealer Steve Ivy contends that the difference in price between an MS-68 and an MS-69 is usually about 20 percent.

Mint State-67. An MS-67 is a wonder coin that you need not wonder about. Its luster, strike, and meticulously preserved surfaces leave the viewer in a state of euphoria. Intense luster usually emanates from immaculate surfaces.

There is room for a detraction or two visible with a 5-power glass. MS-67 examples are truly elusive ones. Even though there now exist grades of MS-68 and MS-69, you really can't expect better than MS-67.

Mint State-66. The MS-66 coin is in equally as high a level of preservation as its MS-65 counterpart, except that it possesses some unusually superior or MS-67 characteristic.

A coin that has the surfaces of an MS-67, but has the mint luster of an MS-65 might be deserving of the MS-66 grade.

Mint State-65. There is some agreement among dealers that the ANA's definition of Mint-State 67 in *Official ANA Grading Standards for United States Coins* (Western Publishing Company, Inc., 1987) is the proper definition for Mint-State 65.

An MS-65 coin should be "virtually flawless but with very minor imperfections" (the description that ANA has used for MS-67).

*A Bausch & Lomb hasting triplet should be used as the standard in discussions of magnification power. The claims of some brands of magnification power are exaggerated. For example, an unreliable magnifying glass manufacturer might represent a certain magnifying glass to be 10-power, when the glass is only 7-power.

The MS-65 coin cannot be lackluster or weakly struck. If either characteristic exists, the marketplace has dictated that a downgrading to 64 be considered.

An MS-65 cannot have excessive nicks, scratches, marks, or flaws of any kind. But it is by no means a perfect coin; and there is room for minor detraction visible with a 5-power glass.

An MS-65 should have an overall pleasing appearance, free from marks and rich with luster and detail.

Mint State-64. In *Rare Coin Investment Strategy* (Prentice Hall Press/Simon & Schuster, Inc., 1986), I define MS-64, in part, as follows: A cursory glance at a coin deserving this grade would indicate that a grade of MS-65 is in order.

Close inspection of the MS-64 reveals a detracting overall characteristic, such as the lack of full mint bloom or too many surface marks.

What sets the MS-64 coin apart from its MS-63 counterpart is its nearly convincing claim to MS-65.

The grade of MS-64 has become an important *marketplace* grade. The marketplace has determined that if an MS-65 of a certain coin is valued at, say, $10,000, but its MS-63 counterpart is only worth $500, then the coin valued at $3,000 has to be graded MS-64.

The MS-64 coin can be lightly fingerprinted or exhibit weakness of its strike in important areas.

The MS-64 coin is indisputably better than an MS-63 but not deserving of the MS-65 grade and, usually, the accompanying high MS-65 price.

Mint State-63. An MS-63 will often have claims to 65, except there are noticeable marks visible to the unaided eye.

An MS-63 may have toning that is not universally appealing and be nearly fully struck, but, perhaps, not 100 percent fully struck.

MS-63s are often found with fingerprints whose darkening are of varying degrees.

Copper and nickel coins which grade MS-63 will often be spotted with dark toning areas which penetrate the surface of the coin. If these spots are deemed too detracting, a downgrading to MS-62 might be necessary.

Mint State-62. An MS-62 is an above-average Mint-State example. It is a coin which does not overwhelm the viewer with scratches, abrasions, and other detractions.

Coins in this category possess all of the characteristics of their 63 counterparts, except that they lack—and only slightly—quality of surface or mint bloom.

Mint State-61. A Mint State-61 coin must have no wear on its highest points. It must not have been circulated.

Scratches, abrasions, and other imperfections will appear on coins of this classification.

The primary distinction of the MS-61 which separates it from its MS-60 counterpart is the 61's lack of that primary detracting gash or imperfection in the grade-sensitive area.

Although the MS-61 might have numerous and multiple marks, imperfections, and other flaws, none will be of such a magnitude that it will become a primary focus of the coin; and the MS-61 will not nearly qualify for the status of "damaged."

An MS-61 can be lackluster or dull as well as have unattractive toning.

Mint State-60. A Mint State-60 coin must have no wear on its highest points. It must not have circulated.

The MS-60 example will come just short of being classified as a damaged coin.

Scratches, abrasions, imperfections visible to the unaided eye, and major detractions will characterize coins of this grade.

Large coins, such as silver dollars and double eagles, will have, in addition to the multiplicity of scratches and nicks, at least one major gash, flaw, or other imperfection in grade-sensitive areas (e.g., Ms. Liberty's cheek on the Morgan dollar).

Copper and nickel coins of this grade, in addition to the surface imperfections, might have problems of corrosive porosity that deeply penetrate the surface.

An MS-60 can be lackluster or dull, as well as have unattractive toning.

NOTE: Occasionally, an MS-60 will be found without that one particularly detracting flaw, but the coin will possess multiple horrendous flaws, pits, and deep scratches.

About Uncirculated-58. An AU-58 coin must appear Mint State at first glance.

Upon close examination, light friction will be visible on the highest points. (Imagine a perspiration-soaked thumb rubbing the coin; and envision the aftermath.)

The AU-58 would ordinarily qualify for the MS-63 grade. However, the light rubbing would remove it from technically being classified as Mint State.

Sometimes, these coins trade among dealers at the MS-63 price (or close to it) because of the overall aesthetic quality of the coin.

A PHOTOGRAPHIC GUIDE TO PRECISION GRADING

If your coin purchases are for trading, you should buy only coins graded by grading services listed in the *Certified Coin Dealer Newsletter*. THERE ARE NO EXCEPTIONS TO THIS RULE. EVEN THOUGH SOME OTHER COINS MIGHT BE GRADED CORRECTLY BY AN UNKNOWN SERVICE, USE ONLY THE SERVICES LISTED IN THE CCDN. OTHERWISE, YOUR INVESTMENT'S LIQUIDITY COULD BE JEOPARDIZED.

Morgan Dollars

Let's start by looking at Morgan dollars. The 1880-S illustrated in Figure 5-1 trades as an MS-66. The single tiny mark on Miss Liberty's cheek, between her nose and lips, keeps this coin from being assigned the MS-67 grade.

Figure 5-2 shows another 1880-S Morgan dollar, this one grading MS-65. Here a detraction appears in the same area as in this coin's MS-66 counterpart. The photographic lighting slightly exaggerates this imperfection, though. Notice the uninterrupted luster and freedom from flaws.

Figure 5-1. MS-66 1880-S Morgan dollar. (Courtesy of the Museum of the American Numismatic Association)

Figure 5-2. MS-65 1880-S Morgan dollar. The lighting exaggerates the tiny facial nick. (Courtesy of the Museum of the American Numismatic Association)

Figure 5-3. MS-64 1880-S Morgan dollar. This coin grades MS-64 under the standards of PCGS and NGC, but NCI might well grade this piece MS-65. (Courtesy of the Museum of the American Numismatic Association)

Figure 5-4. MS-63 1881-S Morgan dollar. (Courtesy of the Museum of the American Numismatic Association)

The 1880-S Morgan dollar illustrated in Figure 5-3 also displays stunning, satiny luster. However, various interruptions of the frost remove it from the MS-65 category. This coin really is a lovely MS-64, though; and the whitened high points are *not* wear, merely breaks in the frost.

The 1881-S Morgan dollar grading MS-63 (Figure 5-4) possesses more scratches and abrasions than the coins that are assigned higher grades. But the 1881-S graded MS-62 (Figure 5-5) has scattered imperfections, thus preventing even the MS-63 grade. However, by far the most hideous looking coin of the group is the coin assigned MS-60 (Figure 5-6)—the minimum Mint State grade.

Walking Liberty Half Dollars

Another popularly traded coin type is the Walking Liberty half dollar. In Figure 5-7, a 1947 Walking Liberty half dollar grading MS-65 is displayed. Notice the lovely lustrous surfaces and lack of any significant marks. The 1939 specimen (Figure 5-8) is of nearly equal beauty except for a few minor detractions. The most obvious flaw is the hit on the leg. The 1946 example (Figure 5-9) grades MS-63 and has marks visible to the unaided eye in the right obverse field.

Figure 5-5. MS-62 1881-S Morgan dollar. (Courtesy of the Museum of the American Numismatic Association)

Figure 5-6. MS-60 1897 Morgan dollar. This most unattractive piece earns the minimum grade of Mint State. (Courtesy of the Museum of the American Numismatic Association)

Figure 5-7. MS-65 1947 Walking Liberty half dollar. Lovely, satiny luster on peerless surfaces. (Courtesy of the Museum of the American Numismatic Association)

Figure 5-8. MS-64 1939 Walking Liberty half dollar. PCGS and NGC would assign the MS-64 grade to this coin. (Courtesy of the Museum of the American Numismatic Association)

Figure 5-9. MS-63 1946 Walking Liberty half dollar. (Courtesy of the Museum of the American Numismatic Association)

Figure 5-10. MS-64 1928 Saint-Gaudens double eagle. Both PCGS and NGC would opt for the MS-64 grade, but NCI might assign it MS-65. (Courtesy of the Museum of the American Numismatic Association)

Figure 5-11. MS-63 1924 Saint-Gaudens double eagle. (Courtesy of the Museum of the American Numismatic Association)

Figure 5-12. MS-62 1923 Saint-Gaudens double eagle. (Courtesy of the Museum of the American Numismatic Association)

Saint-Gaudens Double Eagles

The Saint-Gaudens double eagle enjoys great popularity, but many persons are confused about how to grade this series. The "Saint" grading MS-64 (Figure 5-10) displays attractive luster but possesses too many surface abrasions to qualify for the MS-65 grade. The MS-63 example (Figure 5-11) is not nearly as lustrous and displays marks more prominent and deeper than its MS-64 counterpart. The MS-62 Saint (Figure 5-12) is heavily abraded, but it's not a borderline problem coin like the MS-60 Morgan dollar displayed earlier (Fig. 5-6). The 1923 Saint (Figure 5-13) has light wear on its highest points and grades About Uncirculated-55.

Liberty Head Double Eagles

The Liberty Head double eagle is another heavily traded coin type. But despite these coins' large size, many people have difficulty grading them. The temptation is great to grade many of these coins MS-64 or above, especially since gold retains its original luster. But a great number of them deserve only MS-63 or lower grades. In fact NGC and PCGS have not assigned the MS-65 grade to very many Liberty Heads.

Figure 5-13. AU-55 1923 Saint-Gaudens double eagle. This coin has passed from hand to hand and has circulated. (Courtesy of the Museum of the American Numismatic Association)

Figure 5-14. MS-63 Liberty Head double eagle. PCGS and NCG grade very few coins of this type MS-65, although MS-64s are available. (Courtesy of the Museum of the American Numismatic Association)

Figure 5-15. MS-62 1904 Liberty Head double eagle. (Courtesy of the Museum of the American Numismatic Association)

Figure 5-16. Low-end MS-61 Liberty Head double eagle. NGC's internal grading would read "MS-61C." (Courtesy of the Museum of the American Numismatic Association)

The 1900 $20 Liberty graded MS-63 (Figure 5-14) has great luster and eye appeal but is marred by abrasions on the neck. The 1904 $20 Liberty assigned the grade of MS-62 (Figure 5-15) has a prominent scratch on the cheek, a grade-sensitive area. The 1907 $20 Liberty (Figure 5-16) is not a borderline problem coin but is substantially abraded and just makes the MS-61 grade, although the MS-60 designation is tempting.

How to Identify a Circulated Coin

Locating wear on a coin's high points requires a pinpoint light source and your ability to tilt and rotate the coin. The close-up of the Liberty Seated figure (Figure 5-17) reveals signs of this coin having passed from hand to hand. Examine the arm, knees, and breasts.

THE MOST DIFFICULT COINS TO GRADE

I authored the following article, which appeared in *NGC News*, NGC's in-house dealer-only newsletter.

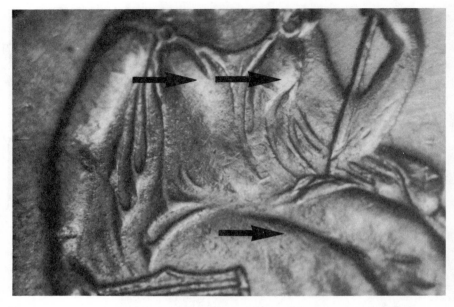

Figure 5-17. Lightly circulated Liberty Seated figure. (Photo courtesy Bill Fivaz)

The "Tough 7"—the Coin Types Most Difficult to Grade

At NGC, all coins submitted for grading are treated equally. By their very nature, though, some coins are harder to grade than others.

Based on my experiences as an NGC grader, I've compiled a list of what might be called the "Tough 7"—the seven coin types that I have found most difficult to grade.

I'd like to extend special thanks to Maurice Rosen, a fellow NGC grader, and John Albanese, NGC's founder and president, both of whom lent a helpful ear while I was preparing this article.

(1) Line Coins.

"Line coins" are coins that qualify to be graded, say, either MS-64A or MS-65C. Either grade would be fair—but with many such coins, traders have paid a price commensurate with the lower grade and are hoping to receive the higher grade from NGC.

On business strikes, it usually comes down to the quality of the surfaces; this is what determines whether a line coin gets the higher grade—although impaired luster can reduce the coin's chances for the next grade.

(2) Law-Breakers.

If you were to assign a technical grade of MS-67/64 to a coin, any old-timer would tell you that the overall grade would have to be MS-64, for it used to be conventional wisdom that a coin couldn't be assigned an overall grade that was higher than the lowest grade of any one side.

Wrong! The overall grade might well be MS-65, since the obverse can "carry" a coin. But if it were the other way around—an MS-64/67—the final grade probably *would* be MS-64.

An MS-65/65 coin with some weakness of strike might be graded MS-64—or lower—at NGC to reflect marketplace standards. NGC grades in such a way that coins can be traded sight-unseen, and a weakly struck coin graded MS-65 could restrict the fluidity of the system.

(3) Incuse-Design Gold.

Coins with incuse designs are difficult enough to grade. With gold coins, this problem is compounded. Gold retains its mint luster indefinitely, and gold coins with incuse designs—like the Indian $5 and $2½—have characteristics that make it hard to tell whether or not there is wear on the high points.

(4) Coins with Sensational Eye Appeal.

If you have a magnificent Barber quarter—one with a cameo contrast between its watery fields and snow-white devices—but the coin has a tiny hit on the *obverse*, can you still grade it Proof-65? Probably. Personally, I don't like seeing the 65 grade assigned to such coins, but it's the consensus that rules.

If you have a proof Seated Liberty half dollar with light hairlines that make it a technical 63A, can phenomenal toning make it a 64? Yes, as long as the eye appeal isn't counted for more than ¼ of a point.

(5) Rare Dates.

If you come across a shimmering proof 1936 Walking Liberty half dollar and it is identical *in every respect* to 50 1942 Walking Liberty halves which were just graded Proof-64, does the 64 grade apply to the 1936, as well? If the '36 is a technical 64A, compensation for the date by ¼ of a point is acceptable. Thus, the Proof-65 designation is acceptable.

Compensation for rarity is satisfactory, as long as you don't go overboard and upgrade a technical MS-62 coin to MS-65.

(6) Small Coins.

Graders spend more time examining small coins than any other kind. We have to be extremely careful about looking for imperfections, and even have to exercise more care in holding these coins. This is not to say that larger coins don't get complete consideration; it's just that smaller coins require closer scrutiny.

A tiny mark on a silver three-cent piece is weighted differently from a mark of the same size on a Morgan dollar. The three-cent silver is tiny *itself*, and even a *tiny* mark can be a considerable detraction.

(7) Problem Coins.

Coins with PVC [polyvinyl chloride] on them, or coins with imperfections, or coins that are bent or tampered with—these are problem, or "no-grade," coins.

Sometimes, however, it becomes a problem to determine whether a coin is, in fact, a no-grade—or whether it simply should have its grade lowered to reflect the imperfection.

For example, a Morgan dollar which under normal circumstances would grade MS-64 might be assigned a grade of MS-62 or MS-63 because of a rather eye-catching ding on its rim. But a Walking Liberty half dollar which normally would grade MS-67 but has a deep gouge on the obverse —a gouge so deep that it nearly travels through to the other side—would be no-graded.

Some coins are, indeed, tougher to grade than others. But the grading process at NGC is designed to maximize the use of *independent*, arm's-length grading to assure equitable grading opinions for everyone.

It may be tough, but it's certainly fair!

Chapter

6

"INSIDER TRADING"
OF RARE COINS

Honest, if you buy this coin I promise I'll bid that coin to three times the level that it's listed on the sheet for now. It's the only one known. I can bid it up to any level you want. What level would you like me to bid it up to?

*Well-known market-maker with a coin
listed in a certified coin population
report as the only one graded for that grade.*

During my years as a coin trader, I've witnessed many examples of insider trading and observed very closely the way that information is disseminated—its ethical use, unethical use, and uneven distribution in this field.

RARE COIN INSIDER TRADING

Just what *is* rare coin insider trading? Outsiders perceive it as the manipulation of the coin market for material gain by people who take advantage of their knowledge of inside information, knowledge not available to the general coin-buying public. In point of fact, however, "insider trading" is a nebulous term not only in the coin market, but also in the securities industry. There is no universally accepted or court-sanctioned definition for Wall Street insider trading, so no one should expect a specific definition for rare coin insider trading either.

A number of prominent coin dealers capitalize on their knowledge of insider information to make advantageous deals. In fact this goes on so routinely that even Ivan Boesky would be impressed. The methods of market manipulation in this field are almost endless. Yet up to now few investors have tapped the profit potential inherent in this freewheeling situation.

The government doesn't regulate the coin market; people in this field don't have government agencies monitoring their day-to-day activities. For this reason, and because the coin industry is relatively small in size, savvy investors can put themselves in the same advantageous position—the same insider position—as major dealers.

For example, an investor can purchase a coin that he or she knows is the only one of its kind to which a certain grade has been assigned by a given grading service, and then make arrangements to have a dealer bid up the value of that coin.

An investor can get friendly with a dealer and learn from that contact, on a confidential basis, that five rare coins of a certain type and date were submitted by the dealer for grading and will be coming onto the market soon.

INSIDER INFORMATION AND RARE COINS

Insider information is used routinely, of course, in many different aspects of daily life. And it's used in ways that are legal and ways that are not.

Suppose your local congresswoman knows that certain property will soon be the site of a major development, and suppose she tips off her cousin, who then makes an investment in the area. That's leakage of insider information.

Suppose the chairman of the Federal Reserve Board is drafting a statement on interest rates that's likely to have a dramatic effect on the securities industry. Any number of his colleagues or associates might conceivably be aware of what he's preparing to say, and this insider information might enable them to make—or advise their friends to make—some highly lucrative deals.

Although this kind of insider information permeates the coin field, I don't believe it to be a major problem. There are mechanisms in place that will limit to a great degree, or even prevent, insider trades. And as I have noted, this industry is relatively small; insider information doesn't remain secret very long.

With that said, I must point out that there *are* certain types of insider information that have put some people at a tremendous advantage in the coin field and have left others at a great disadvantage.

Selling Off Right Before a Massive Downturn

We saw a good example of this phenomenon in July 1988, when coin dealers at the annual convention of the American Numismatic Association were stunned by the announcement that coins supposedly certified by the Professional Coin Grading Service had turned up in counterfeit plastic slabs. Apparently some dealers learned of the situation before the announcement was made—and based on this information, gained through insider contacts, they immediately sold many of their PCGS-graded coins. Some of the coins they sold were in counterfeit slabs and, like virtually all the coins of this type, these were overgraded and therefore overpriced. But even the coins in genuine slabs were worth substantially less following the announcement, because the scandal shook market confidence (at least for a short time) in PCGS coins as a whole. This was a clear instance where knowledge of insider information helped certain dealers significantly.

Price Manipulation

Another common use of insider information in the coin market is price manipulation. Often this involves coins with very low populations, coins that have been graded in very small quantities in a given grade by a particular grading service.

From the insider's standpoint, the ideal population is *one*. The chances for price manipulation are maximized when a dealer owns the only coin of a certain kind to which a given grade has been assigned. This information can be obtained by studying the population reports issued by the major grading services. So long as the dealer is certain that no other coins of that type and that grade are available, he or she can bid up the price of that coin on the teletype system. (If another example happened to exist, the dealer would be obliged to purchase it at his or her bid price if the coin's owner belonged to the same trading network and chose to accept the bid.)

Suppose this coin is listed initially at $2,500 in the *Certified Coin Dealer Newsletter* or Blue Sheet, the standard weekly price guide for coins that have been independently certified. And suppose the dealer offers progressively higher bids, upping the ante to $5,000, to $6,000, and finally to $7,000. After $7,000 has been offered for several weeks, the publishers of the Blue Sheet may raise the coin's listed price from $2,500 to $7,000. At that point the dealer will sell it to someone who is unaware of what has been going on, perhaps another dealer unschooled in the ways of such games or perhaps to an unsuspecting collector or investor. The dealer may even offer a "discount": With the Blue Sheet price at $7,000, maybe the coin will be offered for "just" $6,000. And then, when the dealer stops bidding $7,000 for the coin and has sold it for $6,000, its price will go back down to where it was before and where it belongs: $2,500.

The Inner Circle

Collectors and investors can avoid this type of manipulation by doing business with dealers who are not only honorable, but also members of the coin market's inner circle—that is, dealers who know the ins and outs of population reports and will not themselves fall victim to this kind of scam.

Keep in mind that dealers themselves can be victimized if they don't stay fully informed on all the factors involved in determining the value of a coin. If they don't pay close attention to population reports, they too can be deceived by price lists where the value reflects manipulation rather than real demand. They may think they're getting a bargain when someone comes up to their table at a show and offers them such a coin at a price well below the Blue Sheet level. And they'll pass this "bargain" on to a customer, not because they too are trying to take advantage of someone, but because they themselves aren't very knowledgeable.

In many cases it is wise to do business only with someone who is an authorized dealer of NGC or PCGS or both. On request, both organizations will provide a current list of their authorized dealers.

Collectors, investors, and dealers, too, should watch closely for signs of volatility in any specific area of the market. This is especially true of areas where few coins have been certified and where, for that reason, one dealer can control a complete population. Great volatility in any particular area doesn't always mean that coins are being traded rapidly; it may mean that a dealer has manipulated that portion of the marketplace—manipulated it upward and then sold the specific coin or coins, causing bid levels to drop precipitously.

PCGS has the following anti-self-interest policy posted in its grading room.

GRADERS !!!!
PCGS ANTI-SELF-INTEREST POLICY

PCGS graders *cannot* do any of the following:

1. Grade their own coins.
2. Grade coins they submit for clients or other dealers.

3. Grade coins they have a financial interest in (split-profit deals, etc.)
4. Verify any of the above coins.
5. Participate in *any* discussion whatsoever—inside or outside of the grading room—either before, during or after the coins are in the grading process.

FIDUCIARY RESPONSIBILITY

PCGS graders *cannot* use any information obtained inside the grading room before the information is available in the general market place. More specifically graders cannot do any of the following:

1. Buy coins from a dealer based on information obtained in the grading room. If a grader finds out who a coin or group of coins belongs to while the coins are in the grading process, that grader cannot contact the submitting dealer for the purpose of purchasing the coins (or obtaining first shot, etc.) until *10 days after* the dealer has received his coins back from PCGS.
2. Sell or buy coins and/or coin positions based on information obtained in the grading room.

Any grader who has one substantiated violation of item #1 or who shows a consistent pattern of violating item #2 will be immediately terminated.

THE BAD OLD DAYS

In the early 1980s we witnessed market practices that were far less ethical than those we have today. Dealers at that time often drove up bid levels in the *Coin Dealer Newsletter* or Grey Sheet, the standard weekly price guide for all U.S. coins. They did this on a constant basis. And they didn't have to concern themselves with rules and regulations requiring them to buy such coins if those coins were offered.

Circa-1980 dealers could take a coin listed for $400 in the *Coin Dealer Newsletter*, bid $600, $700, $1,000—and keep bidding higher and higher amounts on the teletype system. In those days they had no real obligation to purchase any coins that people sent; coins were not certified then, and we didn't have a sight-unseen system. The dealers would simply send the coins back, saying they didn't meet their high grading standards.

Dealer promotions and price manipulation played a big part in the marketplace confusion over grading standards. In driving up prices, dealers were looking to make bigger profits on coins they already had; they had no interest in buying such coins from anyone else. Thus, as people sent them coins, these dealers just shipped them right back. A number of people would then submit coins of the next higher grade, since the artificially inflated price levels were high enough to justify selling even these at the quoted bids. Again the dealers would send the coins back. In some cases dealers were offering to buy coins graded MS-65 at a certain price, and people were sending them coins graded as high as MS-67; even then the coins were returned.

Today's Improved Market

Although manipulation does occur today, it's much more difficult to drive up price-guide levels—especially those of certified coins, since dealers must be willing to buy any coins that are offered. This discourages the unscrupulous from trying to manipulate prices of the more common certified coins, where hundreds or even thousands of examples may exist.

As growing numbers of coins are certified, population reports will list far fewer one-of-a-kind coins. Already the number is dwindling, even among super-grade coins bearing the very high MS and proof numbers that grading services assign quite sparingly. In most cases enough coins are available to protect against price manipulation. Today super-grade commemorative coins appear to offer the best opportunities for manipulators—and the greatest risk for potential victims— because these coins exist in very limited numbers in certified grades of MS-66 and above.

Clearly the coin market doesn't have a perfect trading system. But in a world where no system is completely perfect, today's system is certainly far better than yesterday's.

PROMOTIONS OF COINS IN NEWSLETTERS

Newsletters serve as yet another way to promote coins and influence their prices. Some mass-market coin dealers publish their own newsletters and use them on a regular basis to promote the coins they have for sale.

Often it's possible to anticipate such promotions—even without being a true market insider—simply by analyzing which coins these dealers have promoted in the past.

When dealers send newsletters to thousands upon thousands of collectors and investors, obviously they can't use them to promote coins of which just three examples, or even 300, are known. They have to select coins that exist in more promotable numbers. Among the series that combine sufficient numbers with broad-based popularity are Morgan silver dollars, Saint-Gaudens double eagles, and commemoratives.

Dealers stage promotions for these and other popular coins on a regular, systematic basis. They may promote Saint-Gaudens double eagles one month, Morgan dollars the next month, and commemoratives the month after that. If you haven't seen the Morgan dollar promoted in one of these newsletters in a while, you can be quite certain that its turn will be coming very soon. And that might be a good time to buy Morgan dollars—before the promotion hits, with all its attendant hype, and prices go up in response.

I recommend that you get on the mailing lists of all the large dealerships that publish and distribute such newsletters. Often they're quite informative and even entertaining, and they can help guide you in charting the direction of the market.

INSIDER ECONOMICS

Paul Taglione, a former principal of the now defunct New England Rare Coin Galleries, has written a number of valuable books and articles analyzing the coin market's inner workings. Taglione and his company became targets of a Federal Trade Commission lawsuit charging them with unfair or deceptive acts or practices in or affecting commerce. Despite this, and to some extent *because* of this, his insights on the market are fascinating and illuminating.

The following is an excerpt from Taglione's book, *An Investment Philosophy for the Prudent Consumer* (Numismatic Research and Service Corporation, Boston, 1986).

———————

Across the expanse of market actors currently active in the Numismatic Markets, technical numismatic knowledge and comprehension of the economics of the various Numismatic Markets is, in my view, extremely variable in depth and quality. An amazing number of market actors do not possess adequate technical knowledge of areas in which they trade. Incredibly enough, very few market actors seriously study the economics of the Numismatic Markets in which they participate. Any private numismatic investor can obtain an edge in a specialized area and, I am perfectly convinced, any private investor can obtain a general edge in even wider areas of the Numismatic Markets. **The "investment edge", as I see it, involves a wide-ranging knowledge of the economics of the area in which one wishes to invest.** A first step in obtaining this knowledge is researching and examining the supply side of an area. How many examples of this coin exist? How many come to market? Is the supply of this particular coin or class of coins inelastic to increased demand? The next step is obtaining a knowledge of the size, intensity and quality of demand. This step *must* begin at the level of the individual buyer. What sort of market actor demands and desires this coin? Does the acquisition of this coin *satisfy* a preference or does it *stimulate* a preference to acquire more coins? In my opinion, the quality of demand is much more important than its size or intensity. The size or intensity of demand can be the result of dictated preference and if quality of demand is taken to include endurance and continuity (which I take it to include), then it becomes obvious that demand which derives from dictated preference is markedly lacking in these qualities. Another step in obtaining the investment edge is investigating the parameters of price at which buyers can and do acquire material. Obviously the demand for a common coin is much more sensitive to price than is the demand for a rare coin. An investor must exercise a great deal more caution in acquiring a common coin in terms of price than is required for obtaining a rarity whose market appearance in and of itself generates a value for the acquisition opportunity. Perhaps the best investment edge of all is the recognition that the edge is complicated and varies from area to area and from time to time. Part of this recognition is an awareness that choosing the elusive and storied "right dealer" might not be an edge at all; it might be a disadvantage!

INSIGHTS FROM A LEADING INVESTMENT BANKER

One of the most brilliant coin collectors I know is a vice president at a world-famous conservative investment banking house. This numismatist holds an M.B.A. from the University of Chicago and a B.S. from the University of Pennsylvania's Wharton School of Finance. Although he spends a lot of time coordinating multibillion-dollar deals in traditional capital appreciation areas, he has carefully scrutinized and studied the investment rare coin market for over 20 years. I can personally attest to his grading ability and market timing: It's far superior to most savvy professional coin traders'. The genius of his analytical investment mind applied to the coin market's structure and direction is presented here for the first time. He has requested anonymity.

Here are my questions and his responses:

Q. What do you think about the efficiency of the rare coin marketplace?

A. Let me discuss efficiency from a couple of perspectives. Certainly, with certification, the rare coin marketplace is more efficient than it used to be, particularly for low-end coins within a given grade. However, unlike many other investments that are fungible, such as stocks or bonds, rare coins are all pretty much unique. Certain individuals in the market possess superior knowledge and skills, particularly grading skills, and can use these to make money that the average market participant cannot. In addition, subjectivity and perception can affect a coin's value because two individuals may find a given coin more or less desirable, which will affect their respective valuations. What this says is, even with the standardization of grading there will always be an opportunity to improve upon your investment returns by becoming more knowledgeable about grading. Moreover, since not all coins are certified yet, this adds yet another layer of inefficiency relating to raw coins and those not graded by PCGS or NGC.

There is also a source of inefficiency built into the marketplace because of the quality of the information flow, particularly as it relates to prices. Putting aside differences in values due to grade, eye appeal, etc., the current reporting system leaves a lot of room for uncertainty. The actual marketplace includes the electronic information/trading system called the American Numismatic Exchange, teletype networks, major coin conventions, auctions, and private transactions. The reporting is done by price guides such as the *Coin Dealer Newsletter* and *Coin World's Trends*, auction prices-realized lists, and word-of-mouth. Gathering useful information from these diverse sources and presenting it in a timely and accurate fashion is a most difficult task. To the extent that some market participants don't have the best information as to value levels (because the price guides come out only weekly or they don't have accurate values in the first place), they can be taken advantage of. Furthermore, the inefficiency is exacerbated should any manipulation take place within the reporting system.

Q. Based on your knowledge of conventional financial investments, what aspect of the rare coin field needs the greatest refinement in order for this industry to attract the greatest number of investors?

A. If you had asked me this question a few years ago, I would have said grading. But with the use of the 70-point grading system and PCGS and NGC, grading has become very much refined. I believe the area that must be improved next is the information reporting system. With values at high absolute levels and a good deal of price volatility, there must be more accurate, up-to-date information on values for the great majority of investors to be comfortable in participating in the marketplace. This means better price guides and some source of more timely information. For instance, I know that oftentimes the major coin conventions represent the truest marketplaces and best indicators of values at a given point in time. Yet it can take a couple of weeks for any price movements emanating from one of these shows to be reflected in the price guides. Some sort of electronic service that captures and distributes this information on a real-time basis would be of immense value. The practicalities of how the coin market works may prevent the realization of this, but we certainly can use some improvement.

Q. Do you feel that "insider trading" in rare coins—which presently are not regulated as securities—is fair? Why?

A. Obviously, any use of information that is not widely available for personal gain has the potential to be deemed unfair. As it relates to rare coins, there ought to be far fewer types of information that could lead to this, and these should mainly be associated with things affecting the supply of or demand for coins, technical as opposed to fundamental information. (There aren't takeovers or earnings announcements in the coin market.) For example, suppose a dealer buys a hoard of five coins, all graded the same, which doubles the known population. If he distributes them in a way that allows him to sell to others at the current high value because each purchaser doesn't know about the remainder of the hoard, most would agree that this dealer has used his trading expertise in a proper way. On the other hand, if this dealer finds out about the hoard from one of the grading services (maybe he submitted the coins on behalf of a customer) and sells a similar coin from his inventory on the wholesale market before the news of the new five coins is generally available, this is much closer to insider trading and clearly unfair.

Q. There clearly are a number of inner-circle dealers who have access to information that might help these dealers and their clients profit tremendously. Should industry leaders restrict this flow of information or attempt to release it on an equitable basis?

A. In general the more information the market has, the better. Industry leaders should develop a set of rules as to what information is appropriate to release and what is genuinely proprietary. After all, in many instances a dealer is acting on behalf of a client and is justified in withholding certain information. As long as reporting is accurate and there is no manipulation going on, it is hard to argue that dealers should be compelled to release much technical information (such as a large buyer coming into the market).

Q. Given your understanding of the working of the mechanisms in the coin market, how would this field's structure change if there was a loss of confidence?

A. It is tremendously important for the leaders in the industry to ensure that collectors and investors have confidence that the game is fair. Only then can the base of investors be broadened. Any scandal that causes a major loss of confidence, whether it comes from counterfeit holders, widespread manipulation or collusion, or other significant abuses, can irreparably damage the marketplace.

Q. When rare coins are considered as an investment, what should the coin buyer consider?

A. I believe an investor in coins should consider several things. First, *appreciation potential*, since this is the ultimate goal. Many different factors go into the rate at which a coin appreciates in value, but the key ones are the existence of a meaningful (and hopefully growing) base of collectors and investors who want to purchase coins of this type and the scarcity of a given coin. Many coins are scarce but are relatively inexpensive because they lack a meaningful demand base. Conversely, even coins that are readily available in the marketplace can experience dramatic appreciation if there is a high level of demand. Next, related to appreciation potential, is *timing*. An investor should be aware of relative values and should time his or her purchases of coins in a given category to reflect both valuation in relation to coins in other categories and valuation in relation to where in the value cycle a coin stands. The goal is to try to purchase coins that are relatively undervalued. For example, if an MS66 specimen of a given coin type tends to sell at twice the value of an MS65 and the spread narrows to 50% rather than 100%, an investor should focus on purchasing the MS66 and can reasonably expect it to outperform the MS65. Many coin series, such as Morgan and Peace Silver Dollars, Commemoratives and gold type coins, clearly move in definable cycles. An investor should try to concentrate purchases in series that are well off their peaks and relatively out-of-favor. It is virtually assured that at some point a new up cycle will begin. Third, *grading* is a critical element, meaning both the actual grade levels on which an investor concentrates as well as the confidence in the grades of coins purchased. Over the years, due to relative scarcity and a proportionately growing level of demand, higher grade coins have tended to appreciate faster than their lower grade counterparts. Unless human nature shifts, I believe this will continue. In the past, an investor had to rely on his or her own grading ability and/or that of the dealers who sold the coins. The variability in grading standards experienced in the early 1980's exposed the risks associated with grading as it related to coin values. With the advent of the major grading services, PCGS and NGC, not only can an investor be confident of a coin's grade but also he can have confidence in the standards used to grade the coin remaining stable. Fourth, *liquidity* is important for the investor. The more desirable the coin and the larger the demand base, the easier it is to sell a coin at its true value. The existence of certified coins has helped to broaden the demand base for these coins by bringing in new investors to the marketplace. It has also allowed the formation of an active market in sight-unseen coins, further enhancing liquidity. Next, I feel an investor should have *diversification* in his or her portfolio of coin investments. This will minimize the risk of missing strong performance in coin categories you don't hold. Finally, even for investors, the *esthetics* of the coins purchased can help to make the whole exercise more rewarding. An investor will often be well served in buying coins that he or she finds particularly beautiful and pleasing.

Q. What do industry leaders need to do to get rare coins on Wall Street and traded like stocks?

A. For coins to trade like stocks, there must be widely distributed real-time trading information. Presumably this would focus on generic material that trades actively, like Morgan dollars. Just as in the over-the-counter stock market, the coin trading market would be enhanced if it reported actual trades (last price) in addition to bid and ask levels. The first important step would have to be to get at least one or two major Wall Street firms to begin making markets in coins. The physical settlement of trades would have to be streamlined. It might even be possible to develop an options and futures market in coins. Because an effective coin trading department at a Wall Street firm would need an outlet to retail customers, a sales force would have to be developed. It is likely the staffing for such a department would come from experienced professionals within the coin industry.

Q. Please use your emotions: What do you *really* think of low-end certified coins? Would you buy a low-end MS-66 coin from even the best grading service?

A. I have generally found low-end coins to be undesirable. They usually make the technical grade but have some detracting feature. Oftentimes a high-end coin in the next lower grade is more desirable than the low-end coin in the higher grade. An MS-66 is generally something special, quite rare and pretty expensive. Why spend a lot of money on a low-end MS-66 when for a lot less you may get a nicer MS-65? High-end coins have better appreciation potential.

Q. Let's imagine it's the year 2000. Where will the investment coin market be? (It would be unfair to ask you for anything except a wild but educated guess.)

A. Ten or so years from now I would expect most coins on the market to be certified, whether it's by PCGS and NGC or some firm or firms that have taken their place. I hope that more individual investors, directly and through entities such as limited partnerships, will have begun to look at investing in certified rare coins as a mainstream rather than an exotic investment. Institutions such as pension funds, insurance companies, and trust departments should be investing a small portion of their funds in coins. This will represent a sizable amount of money (billions of dollars). Coins in many series grading MS-65 and up will have seen spectacular appreciation over the past decade. Their true rarity will have become apparent. An inexpensive coin will be one that sells for under $100,000. Coins grading MS-66 and up in many series will trade well into six figures. Certain low-population high-grade coins will have broken the seven-figure barrier. Looking back on prices in 1989, when many high-grade rarities sold for $5,000 to $50,000, many will wish they had taken advantage of the incredibly cheap prices available then.

Q. Are our price guides professional enough to satisfy the "prudent man" standard?

A. Today's price guides can do a lot more to improve their accuracy as to values and their timeliness. In addition, they are too easily manipulated by the deliberate placement of inaccurate information. It is probably time to inject some healthy competition into the arena, which would serve to lift the level of professionalism. At the very least the price guides should beef up their staffing to have more people monitoring the marketplace. Frequent surveys of a large number of dealers and market-makers as to both bid and ask levels and actual transactions would pick up more of the market's activity and true value levels than is currently done.

Q. You recently purchased an NGC Proof-63 coin, which one of the nation's leading coin auction firms cracked out of its holder, described glowingly as a Proof-65, and featured in a beautiful color photograph for prospective buyers to see. Was this fair?

A. Activity such as this is quite common. To the extent that a buyer of such a coin in the auction pays more than it is worth because of the higher commercial grade, there is an element of unfairness. However, the auction company clearly has a different standard of grading than NGC, and its coins are available for viewing prior to the auction. Over time this activity should wind down as more and more coins become certified by NGC and PCGS. These two services should garner the bulk of the certified market and will come to be viewed as the only type of coins to be safely purchased. As those who have purchased coins in these auctions get them certified by NGC and PCGS, it will become clear what the true grades and values are, as well as the risks of purchasing non-NGC and non-PCGS coins at auction.

Q. How has this market's inefficiency allowed savvy investors to profit?

A. By purchasing high-end certified coins at prices close to the sight-unseen levels (through a knowledge of grading), an investor can often sell these coins at a significant profit, both at auction or in a private sale and both in or out of the holder.

Q. Will a more efficient market improve or impair the informed investor's ability to profit?

A. Opportunity for abnormal profits declines as a market becomes more efficient. I doubt, however, that many of the new players in the certified market will have the ability to determine or care about high-end versus low-end. Unless these players end up with all the low-end coins and the players with grading knowledge end up with all the high-end coins, there will continue to be profit opportunities of this sort.

Q. Who is the ultimate consumer of coins? Why?

A. I believe that the conventional wisdom has been that collectors are always the ultimate consumers of coins. High prices presumably cannot be sustained unless collectors are willing to pay them. I think you can add to this demand base the collector/investor and even an outright investor. To the extent that these latter players reinvest any disposition proceeds back into coins, or other players step in to take their place, this new demand base is solid and can sustain extant price levels. Investors in coins must be willing to take the long view. If large numbers bail out when there is weakness, and if new investors don't step in when prices decline, then the conventional wisdom will hold true and prices will be effectively capped. I do not believe that this is the case.

Q. We're seeing limited partnerships becoming part of rare coin investing. How do you see this form of coin trading impacting the marketplace? What might happen after one or two funds come into the U.S. market and spend $75–100 million? What will be the end result?

A. There has been a lot of discussion about the impact of large new investment funds coming into the rare coin market. I would bet that it happens in a way and on a time schedule that is somewhat different from what everyone expects. It will probably take longer than people think. When this money does come in, the trick will be to determine what parts of the market will be affected the most. If someone tried to invest $100 million quickly in super-grade or even high-grade material, all of the available coins would be swept off the market long before a quarter of the money was invested. Clearly, material that can be bought in quantity will have to represent a large part of these funds' portfolios—things like common to better-date Morgan dollars, gold type coins, commemoratives, all grading MS-63 to MS-65. As market participants sell to the funds, they will have to reinvest the proceeds in other areas. This will drive the entire coin market higher. As prices rise on generic material, the funds will be willing to pay substantially higher prices for the occasional MS-66 that they are offered.

Q. What needs to be done to make coin investing attractive to the *average* person?

A. Better marketing, information, and public relations concerning the certified rare coin market has to occur before the average person is comfortable investing in rare coins. The awareness level of this market must increase markedly. Something like the entrance of one or two major Wall Street firms into coin trading or the tracking of certified coin values on some electronic information network such as Reuters or Telerate will have to happen. And of course all the things I mentioned earlier are important prerequisites: accurate up-to-the-minute information reporting, confidence in the integrity and fairness of the marketplace, value-added packaging of the investment, and enhanced liquidity.

Chapter
7

HOW TO BUY LOW
AND SELL HIGH

To buy coins at the lowest possible price, you must choose a method of acquisition that minimizes your risks or eliminates them altogether. To sell high, you must choose a method of sale in which the risk is assumed by somebody else: either the ultimate buyer or the dealer who is handling the transaction.

The best way to ensure that you're really buying low is to purchase an independently graded coin. At the time of this writing, you stand to do quite well if you buy a coin graded by the Numismatic Guaranty Corporation of America (NGC). NGC standards are consistent and generally quite tight. The Professional Coin Grading Service (PCGS) also has maintained rigid standards.

The best time to buy is when it appears that the market is coming apart. If you read in the *Coin Dealer Newsletter* (CDN), the popular weekly price guide of the entire coin industry, that dealers are bearish on certain coins and don't want them, then that's a good time to buy those coins yourself.

MANAGED NEWS

You've heard the old expression, "Don't believe everything you read in the papers." That applies a hundredfold to what you read in coin-market publications such as the *Coin Dealer Newsletter* and the *Certified Coin Dealer Newsletter* (CCDN), a weekly price guide for coins that have been independently graded.

To show you what I mean, I'm going to cite some headlines from issues of the *Certified Coin Dealer Newsletter* published in the late summer and fall of 1988—and I'm going to help interpret what was really going on.

First, a bit of background: The coin market developed a very significant weakness at the end of the July 1988 American Numismatic Association (ANA) convention in Cincinnati. The CCDN—traditionally slow to react to both upturns and downturns—was even slower than usual in reporting this particular slump.

Here's the succession of CCDN headlines:

- July 22, 1988: "ANA Convention Off to Roaring Success on PNG Day."
- July 29, 1988: "Gold and Walkers Take Roller-Coaster Ride at ANA." ("Walkers" are Liberty Walking half dollars, popular coins produced by the U.S. Mint from 1916 to 1947.)
- August 5, 1988: "Volatility Hits Walkers and Gold; Overall Market Remains Lively."
- August 12, 1988: "Top-Quality Type Receiving Extensive Measure of This Week's Advances." ("Type" refers to a method of collecting in which a person acquires one coin from every different series, rather than every coin from just one series.)
- August 19, 1988: "Bidding Activity Slows, But Market Generally Steady." In my opinion, the market had actually collapsed by August 19. Apparently however, the *Certified Coin Dealer Newsletter* was giving dealers the opportunity to cash out their positions; the fact that investors subscribe to the CCDN may explain why its publishers didn't want to create a panic.
- August 26, 1988: By this time there was very little trading; the bottom had fallen out and coins were trading substantially below the levels in the CCDN. But on August 26, this was the headline: "Market Mostly Upbeat; Some Corrections Found."
- September 2, 1988: Now the CCDN had no choice but to acknowledge that a correction—or rather, a substantial downward adjustment—was occurring in many areas. The headline: "Certified Market Lively Despite Weakness in Obvious Areas."
- September 9, 1988: "Rare Coin Industry Exhibiting Reforms Which Indicate Long-Range Progress."
- September 16, 1988: "Dealers Feel Selectivity Is Responsible for Current Mixed Market." The market wasn't really all that mixed. The only things that were mixed were the percentage decreases that coins were experiencing in actuality.
- September 23, 1988: "Type Market Continues Displaying Upward Support."

- September 30, 1988: "Lower Bids Create Buying Opportunities for Ready Buyers."

The *Certified Coin Dealer Newsletter* is not *The Wall Street Journal*. By tossing around these euphemistic phrases, the editors clearly were appeasing their coin dealer readers as well as the marketplace as a whole. On occasion, a slight weakness reported promptly can lead to rapid deterioration of the market. If such a weakness goes unreported, the market often strengthens on its own, and losses are minimized. This is a sensitive marketplace.

But as the 1988 market skid continued, pressure on CCDN became too intense. The publishers could no longer dance around the situation; they just had to say it.

- October 7, 1988: "Lower Buys and Discounted Sells Cause Major Market Correction." And people, of course, could see this "major correction" in the value listings.
- October 14, 1988: "Certified Market Softens Further; Sight-Seen Current Trend."
- October 21, 1988: "Spreads Widen Between Sight-Unseen and Sight-Seen." By this time, there were virtually no sight-unseen bids on the ANE system or the Teletrade system, and people selling on sight were asking more for their coins.
- October 28, 1988: "Commems and Dollars Show Some Improvement."
- November 4, 1988: "Dollars Rebounding; Dealers Hopeful Slide Is Over."
- November 18, 1988: "Sight-Seen Auction Action Accentuates Slabbed Sales."

Later that month the market picked up a little bit, and CCDN was quick to pounce on the upturn.

- November 25, 1988: "Certified Coin Market Strengthens in All Areas."

Real Sales, Real Prices

The moral of all this is that people should read between the lines. If you follow this type of publication and you see it trying valiantly to be upbeat, *pay attention to the trend of the market*, not to what some editor is saying. Remember, these publications do not determine how much coins are worth! The values are determined on the bourse floor, where the coins are traded; it's the actual transaction price in every single case that determines how much a coin is worth.

If the *Certified Coin Dealer Newsletter* (see Figures 7-1 and 7-2) reports that a certain type of coin is worth $11,000, and 30 examples like it are trading on the bourse floor for $20,000, how much is that coin really worth? If it's trading for $20,000, that's what it's worth! Weekly price guides can be thrown away the day they're issued, because literally that very day they are out of date. Up-to-the-minute bids for sight-unseen coins are available on the ANE system, on the Teletrade system, and on bourse floors throughout the nation. Don't make the mistake of putting too much emphasis on valuation listings.

Just as these publications are slow to react when the market is in a downward phase, they're often slow to react when the market is headed upward. Again you have to read between the lines, as well as ON the lines, to see whether the prices are followed by plus or minus signs.

If you see a lot of minus signs accompanied by a very hopeful headline—say, "Dealers Optimistic That Decline Will End Soon"— chances are good that you're still in a decline phase; the market is still going down.

HOW TO MINIMIZE ACQUISITION COSTS

When the market is at or near the low, as reflected in the *Certified Coin Dealer Newsletter* or the regular *Coin Dealer Newsletter*, often you can buy coins at a discount—that is, at a price below what the newsletters indicate. That's when you're in your ideal acquisition phase.

In many cases dealers may be willing to tell you how much they paid for a particular coin (and again I urge you to buy only certified coins). If so, you may be able to negotiate an advantageous price.

It's risky to buy uncertified coins at auction. You may find yourself buying into a trap. You may be buying a coin that was graded only Proof-63 or Proof-62 by a certification service, but then was broken out of its plastic holder and put into the auction as a Proof-65.

Time after time after time, I serve as a consultant to institutions and individuals who have coins that were "no-graded" by NGC or PCGS, coins with defects so serious that they couldn't be certified and encapsulated. Yet many leading auction houses (the finest in the nation, in some instances) are willing to take these coins and put them in their sales and give them glowing descriptions.

MORGAN DOLLARS

PCGS DMPL and NGC DPL Bids are for fully Deep Mirror Prooflike coins. Bids for PCGS PL and NGC PL dollars (semi-prooflike or one-sided PL) will be listed monthly in a supplemental insert. CDN *(Greysheet)* Bids have always represented fully, deep mirror prooflike specimens.

	MS61	MS62	MS63	MS63 DMPL	MS64	MS64 DMPL	MS65	MS65 DMPL	MS66	MS67
						P C G S				
1878 8TF	37	60	100	195	720	1,100	2,365	5,200	7,500	14,000
1878 7/8TF	45	65	116	230	1,600 +	3,025	8,500	9,600	22,500	
1878 7TF	35	45	95	205 −	310	630 +	2,220	4,500	6,900 −	11,000
1878 7TF (Rev. 79)	35	42	130	220	530	950 +	4,600	11,000	11,000 −	21,000
1878 CC	65	70 +	126	265	450	690	2,660	5,000 +	5,315 +	10,750
1878 S	24	30	50	125	130 +	300 +	660 +	4,000 +	3,375 +	8,250
1879	24	25	80	150	435 +	640 +	2,535	6,115	9,000	
1879 CC	800 +	1,110 +	2,210	3,100	4,795	7,000 +	17,250	NB	31,600 +	55,000
1879 CC Capped Die	700 +	910	1,400	4,200	7,195	17,500	16,600	NB	22,000 −	27,000
1879 O	29	35	200	325	650	1,250	4,995 +	11,500	8,500	24,000
1879 S (Rev. 78)	135 −	210	410	800	1,920	2,750 +	14,650	16,600	21,000	41,000
1879 S	25	30 +	45	120	100	225 +	328	1,325	800 +	2,635
1880	24	25	72	225	465 +	630 +	2,610 +	9,000 +	5,915	13,750
1880 CC	125 −	130	186	315	330	650	1,550	3,850 +	5,315	9,700
1880 O	25	38 +	255	355 +	2,300	4,125 +	22,500	NB	45,000	70,000
1880 S	24	27	45	120 +	102	225 +	328	1,200 +	800 +	2,635
1881	24	25	72	175	400	750	2,400 +	7,000 +	5,200	10,600
1881 CC	122	140	190	360	355	540	880 +	3,200 +	3,150	7,550
1881 O	24	25	80	145	395 +	660 +	2,610 +	7,000	6,600	16,750
1881 S	24	27 +	45	120 +	102	225 +	328	1,250 +	785	2,550
1882	24	25 +	60	125	250 +	360 +	1,200	5,000 +	4,015	10,000
1882 CC	61	80	107	230	190	340 +	815 +	1,950	2,900 +	13,250
1882 O	24	25	80	135 +	400 +	660 +	2,700 +	9,000 +	5,775	12,600
1882 S	24	31	45	125 +	102	225 +	328 +	2,150	925	3,000
1883	24	25	46	125 +	102 +	300	565 +	2,600 +	1,950	4,750
1883 CC	70	75	110	170 −	180	320	635	1,700	2,850 +	9,250
1883 O	24	25 +	45	125	105 +	275	475 +	2,200	2,400	10,750
1883 S	275	430	1,300	1,700	5,000	NB	22,000	NB	44,000 +	70,000
1884	24	25 +	50	125 −	120 +	330	650	4,250	2,810	11,300
1884 CC	60	80	110	175	175	310 +	655	1,550	2,900	9,100
1884 O	24	27 +	45	125 +	102	250	350	1,300	2,225	7,000
1884 S	2,315 +	5,100 +	9,550 +	NB	17,100	NB	40,600 +	NB	72,500	100K
1885	24	25	50	125 +	102	200	332	1,300 +	1,830 +	6,300
1885 CC	162 +	176 +	232 +	340	390 +	575 +	1,175	2,600	3,360 +	8,700
1885 O	24	27 +	45	120 +	102	225	335	1,300 +	1,525	5,275
1885 S	60	70	140	350 −	425	725 +	2,650	6,500	6,000	15,600
1886	24	25	45	125 +	102 +	250 +	335 +	1,550 +	1,750	4,900
1886 O	210	450 +	2,000	2,700	6,100	6,500 +	22,500	NB	41,000	68,000
1886 S	60	100	200	410 +	1,025	1,200 +	2,825 −	7,500	8,250	20,000
1887	24	25	45	120 +	102 +	250	335 +	1,550 +	2,575	5,300
1887/6	50	90 +	300	NB −	1,150 +	2,900 +	3,300 +	4,600 +	7,250	9,500
1887 O	32	40	165	225	900	1,600	8,250	14,000 +	14,500	25,000
1887/6 O	90	115 +	525	600 +	2,100	2,500 +	14,000	NB	16,000 −	22,000 −
1887 S	50	60	160	350	750 +	1,400 +	5,100	10,000	11,450	24,000
1888	24	25 +	45	125	120 +	330 +	610 +	4,100 +	3,460 +	9,000
1888 O	24	27	60	125	190 +	400	1,585 +	6,000	6,215	14,100
1888 S	62 +	82	250	425	930 +	1,800 +	4,500 +	9,200 +	7,250	22,750
1889	24	25 +	50	125	155	500	1,725	5,000	4,600	9,100

Figure 7-1. A page from the *Certified Coin Dealer Newsletter*, the essential bid sheet for every coin trader. (Courtesy Certified Coin Dealer Newsletter)

	NGC									
	MS61	MS62	MS63	MS63 DPL	MS64	MS64 DPL	MS65	MS65 DPL	MS66	MS67
1878 8TF	40	50	105	NB	650 +	1,000	2,400	5,000	7,500	15,000
1878 7/8TF	45	65	145	200	580 +	1,400	3,000 +	8,350	9,600	20,000
1878 7TF	30	45	96	180	300	590	2,250	4,300	7,500	13,000
1878 7TF (Rev. 79)	35	55	101	190	530	900	4,100	10,000	9,000	16,000
1878 CC	65	80	140 +	250	460	690	2,500	4,800	5,000	9,000
1878 S	26	35	45	105	135 +	250	750 +	3,500	3,025	7,750
1879	24	25	90	130	435	500	2,525 +	5,500	5,900	8,200
1879 CC	860	1,160	2,250	NB	4,600 +	6,500	14,800	17,500	33,500	57,500
1879 CC Capped Die	805	1,025	1,450	NB	− 7,200	NB	16,600	NB	22,000	30,000
1879 O	30	40	180 +	300	700	1,200	5,500 +	10,500	8,750	26,000
1879 S (Rev. 78)	160	220	400	700	1,750	3,850	13,500	NB	18,750	41,000
1879 S	24	32	45	110	110	200	340	1,200	975	2,600
1880	24	25	70	200	450 +	550	2,800 +	8,250	5,525	13,750
1880 CC	120	130	170	275	380	600	1,950 +	3,600	5,600	9,700
1880 O	25	40	285	325	2,100	4,000	21,000	NB	45,000	62,500
1880 S	24	27	47	110	110	195	340	1,000	950	2,550
1881	24	25	75	160	380	500	2,225 +	5,500	4,400	9,250
1881 CC	120	140	190	350	340	510	1,150 +	2,750	2,900	7,700
1881 O	24	25	90	NB	400	500	2,600 +	5,500	6,500	16,750
1881 S	24	27	47	110	110	200	340	1,000	900	2,550
1882	24	25	60	110	260	300	1,200 +	4,000	4,000	8,500
1882 CC	70	85	95	210	200	350	750	1,925	2,600	11,800
1882 O	24	27	80	135	375	500	2,425 +	8,000	5,800	12,600
1882 S	24	32	47	110	110	205	340	1,800	1,000	3,000
1883	24	25	45	125	110	230	600 +	2,250	2,100	4,800
1883 CC	67	85	100	165 −	180	330	650	1,925	2,525	9,000
1883 O	24	25	47	110	110	230	475 +	2,000	3,500	10,750
1883 S	230	400	1,100	1,600	4,800	NB	22,000	NB	41,000	65,000
1884	24	25	47	110	110	290	775	4,000	3,700	11,000
1884 CC	65	80	105	165	180	325	650	1,925	2,800	8,500
1884 O	24	27	47 −	105	110	230	370 +	1,100	2,150	6,000
1884 S	2,195	3,950	NB	NB	16,750	NB	44,000	NB	72,500	100K
1885	24	25	47	110	110	230	350	1,150	1,750	5,150
1885 CC	160	182	220	325	354	500	1,600	2,400	3,600	8,500
1885 O	24	27	47	110	110	230	350	1,100	1,650	5,750
1885 S	65	85	140	325	440 +	700	2,600 +	5,250	6,000	15,600
1886	24	25 +	45	110	110	230	360 +	1,250 +	1,725	4,850
1886 O	215	480	1,850	NB	5,750	NB	19,250	NB	40,000	68,000
1886 S	60	80	200	380	1,000	1,200	3,100 +	6,500	8,800	20,000
1887	24	27	47	110	110	230	350	1,100 +	2,575	5,200
1887/6	75	100	160	NB	1,000	2,500	2,500 +	4,250	5,500	7,000
1887 O	30	40	165	300	885	1,525	8,000	NB	15,000	25,000
1887/6 O	75	100	275 +	550	1,725	2,600	12,150	NB	16,250	30,000
1887 S	50	70	172	320	775 +	1,300	5,150 +	9,250	11,500	24,000
1888	24	25 +	45	110	110	290	575	3,600	3,250	8,500
1888 O	24	27	60	110	240	NB	1,525 +	5,500	5,900	13,000
1888 S	80	100	250 +	400	915 +	1,500	4,100 +	8,000	6,800	22,700
1889	24	25	55	110	180 +	375	1,675 +	4,500	4,300	8,600

Figure 7-1. (Continued)

Continued

	MS61	MS62	MS63	MS63 DMPL	MS64	MS64 DMPL	MS65	MS65 DMPL	MS66	MS67
1889 CC	+ 5,365	+ 6,765	+ 11,300	NB	+ 20,100	NB	+ 60,000	NB	+ 100K	NB
1889 O	50	60	225	450	+ 750	3,500	4,500	+ 12,500	11,000	25,500
1889 S	70	80	175	400	520	+ 935	+ 2,450	+ 7,200	8,250	18,500
1890	24	27	67	+ 130	600	2,500	4,500	14,000	10,500	17,000
1890 CC	140	165	330	450	1,400	+ 2,750	+ 8,215	13,500	+ 13,750	21,000
1890 O	35	40	100	380	450	+ 780	5,250	13,000	10,750	18,000
1890 S	40	50	+ 100	200	360	+ 525	1,600	+ 6,500	+ 5,500	12,600
1891	40	55	+ 125	325	+ 950	2,000	+ 7,750	13,750	14,000	+ 25,000
1891 CC	155	185	− 310	475	885	1,000	3,965	7,750	9,000	21,000
1891 O	44	60	200	900	1,010	2,500	6,500	15,000	14,500	29,000
1891 S	30	40	+ 128	300	+ 405	605	2,350	+ 7,500	4,640	9,100
1892	60	80	190	450	1,025	+ 1,500	5,000	11,000	10,300	21,100
1892 CC	230	275	700	1,250	1,750	2,850	+ 5,200	+ 12,000	+ 20,000	24,750
1892 O	75	90	225	650	725	1,650	6,300	+ 12,000	+ 11,700	28,000
1892 S	5,425	6,425	+ 11,100	13,000	21,000	NB	50,000	NB	80,000	100K
1893	220	275	425	750	1,600	+ 3,000	6,500	17,000	15,000	25,000
1893 CC	675	950	+ 2,750	6,000	5,500	8,250	+ 26,000	29,000	40,000	77,500
1893 O	800	1,000	+ 2,875	4,800	+ 7,100	16,500	+ 31,000	35,000	+ 55,000	+ 75,000
1893 S	14,125	16,950	+ 27,100	29,500	+ 42,150	NB	90,000	100K	100K	110K
1894	625	725	+ 1,500	+ 1,900	3,150	4,200	14,100	21,000	17,500	39,000
1894 O	280	355	1,400	3,500	6,000	9,250	+ 20,500	22,500	29,500	57,500
1894 S	250	− 400	+ 500	770	1,340	NB	5,150	9,000	13,800	20,300
1895 Proof	11,500	12,500	14,250	—	16,500	—	+ 27,500	—	+ 38,000	55,000
1895 O	1,800	2,600	6,500	8,250	+ 10,100	14,000	41,000	55,000	61,000	100K
1895 S	+ 530	800	+ 1,300	1,700	+ 4,275	5,000	+ 14,000	27,500	+ 24,600	42,500
1896	24	25	45	120	− 115	+ 250	630	2,200	2,510	+ 8,100
1896 O	600	760	+ 3,000	4,000	+ 7,300	8,400	34,600	NB	52,500	+ 85,000
1896 S	425	600	+ 1,275	1,750	+ 3,300	+ 4,200	17,000	22,000	+ 27,500	45,000
1897	24	25	47	125	170	+ 250	+ 1,040	4,400	4,400	+ 8,400
1897 O	+ 450	+ 635	+ 2,100	3,300	+ 6,200	7,750	+ 15,300	25,000	26,000	47,500
1897 S	32	37	+ 77	130	210	+ 300	+ 1,115	+ 3,250	2,725	8,250
1898	24	27	+ 45	125	− 120	+ 300	820	+ 3,250	4,000	8,150
1898 O	24	25	+ 45	125	+ 102	+ 250	340	1,600	+ 2,500	5,000
1898 S	115	145	+ 225	275	490	850	2,635	5,500	+ 8,500	15,000
1899	75	90	+ 112	165	365	+ 660	+ 1,455	+ 4,350	+ 3,615	9,500
1899 O	24	25	+ 45	125	+ 112	+ 250	390	1,800	+ 2,010	6,100
1899 S	65	75	+ 195	275	− 520	900	+ 2,715	+ 7,000	7,650	11,700
1900	24	25	+ 45	140	115	+ 250	+ 670	4,500	+ 3,625	+ 7,250
1900 O	24	25	+ 45	125	110	+ 250	+ 465	3,500	2,375	5,650
1900 O/CC	85	110	+ 195	475	725	1,450	+ 2,950	7,000	6,100	14,000
1900 S	55	70	185	350	− 440	700	2,225	+ 6,000	7,100	16,100
1901	+ 1,885	2,400	+ 5,115	NB	+ 11,750	NB	32,000	38,000	65,000	+ 85,000
1901 O	24	25	53	410	130	700	825	+ 6,500	3,875	12,800
1901 S	+ 180	+ 215	+ 400	575	+ 800	1,375	3,650	+ 8,000	11,500	15,000
1902	24	30	80	400	305	+ 550	1,150	+ 5,500	+ 3,865	8,800
1902 O	24	25	45	320	115	+ 460	765	5,000	4,400	10,000
1902 S	80	90	210	425	700	800	+ 3,600	+ 9,000	7,500	20,000
1903	24	27	55	330	210	+ 540	+ 725	5,000	2,750	9,600
1903 O	150	160	200	375	295	500	− 1,175	+ 5,500	2,500	7,700
1903 S	+ 1,410	1,590	2,100	2,900	2,685	4,000	5,200	+ 11,000	13,600	25,000
1904	37	72	180	450	985	1,850	+ 4,915	10,000	15,500	+ 22,750
1904 O	24	25	+ 45	100	102	225	410	+ 1,650	2,400	+ 5,900
1904 S	580	775	1,500	1,750	2,100	3,500	7,500	17,500	21,000	30,000
1921	22	23	28	350	+ 95	500	+ 455	+ 5,000	+ 2,100	7,500
1921 D	22	28	47	400	− 225	675	1,475	5,000	+ 2,700	11,300
1921 S	22	28	47	500	285	1,400	2,260	+ 11,000	+ 6,850	16,500

Figure 7-1. (Continued)

	MS61	MS62	MS63	MS63 DPL	MS64	MS64 DPL	MS65	MS65 DPL	MS66	MS67
1889 CC	5,075	6,400	NB	NB	16,500	NB	57,500	NB	90,000	10K
1889 O	45	70	255	420	720	3,500	− 4,800	+ 11,000	10,500	26,000
1889 S	NB	NB	180	380	515	825	2,500	+ 6,000	8,500	18,500
1890	24	27	75	NB	600	NB	4,500	13,000	20,500	NB
1890 CC	160	175	350	475	1,350	NB	8,000	13,000	13,100	24,000
1890 O	30	37	95	340	475	600	4,600	12,000	9,100	17,000
1890 S	35	45	93	180	370	440	1,400	+ 5,000	5,000	12,500
1891	35	55	125	300	875 +	1,800	6,500	13,200	11,350	22,500
1891 CC	160	175	270	450	850	900	4,000	7,400	9,000	19,100
1891 O	40	70	225	850	950	2,400	6,500	14,250	12,600	31,500
1891 S	35	50	117	NB	450	NB	2,000	+ 5,500	4,450	8,600
1892	61	91	180	410	1,025	1,300	4,900	10,500	10,250	24,000
1892 CC	215	300	750	1,210	1,700	2,650	5,200	12,000	17,500	27,500
1892 O	55	80	230	600	815	1,600	6,500	11,500	11,650	31,500
1892 S	5,250	6,325	NB	+ 12,750	19,500	19,500	50,000	NB	75,000	100K
1893	215	275	425	700	1,575 +	2,750	6,500	16,250	14,100	25,000
1893 CC	+ 675	950	2,600	5,800	5,200	8,000	25,000	NB	36,000	56,000
1893 O	900	1,250	2,400	4,600	7,500	16,000	29,500	33,000	55,000	80,000
1893 S	13,900	16,500	26,250	27,500	38,500	NB	87,500	100K	100K	110K
1894	650	700	1,395 +	1,800	3,025	4,000	13,750	20,000	20,250	40,000
1894 O	285	305	1,400	3,300 −	6,100	9,000	18,500	21,000	30,000	60,000
1894 S	240	300	480	730	1,300	NB	5,000	NB	12,825	26,000
1895 Proof	11,500	12,000	14,000	—	16,000	—	26,000	—	35,625	52,250
1895 O	1,500	2,800	6,000	NB	11,000	NB	39,500	50,000	62,000	100K
1895 S	550	805	1,050 +	1,625	4,350	4,800	14,000	28,000	25,000	47,000
1896	24	25	47	105	130	260	620	1,900	2,650	7,000
1896 O	625	750	2,600	NB	7,250	8,600	35,000	37,500	57,750	85,000
1896 S	450	550	1,000	NB	3,200	NB	19,000	NB	25,000	45,000
1897	24	25	47	110	170	280	1,000	4,000	4,600	7,700
1897 O	450	650	1,850 +	2,750	5,200	NB	18,000	NB	30,000	52,250
1897 S	34	40	80	110	180	250	1,000 +	2,850	3,000	8,550
1898	24	27	47	110	130	290	750	2,800	3,500	8,000
1898 O	24	27	47	110	110	230	370	1,400	2,350	3,150
1898 S	105	125	205	250	500	770	2,200 +	5,200	6,600	14,250
1899	75	86	115	160 −	375 +	500	1,500	4,100	3,000	9,250
1899 O	24	25	47	110	110	300	400	1,600 +	2,000	5,750
1899 S	55	65	200	240	600 +	850	2,350 +	5,500	7,500	10,000
1900	24	25	47	130	130	300	630 +	3,250	2,650	5,250
1900 O	24	27	47	110	110	230	425 +	2,500	2,000	5,300
1900 O/CC	75	95	175 +	450	725 +	1,400	2,825	6,600	5,300	10,250
1900 S	50	75	170	NB	435	675	2,000 +	5,000	7,025	16,000
1901	1,500	2,125	4,400	NB	12,000	NB	32,000	37,000	65,000	90,000
1901 O	24	25	52 +	375	130 +	650	800 +	5,000	3,800	11,850
1901 S	175	205	380	500	800	1,325	3,500 +	5,500	11,500	14,250
1902	24	32	95	350	300	450	1,200	NB	3,500	NB
1902 O	24	25	55	280	110	400	675 +	4,250	4,250	9,500
1902 S	80	100	185	375	680	755	3,400 +	6,500	6,650	19,000
1903	24	27	47	300	230	NB	675 +	4,250	2,300	9,500
1903 O	120	140	210	335	300	550	1,135 +	4,750	2,750	7,000
1903 S	1,450	1,700	2,100	2,825	2,625	4,000	5,400 +	8,500	13,350	23,750
1904	40	75	160	400	1,000	1,800	5,000	9,750	13,750	23,500
1904 O	24	25	47	105	125	230 +	405	1,100	2,500	NB
1904 S	625	775	1,450	NB	2,050	3,500	8,250	19,000	20,100	32,500
1921	22	25 −	28	300	95	460	410 +	3,500	2,100	7,500
1921 D	22	25	45 +	350	190	630 −	1,450	4,700	3,700	8,500
1921 S	22	25	45 +	475	300	1,350	2,100 +	7,500	6,300	16,000

Figure 7-1. (Continued)   Continued

PEACE DOLLARS   NB—Represents no bid at this time.

PCGS

	MS61	MS62	MS63	MS64	MS65	MS66	MS67
1921	115	+ 160	+ 270	+ 685	+ 2,350	5,800	15,000
1922	20	22	26	95	525	2,850	9,300
1922 D	23	26	75	250	+ 1,330	5,915	− 15,500
1922 S	23	26	95	440	+ 3,400	8,000	+ 18,000
1923	20	22	26	95	470	+ 2,100	8,400
1923 D	23	28	85	310	+ 1,765	8,750	+ 16,750
1923 S	22	28	102	545	+ 6,600	11,350	43,000
1924	21	22	31	+ 96	570	3,000	8,800
1924 S	70	90	+ 330	1,900	+ 8,965	+ 16,750	31,000
1925	22	23	26	95	470	+ 2,100	8,600
1925 S	60	80	255	1,125	5,890	+ 11,850	31,250
1926	25	27	80	240	1,375	5,000	10,500
1926 D	26	37	110	250	+ 1,520	4,000	18,000
1926 S	25	35	− 95	345	1,685	5,440	23,000
1927	45	80	130	+ 990	5,750	13,400	22,000
1927 D	125	165	700	+ 1,600	+ 7,040	+ 11,100	23,650
1927 S	75	110	290	1,645	9,000	+ 15,100	22,650
1928	165	210	360	1,395	+ 5,465	+ 11,300	20,500
1928 S	65	80	− 320	1,725	9,800	15,800	27,600
1934	45	60	145	390	+ 2,260	6,500	15,000
1934 D	70	80	200	470	+ 2,590	6,600	12,800
1934 S	+ 975	+ 1,275	+ 2,125	+ 3,715	+ 6,150	+ 11,200	25,400
1935	40	45	120	300	1,810	+ 4,400	10,250
1935 S	75	105	+ 240	540	+ 1,965	+ 5,595	13,500

NGC

	MS61	MS62	MS63	MS64	MS65	MS66	MS67
1921	125	+ 160	+ 300	700	2,250	6,500	NB
1922	22	24	30	105	625	2,850	9,000
1922 D	24	28	110	200	1,300	5,600	15,000
1922 S	24	28	100	350	3,250	7,800	NB
1923	21	24	30	95	585	+ 2,100	8,500
1923 D	24	30	85	275	1,700	8,000	18,000
1923 S	24	28	99	500	6,500	11,000	41,000
1924	22	24	− 31	− 100	650	3,200	8,500
1924 S	70	100	275	1,550	8,850	16,500	30,000
1925	22	24	30	95	585	+ 2,050	7,850
1925 S	70	90	270	1,100	6,000	11,500	30,500
1926	28	33	85	250	1,400	5,000	10,250
1926 D	30	40	140	230	1,450	4,100	NB
1926 S	26	40	90	305	1,650	5,500	20,000
1927	45	75	150	1,000	5,400	13,000	20,000
1927 D	120	160	625	+ 1,400	7,250	10,750	22,325
1927 S	85	100	290	1,550	8,600	15,000	22,000
1928	165	210	380	1,300	5,750	11,000	19,000
1928 S	75	90	325	1,650	9,650	15,000	26,500
1934	55	− 65	150	400	2,200	6,250	NB
1934 D	70	80	200	430	2,500	6,750	12,500
1934 S	900	1,315	1,850	3,300	7,000	10,000	24,900
1935	42	45	125	300	1,725	4,400	10,250
1935 S	75	100	250	550	1,900	5,500	13,500

Figure 7-1. (Continued)

Page B *CERTIFIED COIN DEALER newsletter* **February 3, 1989**

MORGAN DOLLARS

	ANACS					NCI		
	MS62	MS63	MS64	MS65	MS67	MS64	MS65	MS66
1878 STF	50	− 100	+ 650	− 2,400		− 160	− 800	
1878 7/8TF	65	145	600	− 3,000		− 170	− 1,000	
1878 7TF	− 45	95	315	+ 2,250		+ 115	+ 700	
1878 7TF (Rev. 79)	− 55	+ 130	530	+ 4,000		+ 165	+ 1,300	
1878 CC	− 80	140	− 460	2,600		150	825	
1878 S	− 33	50	− 135	− 750		+ 70	230	
1879	− 28	140	+ 435	2,550		140	700	
1879 CC	− 1,150	− 2,250	4,750	NB		NB	NB	
1879 CC Capped Die	1,025	1,450	− 7,200	NB		NB	NB	
1879 O	− 42	− 200	700	NB		− 235	1,100	
1879 S (Rev. 78)	200	400	+ 1,875	+ 14,000		+ 600	3,500	
1879 S	31	45	− 110	− 340		65	140	
1880	− 27	135	− 475	− 2,800		150	− 925	
1880 CC	− 130	180	380	+ 1,800		− 180	+ 550	
1880 O	− 38	270	2,200	NB		+ 400	2,900	
1880 S	− 27	45	− 110	− 340		65	− 145	
1881	− 25	+ 130	+ 400	2,300		+ 125	600	
1881 CC	− 150	− 190	350	+ 1,100		− 190	+ 350	
1881 O	− 25	150	+ 400	+ 2,600		+ 125	+ 825	
1881 S	− 27	45	− 110	− 340		65	140	
1882	− 25	120	− 260	− 1,200		75	425	
1882 CC	81	110	200	+ 775		+ 120	− 275	
1882 O	− 27	130	385	+ 2,500		− 130	700	
1882 S	31	46	− 110	− 340		65	− 145	
1883	− 25	50	− 120	550		65	180	
1883 CC	81	110	− 180	650		+ 120	− 230	
1883 O	25	46	− 110	− 475		65	− 160	
1883 S	420	+ 1,300	4,950	NB		+ 1,150	NB	
1884	− 25	− 50	− 125	650		65	210	
1884 CC	− 80	110	− 180	650		120	− 230	
1884 O	− 25	46	− 110	− 340		65	− 145	
1884 S	+ 4,000	+ 8,500	NB	NB		NB	NB	
1885	− 25	46	− 110	− 340		65	140	
1885 CC	210	230	+ 390	+ 1,300		− 230	400	
1885 O	− 25	45	− 110	− 340		65	+ 140	
1885 S	− 85	190	− 425	+ 2,600		− 140	+ 825	
1886	− 25	45	− 110	− 340		65	− 145	
1886 O	+ 410	1,850	− 6,000	NB		1,600	NB	
1886 S	− 100	− 200	1,000	3,100		− 250	930	
1887	− 25	46	− 110	− 340		65	− 145	
1887/6	100	+ 225	+ 1,000	+ 3,000		+ 220	+ 800	
1887 O	− 40	230	900	NB		275	1,150	
1887/6 O	100	+ 400	+ 1,850	NB		+ 425	1,500	
1887 S	− 70	170	750	5,150		220	1,600	
1888	− 25	50	− 120	+ 600		65	210	
1888 O	− 27	110	315	1,500		90	500	
1888 S	− 100	+ 250	925	4,250		300	1,250	
1889	− 25	110	290	1,700		75	375	

Figure 7-2. This page from the *Certified Coin Dealer Newsletter* gives values for ANACS and NCI coins. Although the newsletter is a weekly publication, ANACS and NCI coins trade less frequently and are reported monthly. (Courtesy Certified Coin Dealer Newsletter)   Continued

	ANACS					NCI		
	MS62	MS63	MS64	MS65	MS67	MS64	MS65	MS66
1889 CC	+ 6,250	+ 11,000	+ 17,500	+ 42,500		NB	NB	
1889 O	− 70	250	+ 750	− 4,800		250	1,400	
1889 S	− 90	180	+ 520	2,500		180	800	
1890	− 27	145	600	+ 4,500		+ 200	1,150	
1890 CC	170	350	+ 1,400	+ 8,150		+ 400	+ 2,150	
1890 O	− 40	175	− 450	+ 4,850		160	1,400	
1890 S	− 50	95	380	+ 1,475		120	500	
1891	− 55	255	+ 950	+ 6,850		+ 275	2,200	
1891 CC	185	+ 310	850	4,000		+ 270	1,100	
1891 O	− 70	225	+ 1,000	− 6,500		− 260	− 1,500	
1891 S	− 50	− 130	450	+ 2,100		− 140	600	
1892	80	− 190	1,000	4,850		290	1,500	
1892 CC	300	750	+ 1,750	− 5,200		+ 575	1,650	
1892 O	90	− 230	825	− 6,500		− 270	− 1,700	
1892 S	6,250	+ 11,000	− 20,000	NB		NB	NB	
1893	275	+ 425	1,600	6,500		− 450	2,000	
1893 CC	950	+ 2,750	5,250	NB		+ 1,700	NB	
1893 O	− 1,250	+ 2,800	− 7,250	+ 29,000		2,400	NB	
1893 S	+ 15,500	+ 26,500	+ 38,500	NB		NB	NB	
1894	− 750	+ 1,475	3,000	+ 13,250		1,100	NB	
1894 O	− 360	+ 1,400	− 6,100	NB		1,400	NB	
1894 S	+ 330	500	1,300	− 5,100		425	1,500	
1895 Proof	+ 12,500	+ 14,250	− 16,500	NB		NB	NB	
1895 O	− 2,800	6,500	− 11,000	NB		4,500	NB	
1895 S	780	+ 1,275	4,350	NB		1,350	NB	
1896	− 25	48	− 130	600		65	200	
1896 O	− 750	+ 2,850	NB	NB		2,250	NB	
1896 S	+ 600	+ 1,200	3,300	NB		1,100	NB	
1897	− 25	48	170	+ 1,025		65	295	
1897 O	− 650	+ 1,900	+ 6,000	NB		+ 1,750	NB	
1897 S	− 40	− 80	200	+ 1,000		− 80	325	
1898	− 27	50	− 120	− 820		65	250	
1898 O	− 27	45	− 110	− 370		65	− 145	
1898 S	+ 145	220	475	+ 2,500		175	+ 725	
1899	− 90	− 115	− 380	− 1,450		− 135	− 500	
1899 O	− 25	46	− 110	400		65	+ 140	
1899 S	− 90	215	600	+ 2,650		210	+ 750	
1900	− 25	50	− 130	+ 650		65	200	
1900 O	− 27	50	− 110	+ 450		65	+ 140	
1900 O/CC	− 110	+ 175	+ 700	+ 2,850		+ 210	+ 850	
1900 S	− 80	180	450	+ 2,100		150	675	
1901	+ 2,150	+ 4,750	NB	NB		NB	NB	
1901 O	− 25	50	− 250	825		65	− 275	
1901 S	− 210	+ 400	800	+ 3,500		300	+ 1,050	
1902	− 32	160	300	− 1,150		100	− 380	
1902 O	− 25	50	− 115	+ 750		65	220	
1902 S	− 100	215	+ 700	+ 3,450		210	+ 950	
1903	− 27	55	230	− 700		− 80	210	
1903 O	− 175	210	− 300	− 1,150		200	− 380	
1903 S	1,650	2,100	2,650	− 5,200		1,600	NB	
1904	− 70	180	1,000	− 5,000		275	1,500	
1904 O	− 25	50	− 105	+ 400		65	140	
1904 S	− 775	1,500	2,100	NB		800	NB	
1921	25	− 28	− 95	+ 425		50	− 120	
1921 D	28	45	225	1,450		80	400	
1921 S	28	45	300	2,200		110	740	

Figure 7-2. (Continued)

COMMEMORATIVES

	ANACS				NCI		
	MS63	MS64	MS65	MS67	MS64	MS65	MS66
1893 Isabella Quarter	655 +	1,075 +	3,150		550	1,000	
1900 Lafayette Dollar	+ 2,150 −	4,500 −	13,000		− 1,800 −	4,750	
1921 Alabama Centennial 2×2	475	1,380 +	4,900		460	1,540	
1921 Alabama Centennial	350	1,350 +	4,800		400	1,540	
1936 Albany, New York	325	600 +	900		250	425	
1937 Antietam, Battle of	− 470 −	550 −	825		400	450	
Arkansas Centennial Type	100 −	250	850		− 110 −	300	
1935 Arkansas PDS Set	300 −	750	2,550		− 330 −	900	
1936 Arkansas PDS Set	300 −	750	2,550		− 330 −	900	
1937 Arkansas PDS Set	300 −	750	2,550		− 330 −	900	
1938 Arkansas PDS Set	− 460	1,050	3,000		450 −	1,050	
1939 Arkansas PDS Set	900 +	1,450 −	4,275		825 −	1,500	
1936-S Bay Bridge, San Fran.-Oak.	180	230 −	625		170 −	220	
Boone Bicentennial-Type	130	160	450		125 −	160	
1934 Boone Bicentennial	130	170	450		125 −	160	
1935/34 Boone—PDS Set	− 900 −	1,250	2,450		900	1,300	
1935 Boone—PDS Set	390 −	480	1,350		375 −	480	
1936 Boone—PDS Set	390 −	480	1,600		375 −	480	
1937 Boone—PDS Set	625	750 +	1,450		540 −	480	
1938 Boone—PDS Set	1,050 −	1,350	1,800		975	1,275	
1936 Bridgeport, Conn. Centennial	− 160 −	200 −	900		− 150 −	300	
1925-S California Diamond Jubilee	− 300	475 −	1,500		210	480	
1936 Cincinnati Music Ctr-Type	− 310	475 −	1,500		300 −	500	
1936 Cincinnati—PDS Set	− 930 −	1,425	4,850		900 −	1,500	
1936 Cleveland—Great Lakes Expo	110 +	200 −	950		110 −	275	
1936 Columbia S.C. Type	− 290 −	310 −	490		270 −	300	
1936 Columbia S.C.—PDS Set	− 870 −	930 −	1,470		810 −	900	
1892 Columbian Expo., Chicago	150	625	2,500		180 +	850	
1893 Columbian Expo., Chicago	150	625	3,300		180 +	1,000	
1935 Connecticut Tercentenary	280	375 −	1,000		+ 260 −	370	
Delaware Tercentenary	270 −	330 −	950		260 −	320	
1936 Elgin, Illinois Centennial	280	320 −	650		260	310	
1936 Gettysburg, Battle of	305	380 −	1,275		270 −	450	
1922 Grant Memorial with Star	1,400 −	3,800 −	11,500		− 1,400 −	4,000	
1922 Grant Memorial	− 240 −	510 −	1,525		235 −	500	
1928 Hawaiian Sesquicentennial	− 1,400 +	1,900 +	5,200		875	1,750	
1935 Hudson, Sesquicentennial	550	900 −	3,000		500 −	1,025	
1924 Hug—Walloon Tercentenary	210	400 −	1,650		180 −	575	
1946 Iowa Centennial	− 100	135 −	360		105	160	
1925 Lex.—Con. Sesquicentennial	115	375 −	1,600		100	500	
1918 Lincoln—Illinois Centennial	− 165 +	350 −	1,175		− 160 −	400	
1936 Long Island Tercentenary	110	250 −	1,000		110 −	330	
1936 Lynchburg—Sesquicentennial	− 215	260 −	750		200	250	
1920 Main Centennial	− 230	400 −	1,650		200	550	
1934 Maryland Tercentenary	− 190	270	900		180 +	295	
1921 Missouri Centennial 2×4	+ 790	1,550 −	6,500		625	2,200	
1921 Missouri Centennial	− 575	1,550 −	6,500		− 575	2,200	
1923-S Monroe Doctrine	195 +	800 −	3,100		− 260	975	
1938 New Rochelle, New York	− 400 −	430 −	800		350	400	
1936 Norfolk, VA, Bicentennial	550 −	580 −	615		510	550	
Oregon Trail Memorial—Type	− 155	200	475		130	200	
1926 Oregon Trail Memorial	− 155	200	500		130 +	210	
1926-S Oregon Trail Memorial	− 155	200	475		130	200	
1928 Oregon Trail Memorial	200	300 +	800		180	300	
1933-D Oregon Trail Memorial	250 −	300	825		− 250 −	300	
1934-D Oregon Trail Memorial	200 −	300 −	1,100		180 +	350	
1936 Oregon Trail Memorial	− 170	250	475		130	240	
1936-S Oregon Trail Memorial	200 −	300 −	520		190	325	
1937-D Oregon Trail Memorial	− 170	225	475		130	220	
1938 Oregon Trail Memorial—PDS	600	900 −	1,650		570	875	

Figure 7-2. (Continued)

Continued

	ANACS				NCI		
	MS63	*MS64*	*MS65*	*MS67*	*MS64*	*MS65*	*MS66*
1939 Oregon Trail Memorial—PDS	1,400 −	1,725 −	2,400		1,300	1,500	
1915-S Panama—Pacific Exposition	750	1,450 −	3,000		700	1,175	
1920 Pilgrim Tercentenary	125	265 −	1,100		110	300	
1921 Pilgrim Tercentenary	170	360 −	1,550		160	525	
1936 Rhode Island—Type	− 105	275 −	825		110 −	290	
1936 Rhode Island—PDS Set	− 315	825 −	2,475		330 −	870	
1937 Roanoke Island, N.C.	260 −	280 −	700		245 −	280	
1936 Robinson—Ark. Centennial	130	220 −	950		130 −	310	
1935-S San Diego, Calif.—Expo.	120	140	350		110 −	125	
1936-D San Diego, Calif.—Expo.	125	150	350		120 −	130	
1926 Sesquicentennial	− 200 +	1,050	4,400		− 325 −	1,450	
1935 Spanish Trail	− 705 +	850 −	1,425		− 600 −	725	
1925 Stone Mountain Memorial	65	120	575		60 −	190	
Texas Centennial—Type	− 165	200 −	460		140	200	
1934 Texas Centennial	− 165	200 −	460		140	200	
1935 Texas—PDS Set	− 495	600 −	1,380		420	600	
1936 Texas—PDS Set	− 495	600 −	1,380		420	600	
1937 Texas—PDS Set	− 495	600 −	1,380		450	600	
1938 Texas—PDS Set	700 −	800	1,600		660	750	
1925 Fort Vancouver Centennial	425 +	640	1,675		420	580	
1927 Vermont Sesquicentennial	− 240	500 −	1,600		− 240 −	550	
. B.T. Washington—Type	18 −	26 −	130		20 −	40	
1946 B.T. Wash.—PDS Set	54 −	78 −	390		60 −	120	
1947 B.T. Wash.—PDS Set	60 −	78 −	500		60 −	120	
1948 B.T. Wash.—PDS Set	120 −	180	500		− 90 −	120	
1949 B.T. Wash.—PDS Set	135 −	225	510		135 −	150	
1950 B.T. Wash.—PDS Set	135 −	180 −	425		135 −	150	
1951 B.T. Wash.—PDS Set	105 −	150	500		105 −	120	
Wash—Car Type	− 17 −	45 −	350		− 17	160	
1951 Wash—Car—PDS Set	90 −	155	1,670		− 81	580	
1952 Wash—Car—PDS Set	90 −	180 −	1,850		− 81	700	
1953 Wash—Car—PDS Set	90 −	180	2,470		105	850	
1954 Wash—Car—PDS Set	90 −	165	2,125		− 81	740	
1936 Wisconsin Centennial	250 +	330	550		250	300	
1936 York County, Tercentenary	250 +	330	575		250	300	

Figure 7-2. (Continued)

Continued

PEACE DOLLARS

		ANACS				NCI		
	MS62	*MS63*	*MS64*	*MS65*	*MS67*	*MS64*	*MS65*	*MS66*
1921		160	+ 300	700	+ 2,350	250	+ 725	
1922	−	24	30	− 105	− 625	40	160	
1922 D	−	28	110	250	+ 1,300	100	+ 400	
1922 S	−	28	− 100	425	+ 3,300	− 120	+ 875	
1923	−	24	30	− 95	550	40	160	
1923 D	−	30	− 85	300	+ 1,750	− 90	+ 500	
1923 S	−	28	100	+ 540	6,500	− 120	1,400	
1924	−	24	31	− 100	− 650	40	160	
1924 S	−	100	+ 300	+ 1,900	8,800	− 400	2,100	
1925	−	24	− 30	− 95	550	40	160	
1925 S	−	90	275	− 1,125	− 6,000	− 370	1,800	
1926	−	33	− 85	250	− 1,400	− 90	− 475	
1926 D	−	40	− 140	250	+ 1,500	− 140	+ 450	
1926 S	−	40	− 95	325	+ 1,650	− 100	560	
1927		80	150	1,000	5,650	− 320	1,500	
1927 D	−	165	760	+ 1,450	− 7,100	+ 475	2,000	
1927 S	−	110	+ 290	1,600	8,600	525	2,000	
1928	−	210	− 400	1,400	− 5,600	400	1,600	
1928 S	−	90	− 325	1,700	9,600	+ 500	1,650	
1934	−	65	150	400	+ 2,200	− 150	+ 625	
1934 D	−	80	200	+ 450	+ 2,550	200	+ 725	
1934 S	+	1,275	+ 2,100	+ 3,600	− 7,000	+ 1,175	2,250	
1935	−	45	− 125	300	+ 1,750	− 125	+ 575	
1935 S	−	105	250	550	+ 1,925	245	+ 630	

GOLD COMMEMORATIVES

	ANACS				NCI		
	MS63	*MS64*	*MS65*	*MS67*	*MS63*	*MS64*	*MS65*
1903 LA Purchase/Jefferson $1	1,600	+ 2,200	+ 4,300		700	1,100	1,700
1903 LA Purchase/McKinley $1	1,550	+ 2,200	+ 4,100		675	1,100	1,700
1904 Lewis & Clark Expo. $1	+ 3,300	4,100	+ 9,350		1,050	1,900	3,600
1905 Lewis & Clark Expo. $1	+ 3,800	+ 6,850	13,350		1,225	2,750	5,500
1915-S Pan-Pacific Expo. $1	1,325	2,250	+ 4,100		625	1,000	1,675
1915-S Pan-Pacific Expo. $2½	3,000	3,850	+ 6,250		1,500	1,750	2,350
1916 McKinley Memorial $1	1,400	2,100	+ 4,000		650	1,100	1,800
1917 McKinley Memorial $1	+ 1,425	2,100	+ 4,450		675	1,100	2,000
1922 Grant Memorial $1	+ 2,850	+ 3,400	+ 4,600		1,500	1,750	2,200
1922 Grant Memorial with Star $1	2,900	3,425	+ 4,850		1,600	1,800	2,300
1926 Sesquicentennial $2½	950	+ 2,100	+ 9,000		500	900	3,450
1915-S Pan-Pacific $50 Round	+ 39,000	+ 51,000	+ 87,000		NB	NB	NB
1915-S Pan-Pacific $50 Octagonal	+ 33,000	+ 43,000	+ 77,000		NB	NB	NB

Figure 7-2. (Continued)   Continued

EARLY GOLD TYPE COINS

	ANACS				NCI		
	MS60	*MS63*	*MS64*	*MS65*	*MS63*	*MS64*	*MS65*
Two & One-Half Dollar 1796 N/St	38,000	+ 56,000	NB	NB			
Two & One-Half Dollar 1796–1807	13,500	+ 21,500	51,000	100K			
Two & One-Half Dollar 1808	38,000	55,000	NB	NB			
Two & One-Half Dollar 1821–1827	13,500	23,000	30,000	62,500			
Two & One-Half Dollar 1829–1834	10,000	15,500	26,000	51,000			
Two & One-Half Dollar 1834–1839	1,300	6,000	14,000	40,000			
Five Dollar 1795–1798	18,000	+ 30,250	+ 70,000	+ 120K			
Five Dollar 1797–1807	− 6,750	13,000	30,000	+ 77,500			
Five Dollar 1807–1812	5,000	12,500	30,000	75,000			
Five Dollar 1813–1829	7,000	15,000	35,000	80,000			
Five Dollar 1829–1834	− 6,500	16,000	− 37,000	− 76,000			
Five Dollar 1834–1839	+ 1,800	+ 9,350	24,000	55,000			
Ten Dollar 1795–1797	21,500	+ 40,000	80,000	+ 150K			
Ten Dollar 1797–1804	9,500	15,000	− 40,000	100K			
Ten Dollar 1838–1839	6,000	17,500	35,000	+ 70,000			

Figure 7-2. (Continued)

VOLATILITY IN THE COIN MARKET

Wall Street Money Brings Wall Street Volatility

The rare coin market learned that lesson in June 1989, when a surge in prices, fueled by excitement over Wall Street's involvement with coins, suddenly gave way to a sharp decline.

This was just a taste of things to come. As more and more Wall Street money is invested in rare coins, the coin market will undergo still more price swings similar to those in commodities markets. It will be a time of unprecedented volatility in the marketplace, with ups and downs more frequent and perhaps more drastic than coin buyers and sellers have ever known.

The big investment funds now entering the coin market are in a position to buy and sell many millions of dollars worth of coins. For example, Kidder, Peabody & Co. Inc. went into the market in 1989 with $40 million to invest. That kind of leverage gives these funds the capacity to push coin prices higher within a short period of time. Conversely, a sell-off of millions of dollars worth of coins—or even the rumor of such a sell-off—can push prices down in an equally short period. If funds of this magnitude sell off into the marketplace, market values are likely to fall quickly and dramatically.

In a sense, the rare coin market is now at the mercy of the major players. They possess the power to push levels up by buying large quantities of coins, or to push levels down by selling coins.

The anticipatory factor should never be underestimated in this industry. The mere rumor of a new $100-million Wall Street fund can send prices soaring. And the mere rumor of a Wall Street fund about to sell its coins can cause prices to plummet.

The rare coin industry has undergone a basic restructuring. Because of the greater volatility, buyers must be prepared for sharper, more frequent changes—down, as well as up—in the value of their coins. Tremendous infusions of new investment money may very well push prices to record highs, but the trip to the top will be bumpy as this great new demand is applied to, or withdrawn from, the small, pressure-sensitive supply of investment-quality coins.

In the rare coin market of the early 1980s, the biggest potential pitfall was an acquisition risk, or "buy risk"—the risk that a coin buyer wouldn't get the quality he or she paid for. During that period, unknowledgeable buyers might well have paid $5,000 for a coin and ended up with something worth no more than two or three hundred dollars.

Today, the greatest risk is a marketplace risk—the risk that a coin acquired at its current market price may drop in value substantially after the purchase. The market volatility heightens this risk. But, on the other hand, it also enhances the prospects for rapid gains.

In its effort to attract Wall Street money, the coin market set up a number of new mechanisms calculated to make it more appealing to traditional investors. One of these is the American Numismatic Exchange (ANE), an Atlanta-based electronic trading system on which certified coins—those graded and encapsulated by an independent third-party grading service—are traded sight-unseen. ANE has indeed helped make Wall Street companies more comfortable with the concept of buying and selling coins. At the same time, however, it facilitates volatility by leaving the market more vulnerable to price manipulation and sudden, sharp movements up or down.

The rare coin market is a liquid market, but it's not *continuously* liquid. The coin field is composed of thinly capitalized entrepreneurs who control the field's liquidity based on their collective ability to buy or sell a coin at any given time. As late as the mid-1980s, if a dealer didn't have the need or desire to buy a particular coin during a particular time period, the owners of the coin would hold it until that dealer (or another dealer) could pay a fair price. But today, as a result of the ANE system, the price that the dealer is willing to pay has become public knowledge. Consequently, a small cash crunch of a few market-makers unable to post bids can snowball into a major panic.

The coin market tailspin of June 1989 illustrates how quickly and thoroughly rare coin prices can be altered by volatility, and it also shows how ANE can further this process.

Before the downturn, certified coins graded by either the Professional Coin Grading Service (PCGS) or the Numismatic Guaranty Corporation of America (NGC) were trading at very substantial premiums over the prices listed on ANE. Just a few days later, ANE prices had plunged 40 percent or more in some cases, and many coins were trading for even *less* than the new, depressed ANE levels.

Because the coin marketplace is so thin, four or five dealers were literally supporting the sight-unseen market, and when some of these dealers pulled their bids off the system, prices collapsed.

Prior to the turnaround, dealers were routinely paying $6,000 for super-grade coins listed on ANE at $5,000 sight-unseen. The dealers, in turn, were selling those coins to investors for $7,000. Coin dealer Maurice Rosen, publisher of the *Rosen Numismatic Advisory*, refers to this as a "market premium factor." It reflects the fact that in a rising market, coins that are in demand bring prices in advance of ANE or price-guide levels.

When a few key dealers withdrew or reduced their ANE bids and ANE levels started to decline, these coins were hit with a double whammy: They lost not only a substantial percentage of their bid value, but also the extra premium. Their ANE levels skidded from $5,000 to $3,000, and since people sell their coins for less than ANE levels in a declining market, their actual market value at the time was $2,800. These same coins had been selling for $7,000 just a few days earlier, so the actual loss in value was a staggering 60 percent.

It's important to remember that ANE is only one of a number of market indicators, and that a drop in a coin's ANE level may not represent an accurate reflection of its true market value. Auction prices constitute another important barometer. So do the levels in dealer-to-dealer transactions.

ANE levels were thoroughly depressed at the time of the Dallas Coin and Stamp Exposition, a major Southwestern coin show, in mid-June 1989. Nonetheless, prices were strong—much stronger than ANE levels—at a public auction held at the same show by a leading Dallas coin firm, Heritage Numismatic Auctions. To cite one example, common-date S-mint Morgan silver dollars graded MS-65 were listed at the time for $325 on the ANE system, but were selling for $550 or more at the auction.

Lower ANE levels don't necessarily signify actual sales at those levels. When ANE prices plummeted in June 1989, few coins were available at the new, depressed levels. That's not to say an occasional coin couldn't have been bought; if a dealer had been forced to panic-sell a coin, he might have let it go at the lower price. But the lower

ANE prices were really not a product of supply and demand. Rather, they resulted from the withdrawal of a few dealers' bids—and that points up how thin the coin marketplace is.

The volatility now being seen is a new phenomenon for the coin market. Already, though, the market is demonstrating resiliency and showing it can bounce back quickly when prices plunge.

In April 1989, a story in *The Wall Street Journal* raised doubts about whether Shearson Lehman Hutton would enter the rare coin market, as previous published reports had said it was ready to do. This triggered a sharp decline in the value of MS-65 Saint-Gaudens double eagles, since these are the kind of fungible coins that Shearson was expected to buy and sell extensively. Almost overnight, these $20 gold pieces dropped in price from $4,200 to $2,900. But within a matter of days, they had rebounded to $4,300. This was clear evidence not only of the heightened volatility that will characterize the coin market from now on, but also of the marketplace's underlying strength.

In these new times of turbulence and volatility created by Wall Street money, do not panic and do not use ANE levels as the primary determinant of value for your coins. ANE levels don't necessarily reflect a coin's true value; rather, they show what certain dealers are willing to pay for the coin at a given time, and this may be skewed by marketplace volatility and dealer illiquidity. At times of dealer illiquidity, ANE levels can deteriorate rapidly, and at such times they won't provide an accurate picture of true market values.

Even if the ANE system hadn't been created, volatility would still be a fact of life in today's coin market. It's inevitable, with so much buying (and selling) power concentrated in the hands of a few investment funds. ANE simply makes it easier to measure the impact of all this volatility.

The sharp decline in prices in June 1989 wasn't a sign of fundamental weakness in the coin market. What it really signaled was that new forces, unleashed by Wall Street's involvement, are operating now in the marketplace.

As time goes by, both Wall Street money and Wall Street volatility will play increasing roles in shaping the rare coin market. That will make the market much stronger, but also much more volatile.

HOW TO SELL HIGH

The way to sell coins high is to take certified coins, crack them out of their holders, and consign them to a dealer for sale at auction.

Chances are, the dealer will take attractive color photographs of those coins, give them a nice display in a glossy, impressive catalog—and indicate they're in a higher grade.

Normally, you shouldn't sell coins at auction during times of climatic extremes—in other words, in the summer or in the winter. Of course, there are exceptions. If the market is heating up, for example, it might be a good idea to sell in the summertime.

In most cases it's not a good idea to sell in the wintertime, even if the auction is taking place at a coin show in an area where it's warm and the show is a popular one. Traditionally, such auctions haven't produced the absolute highest prices for consignors.

Auction-House Grading

Not all auction catalogs overstate the grades of their coins. Sometimes, in fact, the opposite is true—and in such cases shrewd bidders may be able to pick up real bargains.

Suppose a consignor goes to an auction house and says, "You people are the most competent coin graders in the world; grade these coins the way you want to." The auction house, not wanting to be accused of overgrading and wanting to make its realized prices more impressive, may assign conservative grades to the coins. This has been known to happen in an estate sale. Lawyers representing the estate will consign the coins to an auction house, and you'll find MS-65s being graded in the catalog as MS-63s.

Often, however, the scenario is diametrically different. Someone will go to an auction house with a package of coins and say, "Listen, I know NGC would grade these coins MS-63; but unless you call them MS-64 or 65, I'm not going to consign these coins to you." Even a so-called reputable auction house is likely to take those coins and abide by the wishes of the consignor.

There's nothing unethical about what these auction firms are doing. They don't necessarily grade according to the standards set forth by NGC or PCGS. Auction firms have their own grading standards; therefore they can take a certified coin—a coin that's been graded conservatively by an independent grading service as MS-64 or 63, and for which you've paid a 64 or 63 price—and legitimately grade it MS-65 after cracking it out of its holder.

Maximizing Grades

Recently I was fascinated by a very interesting deal with an auction house. There were coins that NGC had graded About Uncirculated-

58, but when they were taken out of their holders they were cataloged as MS-62s and realized handsome prices of thousands of dollars apiece. As an MS-62, one of these coins sold for $5,400 plus a 10-percent buyer's fee. When it was in its slab as an AU-58, dealers did not want to buy it. One dealer refused even to make an offer on this coin; he said he wasn't interested.

In another case, an institution took dozens of MS-63 gold coins that were no-question 63s to an auction house that cataloged many of them as 65s. The coins did not bring big prices though.

Another coin group involved PCGS MS-64 Premium Quality Morgan dollars. A very large grouping of these coins was presented to an auction firm that was willing to crack them out of their holders, grade a number of them as high as MS-66, and include color photographs in its catalog. With very few exceptions, the remainder of the coins were cataloged MS-65. An auction firm that maximizes grades is still not an assurance of high prices realized.

THE GRADING CONTINUUM

Coins are graded on a continuum. If you own a coin graded MS-64, you may have a 64.9; on the other hand, you may have a just-made-it 64. If you're buying a coin graded MS-64, you want the coin that's an almost-made-it 65; you don't want a just-missed-it 63.

NGC recognizes this continuum. It recognizes that a coin graded MS-64 can be 64.9 or 64.1, so for internal purposes NGC graders have the option of using the letters A, B, and C. An MS-64A is a coin that might qualify for the next highest grade, MS-65. In many cases you can take an MS-64 coin to which NGC internally has assigned the letter A, crack it out of its NGC holder, and consign it to an auction house as an MS-66. As a 66, the coin could bring $1,500—not bad for a coin that may have been available from a dealer for $100.

For now, the letters A, B, and C are not disclosed to buyers of NGC coins. But as we approach the time when coins are bought and sold on a sight-unseen basis like stocks, it's my opinion that the A, B, or C designation will be revealed on the grading insert of each coin.

Coins Grading MS-63 to MS-67

The grading band between MS-63 and MS-67 is the one of greatest concern to consumers. We're likely to see a trend toward fuller description within that one small area than in all the rest of the spectrum.

Grades 1 through 62 are almost a non-issue compared with that part of the spectrum between 63 and 67.

A high-quality 65—one that almost grades 66—is clearly worth more than a minimum 65 price. In all cases investors should stick with Premium Quality coins, but try not to pay the price for the next higher grade; try to keep the premium down to no more than halfway between the two levels. If the 64 price for a coin is $100 and the 65 price is $300, it's not wise to pay $290 for a Premium Quality-64. You wouldn't want to pay more than $200 for the coin.

INNER-CIRCLE DEALERS

Finding bargains in certified coins involves a great deal of judgment, and I don't like making generalizations in this area. You really need to consult your coin advisor and find someone you can trust implicitly. Many coin dealers are reputable, but not all are knowledgeable enough to help you in this area of the market. When it comes to these particular types of coins, you really need a dealer who's a member of the inner circle.

You can find inner-circle dealers by checking ads in coin publications and noting which ones are affiliated with both the Professional Coin Grading Service and the Numismatic Guaranty Corporation. Determine who these authorized dealers are; there are listings. Both organizations scrutinize their dealers for financial integrity and trustworthiness. In fact, dealers who are members of NGC are pledged to arbitrate any dispute regarding NGC-related coins through that service; so if you deal with an NGC-authorized dealer who's listed in the ads, you can be certain the dealer has been prescreened closely and will arbitrate any dispute.

A WINDOW OF OPPORTUNITY

The coin market today is somewhat inefficient, and this allows people to make exceptional profits. As I have shown, it allows people to buy coins that are certified, crack them out, and consign them to auction companies. As we become a more efficient market, it may be difficult to do this because everybody may want certified coins.

It's my contention that right now we have a window of opportunity for people to sell coins this way. This window may last another five, six, or seven years. But the more efficient we become, the less able consumers will be to capitalize on this liquidation process.

COST AVERAGING

Cost averaging is a technique familiar to people in financial fields. Essentially, it's a way of cushioning a loss when one investment goes down in value by purchasing a second example of the same item at the lower price.

Suppose you buy a coin for $10,000 and it plunges in value to $1,000. To cost average, you buy another coin just like it—a coin of the same denomination, date, and grade—for $1,000. What you are doing, effectively, is splitting the difference. Now you can take the attitude that you really paid $5,500 apiece for the two coins: the sum of their prices ($11,000) divided by two. It's unlikely that the market value of either coin will rebound all the way to $10,000, but chances are good that after dropping in price so sharply, the coins will regain at least part of the lost ground. They may rise to $5,000 or even $7,000 apiece. And at that point you'll break even or come out slightly ahead.

Cost averaging is a psychologically soothing way to rationalize the fact that you overpaid for a coin or bought it at the top of the cycle.

WHY COIN INVESTORS ARE UNCOMFORTABLE BUYING AT THE LOW

When their market value is at the lowest point, coins frequently are the focus of a great deal of negative publicity. You'll read stories in the press about how they're not very good investments or the fact that there's no end in sight to their decline. Shrewd investors know that often this is the best time to buy; things are always darkest just before the dawn, so to speak. But many people feel uncomfortable buying at the bottom. If anything, they're more inclined to sell.

We see the same kind of attitude in the stock market. Many investors sold their stock on Black Monday, but in retrospect we know Black Monday was the low for that particular period. The stock market, of course, may take another plunge; I'm certainly not making any predictions. However, it's a fact that more than fifteen months after the Wall Street crash of October 1987, stock prices overall are higher today than they were at that time. So Black Monday—when everybody was talking about there being no end in sight to declining stock prices, talking about a stock market at 1,000, a stock market at 800—that was the market's low.

When coins are receiving negative publicity, when it seems there's no end in sight to falling prices, when everyone's pessimistic, when dealers have no money, *that's* the time to buy. Be gutsy. Be bold. Be brazen. Don't be afraid. Go out and take the plunge. You will be rewarded when the time comes to sell; you will be rewarded for your gutsiness. This kind of risk-taking is a virtue in the coin field. When opportunity knocks, open the door!

One word of caution: This advice applies only to buying coins of proven rarity. When common coins hit low ebb, sometimes they remain there for years. Jefferson nickels, for instance, have been becalmed in the marketplace for more than two decades. To take proper advantage of buying opportunities, you must know coin values well and be able to project future appreciation. Coins that are rare will become rarer. Coins that are scarce will become scarcer and rare. And coins that are common will remain common in the relatively near future. Coins that are common do not increase in value. Don't buy them.

LATE-DATE HYPE

Beware of late-date coins in plastic slabs. Although the rare coin market has benefited greatly from the certification of coins by independent grading services, certification has led to unfortunate abuses in this one area.

The problems involve late-date coins in exceptional condition—coins like proof or mint-state Jefferson nickels, Roosevelt dimes, and Kennedy half dollars. Even in the highest grades these coins are extremely common, but certain unscrupulous dealers have found a way to market them at greatly inflated prices as if they were much rarer and more valuable. They submit the coins to one of the grading services, get them certified and slabbed at a very high grade such as Proof-68 or MS-67, and then sell them for far more than they're really worth—sometimes two or three hundred times as much.

NGC has taken forceful action to combat this type of abuse. Right from its inception, the company refused to certify any coins dated after 1964. Then, in early 1988, it extended this ban to most proof coins dated 1956 to 1964. The only exceptions are Franklin half dollars, which have an established market as certified coins.

Prior to extending its restrictions, NGC studied advertisements for certified late-date coins in major coin periodicals. It compiled a list of 37 certified late-date proof coins that were being offered for sale in these ads. It then asked experts in modern U.S. coins how much they would pay for these as "raw" coins, uncertified and out of their plastic slabs. The total came to $141, an average of less than $4 per coin. But the sellers' advertised asking prices totaled $8,395: an average of nearly $227!

SUPER-GRADE COINS

Super-grade coins, also known as "wonder coins," have risen in value spectacularly during the last few years. These are coins above the grade of Proof-65 or MS-65 in older U.S. series, coins that are genuinely scarce or even rare in such high grades.

Typically, a coin graded Proof-66 or Mint State-66 brings several times as much as a coin of the same type with a grade of Proof- or Mint State-64. And with each higher level above 66, the price may double or triple. To enjoy market acceptance at these prices, the coins ordinarily need to have been certified by one of the major grading services.

To the untrained eye, the difference between one mint-state coin and another may seem slight. However, that slight difference can lead to a disparity of thousands of dollars in value. Consider the case of the 1885 Liberty Seated quarter. In NGC Proof-64 condition, this coin is worth about $2,000. In Proof-65, the price jumps to $4,000. In Proof-66, it soars to $7,000. And in Proof-67, the coin commands a premium of $14,000 or more (see Figure 7-3).

NGC and PCGS together have played a major role in creating the buyer confidence on which these huge price increments are based. The super-grade coins are many times rarer than typical proof or uncirculated coins, but not until the era of professional independent grading did people feel secure enough to pay such spectacular sums (see Figure 7-4).

HOW TO SELL SLABBED COINS PROFITABLY

When liquidating certified coins, an investor must decide whether they are high-end, low-end, or mid-range coins of the designated grade.

Figure 7-3. Proof-67 1885 Liberty Seated quarter. This stunning wonder coin would command $14,000 or more with NGC or PCGS certification. The fields are watery and reflective, and the devices are snow-white frosted.

Figure 7-4. Proof-67 1897 Barber half dollar. This awe-inspiring jewel might fetch well above $20,000 with NGC or PCGS certification. This is a premium quality example, too. Beautiful peripheral shades of aqua and sunset gold fade into sensational brilliant centers.

After this is established, the investor should adhere to the following rules of thumb:

- Coins that are premium quality or high-end and nearly qualify for the next higher grade should be broken out of their certified slabs and sold at public auction at a negotiated higher grade. Sometimes an auction company will guarantee a minimum price. Some auction firms may even agree to reimburse the consignor for the value of the coin at its sight-unseen grade if it should bring a lower price after being broken out of its holder and sold at auction.
- Coins that are low-end—just-made-it coins that might be given a lower grade if they were cracked out of their holders—should be sold on a sight-unseen basis through an American Numismatic Exchange authorized dealer or through the Teletrade Exchange.
- Coins that are in between—neither high-end nor low-end but simply decent, accurately graded coins—can be sold on a sight-seen basis to other dealers at a reasonable negotiated price. These coins can also be sold at public auction in their slabs.
- When selling certified coins that are just-made-it coins, or even reasonably decent coins for the grade but not premium quality, be absolutely certain to deal only with an authorized dealer of the grading service in whose capsules these coins are slabbed. I can document many cases in which individuals have gone to unauthorized dealers with certified coins encapsulated by grading services; resenting the independent services with which they have no working relationship, these dealers have said, "This coin is worthless; I'll give you $50 for it," when the sight-unseen price on the coin was as much as $3,000. Dealing with *reputable* dealers isn't enough; you must deal with dealers who have been screened by the grading services. At press time, both PCGS and NGC are imposing very stringent financial and other requirements on members of their authorized dealer networks.

HOW TO NEGOTIATE AUCTION CONTRACTS

If the time comes to negotiate an auction contract and you find yourself with coins of substantial value to consign, you may want to seek legal counsel about a Uniform Commercial Code filing statement, according to Leonard H. Hecht, a lawyer with Battle Fowler in New York. This can be quite important, and I suggest you consult your attorney for further details.

When you negotiate with an auction house, you also may want a cash advance. All these points are negotiable, depending on how much your coins are worth.

Many coin auction firms use a 10-10 commission structure—that is, they charge the consignor 10 percent of the prices realized for his or her coins and receive a like commission from each of the buyers.

If your holdings are sizable (and most auction firms won't accept a consignment worth less than a couple of thousand dollars), you should negotiate for a lower rate. Auction houses often reduce the seller's fee to 7 percent, 5 percent, or even less. In some cases they have been known to waive a seller's fee altogether in order to get a consignment. And if they want a consignment badly enough, some auction firms will even provide a rebate to the seller, giving him or her a share of the buyers' fees.

Because there's so much room for auction firms to maneuver on their fees, heirs to estates should be especially vigilant and cautious. Suppose you've inherited a coin collection worth four or five million dollars, and you've hired a so-called independent consultant to help you decide how and where to sell it. Quite conceivably, one auction firm may have contacted your consultant with a tempting offer: "Convince your client to auction that collection through us, and in exchange we're prepared to pay you a percentage of the prices realized." Not being a coin collector yourself, you may have limited knowledge of what's involved and may decide to use that particular auction firm based on the counsel of someone who, behind the scenes, has a vested interest in the outcome of this transaction.

AN ANALYSIS OF PRICES REALIZED

Given the same coins, all the top-notch auction firms get about the same price levels from their buyers. Usually the big difference is just how big a chunk of the proceeds you, the consignor, will receive and how much the firm will keep for itself. From your standpoint, how much you get—not what the coins sell for—is the real bottom line.

Let's say one firm wants to charge you a 20 percent fee and won't give you any money in advance. Meanwhile, a competing firm is willing to guarantee you $800,000 on your $1 million collection, willing to give you a check for it up front without interest, and even willing to waive the seller's fee; in fact, this firm is willing to pay *you* a percentage or two of the buyer's fee. It seems pretty obvious which is the better deal from your standpoint. You certainly shouldn't listen to any hype you hear from the firm that wants to charge you 20 percent.

What counts is the financial deal, not how big a name the auction company has. It comes down to a matter of numbers: so pick the best ones. In some cases you can even negotiate for minimums—the minimum prices realized for certain coins. This is especially true in smaller auction sales.

While you're at it, weigh those numbers in judging your financial advisor's advice. You should be suspicious (indeed, you should be downright skeptical) if your trusted advisor tells you, "This is a wonderful firm that wants to charge you 20 percent and not give you any advance on the prices realized. Don't listen to the firm that's willing to give you $800,000 interest-free and willing to pay you a price for the privilege of selling your coins; that's not a very good deal." Your advisor could be in somebody's pocket, and that somebody might not be you.

What it comes down to is negotiation, negotiation, negotiation. And you really have to trust your own instincts. There's no specific formula for getting the best deal except to go out and get the best deal.

QUALITY VERSUS RARITY

Traditionally, coins in the highest level of preservation have appreciated at the fastest rate. In recent years, in fact, collectors have gone crazy over quality. And investors have become so "condition-wacky," as coin dealer Norman Stack so succinctly put it, that they've sometimes lost sight of what really constitutes good value. As I pointed out earlier in this chapter, some dealers have been able to take modern proof coins of relatively little value and sell them for hundreds of dollars because they're in exceptional condition.

The quest for quality coins—the push for perfection, if you will —gained tremendous momentum in 1979 and 1980, when tangible assets were flying high and rare coins came to be viewed as the ideal inflationary hedge. As investors rushed into the market to purchase quality coins, those coins increased significantly in price. But coin investing at that time was really a shot in the dark. A number of people who thought they were buying quality coins weren't.

Ten years ago, investors wanted coins as close to perfection as possible. They still do. But at that time the marketplace wasn't ready to deal with such demand in a smooth, efficient way. We didn't have the kind of strict, consistent, professional grading that's needed to instill buyer confidence in high-condition coins. And we didn't have a commoditized system of trading.

Dealer Uncertainty

Collectors and investors weren't the only ones who lacked total confidence in coin grading back in 1980. Coin dealers, too, had their doubts. And while it's true that coin prices soared astronomically during that period, they would have risen still higher for super-grade coins if it hadn't been for uncertainty over grading.

Suppose $1,000 was the going, legitimate price at that time for a certain coin in MS-65. And suppose a dealer was selling a truly amazing example of this coin that for all practical purposes looked like an MS-69—a coin on the very threshold of perfection. To reflect accurately its true rarity, that particular coin probably should have sold for 20 or 30 times the MS-65 price; but instead, the typical dealer sold it for only four, five, or maybe six times that price. Why? Because the dealers lacked self-confidence. They were not sufficiently sure of their own abilities as graders to feel comfortable charging (or paying) all that much of a premium. Sure, you'd see monster premiums on occasion, but the premiums then were nowhere near the ones being paid for super-grade coins today.

What we have today is a safer environment in which to buy and sell those high-grade, high-priced coins. If a widely respected grading service such as NGC assigns a coin a grade of MS-68, dealers feel comfortable paying an unbelievable—even an unreasonable—premium for that coin, because they don't have to rely on their own abilities. They can rely on the abilities of a top-notch grading service.

Because of this, the premiums paid today for so-called wonder coins are even more dramatic than those paid in 1980. Dealers worry far less today about taking a risk. They don't have to be afraid that if they pay $30,000 for a coin, they'll look at it under a glass half an hour later and say to themselves, "Hey, I didn't see this scratch on the reverse; this coin's worth $20,000 less than what I paid for it." The grading services furnish grading guarantees, and reasonable efforts are made to buy back coins if ever a mistake is made. Thus coin buyers are comfortable with quality today.

With quality coins, by the way, you're really getting rarity as well, so long as you're dealing in U.S. series from the 1800s or early 1900s. Liberty Seated quarters from the middle to late 1800s are legitimately rare. A Liberty Seated dime graded Proof-67 or MS-67 by NGS is a super, monster rare coin, yet it also is a coin in a high level of preservation.

The Three Keys to Value

Three basic factors determine the value of a coin.

* First and foremost is the level of preservation—how many nicks or scratches or flaws a coin has.
* Second is the collector base—how many collectors are interested in a particular coin series. A certain Lincoln cent may have a mintage of 500,000, and that's a lot of coins. But if there are a million collectors of Lincoln cents, then 500,000 becomes a relatively low number.
* Third is the number of coins extant or available. If only 50 examples of a given coin are available, but only 40 people want one, the value of the coin isn't going to be very high.

It's the interrelationship of these three factors that determines how much a coin is worth. Ideally, you want a high-grade, low-mintage coin with a broad collector base. Although mintage figures can guide you, they can be misleading because in many cases significant numbers of coins have been melted or otherwise lost since their manufacture.

In general, the higher the level of preservation, the better off you are. That's not to say you should automatically turn up your nose at all coins in circulated condition. Sometimes the finest known example of a given coin may be in less than mint condition—say, about uncirculated or extremely fine. Certainly you shouldn't reject such a coin simply because it's not MS-68 or 67.

A Winning Combination

For a number of years an emphasis on quality sometimes led the marketplace to lose sight of rarity; in top condition, low-mintage coins in a given series were selling for little more than high-mintage coins. This focus on quality offered sharp contrast to the early twentieth century, when stress was on rarity alone. In those days little attention was paid to grading. A coin was either uncirculated or it wasn't; but if just three examples of a given coin were known, *that* was extremely important.

Today we see a more balanced approach. Circa-1990 collectors are seeking a combination of quality and rarity. Today it's important that a coin be MS-68 *and* be one of three known. More money is entering this field, and buyers are becoming more selective. They want their coins to have everything. And with the advent of population reports from the grading services (see Chapter 1), they're getting to know more about the coins than they've ever known before.

A note of caution: Population reports (which tell how many coins a service has graded) can be misleading because some coins are resubmitted in quest of a higher grade. I know of instances where coins have been resubmitted 30 or 40 times—and you'll be unable to tell from the population report that this was one coin, not 30 or 40 different coins.

HOW TO GET OUT AT THE TOP

Getting out at the top requires a degree of good luck. However, you can do a great deal to improve your luck if you keep a close eye on the market and develop good instincts.

The signs to watch for here are the opposite of those that enable you to buy at the bottom.

- When you see coins going up in price dramatically and hear people talking about these increases, that's when you should sell.
- If you hear that a limited partnership is buying $50 million worth of coins, that's a good time to sell.
- If you hear there's a limited partnership that now has $80 million and is almost in its acquisition phase and coins are a great investment, but you look and don't see any other limited partnerships behind it, think about this: When these people go to sell all these coins, who's going to buy them? That could be the top; that's the time to sell.

But don't be guided strictly by marketplace signs. From a personal standpoint, the best time to sell is if you've made a profit, or if you want to cut your losses and get into something else. If you buy something for $1,000 and it increases to $10,000, that's fine. What's wrong with taking a small profit? It doesn't hurt. The coin may go up another 10 or 15 percent—but so what? You've sold and you've made a profit, and that's what's important. If you can sell and make a profit, that's the top for you.

THE ABSOLUTE TOP

Don't ever think you can sell at the absolute top, because you can't. The finest experts in this industry can't do it: the people who think they can manipulate the marketplace, control the price guides, bid coins up to whatever levels they want, and then sell them off to unsuspecting customers. In many cases their best-laid plans backfire, and they fail to get out at the top. Sometimes they end up selling off hundreds of thousands—even millions—of dollars worth of coins at the bottom of the cycle because they're in a cash-flow crunch.

You can't predict with any certainty what is going to happen in the coin field, even in the very near future. On the other hand, you *can* make reasonable assumptions based on market activity. And one such assumption seems very safe indeed: If big new money continues to enter the market from limited partnerships and other important sources on or close to Wall Street, the price increases now being seen are likely to continue and even accelerate.

A SURPRISE BULL MARKET

When I tell you that the coin field is unpredictable, I speak from personal experience. Recently, for example, I was making plans to attend a major show—the Dallas Coin and Stamp Expo in December 1988. And I was fully convinced it would be a terrible show. For that matter, that's what everyone thought. But it turned out to be just the opposite.

Prior to the show I telephoned a client and said, "Hey, this show is going to be terrible; this is a great time to buy." I called people in November and told them, "This marketplace is decreasing on a daily basis, decreasing right now by the hour; we're seeing tremendous weakness; I think you all should buy." Many of these people sent me checks. "Okay," they said, "we agree; this is a good time to buy."

A number of big auctions had taken place—including Part III of the Norweb Collection Sale, conducted by Auctions by Bowers and Merena Inc. of Wolfeboro, New Hampshire—and I felt that for this reason dealers would be facing a tremendous cash crunch. Thirty days after the Norweb Sale the auction bills would come due, and the dealers would have to pay them. I figured that I knew exactly what the future held, and I called my coin associates and told them so: "You have to buy at Dallas; that's going to be a terrible show and people are going to be selling coins at distress prices." I thought the auction held in conjunction with the show would be disastrous, even though I had clients with coins consigned to the sale. I was worried about what their coins were going to bring.

What happened at Dallas? It was one of the best coin shows we've ever had! And the coins consigned by my clients did extremely well in the auction. One coin was described in the auction catalog as Mint State-67. I expected it to bring several hundred dollars—but it ended up bringing $3,400 plus a 10-percent buyer's fee. Dallas turned out to be a tremendous success.

No one can predict even short-term trends in this field. There is no writing on the wall. The writing on the wall is the writing of the check for your profits. If you can make money selling off your coins, then do it.

Chapter

8

BIG MONEY IN ANCIENT AND WORLD COINS

The world coin market stretches around the globe and features collectors, dealers and even investors and speculators. Consequently, there are many dollars and a lot of other currencies floating around. And they're being spent in numerous cities in countries outside of the United States. I wouldn't be surprised if there were suitcases full of cash changing hands in exotic lands.

Paul M. Green, renowned numismatic
foreign correspondent

To a great number of mainstream collectors and investors, ancient coins seem as enigmatic as the riddle of the sphinx. Many dealers regard them as museum pieces, far too complex and obscure for the average person to comprehend, much less buy and sell.

It's true that old Greek and Roman coins are much more diverse and require far more study than do any nation's modern coins. But those who take the trouble to learn about these coins find them richly rewarding not only as a source of intellectual satisfaction, but also as components of a coin investment portfolio.

Although they get less publicity and are seldom in the spotlight at major U.S. coin shows and auctions, ancient coins often command impressive premiums. On a number of occasions in recent years, rare Greek and Roman coins have brought six-figure prices. What's more, their performance has been far less erratic than that of modern rarities. While U.S. coins have undergone dramatic ups and downs, ancient coins have tended to rise in value steadily, suffering only minor dips instead of major depressions along the way.

Because it seems to demand greater expertise, U.S. investors have avoided the world coin field in general, and ancient coins in particular, even in boom-market periods. It is simpler to acquire Morgan silver dollars or Saint-Gaudens double eagles than Greek tetradrachms or Roman denarii, even though it may not be less expensive. But analysts familiar with the world coin field believe that its complexity is often overstated.

"Ancient coins, especially, appear to be more difficult than they are," says Michael Hodder, a foreign coin expert at Bowers and Merena Galleries. "They're certainly not as easy to collect as U.S. coins, especially for those who got their start in the hobby by finding Lincoln cents in their pocket change. They're not at all forbidding, though— and once you get into them, they really have tremendous fascination."

LIMITED PARTNERSHIPS

A number of investors have already "gotten into" ancient coins by purchasing shares of Merrill Lynch's Athena Funds I and II. Both of these highly publicized limited-partnership funds include large numbers of ancient coins; in fact, they are the funds' key components.

It is highly probable that ancient coins and foreign coins from other periods of world history will figure even more prominently in future funds of this type. More immediately the stress is likely to be on United States coins; it is anticipated that during the next few years many millions of dollars from limited partnerships and other institutional sources will go into rare U.S. coins. But it's reasonable to assume that if this infusion of money drives up the prices of U.S. coins, as it almost surely will, investors and collectors will then set their sights on an area that was previously unexplored—namely, foreign and ancient coins. And such attention may well touch off a boom in that field too.

NELSON BUNKER HUNT'S MILLION-DOLLAR ANCIENT GREEK COIN

Texas oil tycoon Nelson Bunker Hunt helped drive the price of silver to $50 an ounce in 1980. Around the same time, he demonstrated a taste for silver in a more expensive form—roughly $667,000 per ounce.

Hunt bought a set of nine Greek dekadrachms, large silver coins weighing about an ounce and a half apiece. All but one of the coins were part of a larger collection for which Hunt reportedly paid $20 million. That made it difficult to assign a specific value to each and every coin. But the dealer who negotiated the sale—Bruce McNall, president of Numismatic Fine Arts Inc. of Beverly Hills, California—said the most valuable dekadrachm, the ultra-rare dekadrachm of Athens, was calculated at $1 million.

More recently, McNall brokered a deal for an even more valuable "commodity" when he acquired superstar Wayne Gretzky for the Los Angeles Kings hockey team and signed him to a multimillion-dollar contract. Besides being a prominent professional numismatist, McNall is also owner of the Kings.

MERRILL LYNCH'S ATHENA FUNDS

McNall and other experts at Numismatic Fine Arts (NFA) are serving as consultants on the two Athena funds. Numisarts Inc., an NFA affiliate, is managing general partner of the funds, and NFA is acting as portfolio manager. NFA's role is to oversee the selection, acquisition, and disposition of the funds' components. MLL Antiquities Inc., a wholly owned subsidiary of Merrill Lynch, is administrative general partner. Both funds are seven-year limited partnerships.

The $7.3 million Athena Fund I was formed in the summer of 1986. By the end of 1988 its managers were reporting a 36 percent net gain. Merrill Lynch began selling the $40 million Athena Fund II in August 1988. According to its prospectus, Athena II's objective is to put together "an investment quality portfolio consisting principally of ancient Greek and Roman coins and, to a lesser extent, Greek and Roman antiquities." This parallels the purpose of the first Athena fund.

Athena I and II are pursuing the same kind of seven-year strategy. In each case the first three years are designated as a "trading period," during which the emphasis is on short-term assets—coins and antiquities meant for sale within two years of their purchase. This activity is designed to generate profits from which cash distributions can be made to the limited partners. The fourth year is planned as a "transition period," during which all remaining "trading assets" will be sold and the concentration will shift to longer-term holdings. The last three years are programmed as a "liquidation period," during which dispersal of the assets will be completed through "major public auctions, direct public sales, and private transactions."

A Fast Start for Merrill Lynch

Athena Fund I has enjoyed early success. In March 1987, NFA sold 532 Athena coins (about 29 percent of the fund's portfolio, on a cost basis) for nearly $1.9 million at public auction. After deductions for sale-related costs and commissions, the fund achieved a 41 percent net increase in value on those coins over a seven-month period. In March 1988, NFA conducted a second Athena auction and sold 521 coins (15 percent of the partnership's portfolio) for nearly $1.25 million. This time the net gain in value amounted to 44 percent.

NFA earned similar healthy profits for the fund through private sales of other Athena coins. Most notable of these was a lovely Athenian dekadrachm that was reportedly purchased by an anonymous Beverly Hills businessman for $600,000 (see Figure 8-1). The sale was arranged by NFA and Superior Stamp and Coin Co., which also is based in Beverly Hills.

How the Athena Funds Work

The Athena funds' managers seek to generate profits in three different ways. First, they acquire ancient coins and antiquities at wholesale prices and sell them at retail. Second, they purchase items that historically have risen in value over time and count on the market trend to continue its normal upward path. Third, they attempt to assemble complete sets of related objects because these are often worth more as a whole than the sum of their separate parts.

To become a limited partner in Athena Fund II, an investor must

Figure 8-1. Athenian dekadrachm from Merrill Lynch's Athena Fund I, bought privately from the fund by a Beverly Hills businessman for a reported $600,000. (Photo courtesy Superior Stamp and Coin Co. Inc.)

purchase at least five "units" of interest in the fund. These are priced at $1,000 each, so the minimum investment is $5,000. The prospectus provides for a maximum sale of 25,000 units, or $25 million worth. However, Merrill Lynch may sell up to 15,000 additional units, bringing the overall total to 40,000 units worth $40 million.

Limited partners will receive 100 percent of all cash distributed by the fund up to the point where they have 100 percent of their original investment. In addition they will receive a cumulative, annualized, noncompounded return of 12 percent. Beyond that they will get 85 percent of any additional cash distributions until they have received 200 percent of their original investment. After that point they'll get 76 percent of any further cash distributed by the fund.

KING-SIZE GOLD COINS

Greece and Rome don't have a corner on interesting and valuable world coins from the past. In 1987, collectors were startled when a European auction house—Habsburg, Feldman S.A. of Geneva, Switzerland—announced its intention to sell two truly spectacular gold coins from seventeenth-century Hindustan.

Both coins were rare, but what set them apart from virtually all others was their size: One was about 8 inches in diameter and weighed almost 32 troy pounds, more than 29 pounds of it gold (see Figure 8-2); the other was 3.8 inches in diameter and weighed about 3 troy pounds.

These coins, known as "mohurs," were struck in Hindustan during the reign of India's Mughal emperors. It's believed that these and other coins like them were presentation pieces. David Feldman, managing director of the auction house, suggested that coins of the larger size may have been struck as gifts for ambassadors of Persia, then a powerful ally of the Mughals.

Whether or not they started out as presentation pieces, they certainly ended up as conversation pieces. Part of that conversation took place on NBC's Today Show, where host Bryant Gumbel whimsically flipped the larger piece in his hand like a gilded, overweight Frisbee.

At the going market price of $480 per ounce, the larger coin would have been worth about $169,000 just as bullion. But the auction firm (and presumably the consignor) had set much higher goals: The presale estimates were $10 million for the larger piece and $4 million for its companion.

Either of those figures would have shattered the auction record

Figure 8-2. Hindustani 1,000-mohur gold coin. Weighs nearly 32 troy pounds. Carried a $10 million estimate at a November 1987 auction, but was withdrawn by the consignor. (Photo courtesy Habsburg, Feldman S.A.)

for any single coin (a mark just broken in 1989, when Kidder Peabody's coin fund bought a United States 1804 silver dollar for $990,000). But while both drew bids well above $1 million, both fell short of the preestablished minimums, and the consignor chose to withdraw them from sale.

The auction firm suggested that the coins might appeal to a sultan or a king, or possibly to a wealthy American or Japanese investor. That may yet prove to be the case at somewhat lower prices. But in the meantime, these exotic, remarkable coins have helped stir new interest in world coinage.

COLLECTORS OF FOREIGN COINS

Coin collecting inevitably involves a degree of national pride, perhaps even chauvinism. Hobbyists tend to collect items they associate with their homeland. Thus U.S. coin collectors favor U.S. coins, Canadians prefer Canadian issues, and so on.

There are practical reasons for this, of course, as well as sentimental ones. The source of supply is near, the resale market is close at hand, and it's easier to find collectors with similar interests. But national pride and sentiment can be highly potent forces in the sale of certain coins. In 1986, for example, Japan announced plans to mint 10 million 100,000-yen gold coins to honor Emperor Hirohito on the 60th anniversary of his reign. A lottery was held because of high public demand for the coin, and 20 million Japanese entered. That's a staggering number of coins to mint and to sell, considering that each contains almost two-thirds of an ounce of gold.

The United States Mint had similar success with a 1986 half eagle (or $5 gold coin) honoring the Statue of Liberty. Congress authorized a maximum mintage of 500,000, and the issue was oversubscribed before the end of the so-called preordering period. Again, sales could be attributed at least in part to a strong sense of patriotism evoked by the highly visible, highly popular symbol that appeared on the coin.

The principal collectors of foreign coins, then, are people to whom they are not "foreign": those who live in the country of issue.

Americans' Special Role

Americans occupy a somewhat unique niche in that they are all either immigrants or descendants of immigrants. As a result, many retain a special attachment to the country or countries of their forebears; and those with an interest in coins frequently collect not only U.S. issues, but also coins of their ancestral homelands. This helps explain why Americans are among the most active collectors of "world" or foreign coins.

Some collectors, of course, find foreign coins appealing for reasons that have absolutely nothing to do with national pride, family ties, or ethnic identification. Their interest may stem from intellectual curiosity about the history and the culture of other lands. Or they may simply find the coins themselves attractive. Foreign coins hold particular appeal to hobbyists who collect along the lines of a common theme: coins depicting animals, buildings, ships, monarchs, natural wonders, landmarks, and the like. Diversity, in fact, is one of their greatest lures.

THE RATIONALE BEHIND ANCIENTS

Ancient coins are widely viewed more as works of art than forms of money. People collect them because they are relics of some of the world's most glorious cultures, much as they collect Grecian urns or Roman statues.

Age, of course, is part of their appeal; many date back well over 2,000 years. But age alone isn't a good barometer of value: Base-metal Roman coins often can be purchased in attractive, collectible grades for less than $50. As with modern coinage, the two key factors are supply and demand. Because well-preserved gold and silver ancient coins tend to be the ones in shortest supply, they are in the greatest demand.

The Role of Hoards

Among the most important sources of rare ancient coins, and most significant influences on their price, are the long-concealed hoards that turn up from time to time. Some of these caches date back many centuries and contain multiple examples of the ancient world's rarest coins.

In 1984, for example, three Turkish treasure hunters found what has been described as "the hoard of the century" buried in a field near the town of Elmali, Turkey. There, in an earthen jar, they discovered nearly 2,000 Greek silver coins dating from about 465 B.C. and apparently secreted ever since. The hoard included 14 Athenian dekadrachms, all in mint condition. Until that time only 13 of these coins had been known to exist in the whole world, and not a single one was in mint condition. These alone were worth millions of dollars, and estimates placed the hoard's total value at up to $10 million.

The sudden, simultaneous appearance of so many Athenian dekadrachms had a shock value on the market, depressing the prices of the previously known examples as well as of the newly discovered ones. But while hoards can disrupt the market in the short term, their long-range impact tends to be positive. They stimulate interest, make rare coins available to a wider circle of buyers, and in time push prices even higher as demand catches up to supply.

THE ECONOMIC FACTOR

Beyond all other considerations, foreign and ancient coins appeal to many collectors for reasons of economics. As a group, they're more affordable (that is, they cost less) than U.S. coins.

When the U.S. coin market soared to record heights in 1979 and 1980, many collectors turned to the world coin market instead. They found that prices there were much more reasonable. They also discovered that world coins offer—quite literally—a world of variety and pleasure. And later, when things took a turn for the worse in the U.S. market, collectors learned another very important lesson: Foreign coins were far safer ports in an economic storm.

Why did the price of world coins fail to drop significantly during the market's lean years? The answer is simple; never had they risen excessively high to begin with. Because they hadn't attracted the kind of investor interest that U.S. coins had enjoyed, they hadn't experienced the same dramatic surge.

A World of Difference

Because it is global in scope, the world coin market differs in basic ways from the U.S. coin market. Consider the significance of currency rates, for example.

Since world coins routinely cross international borders, foreign exchange rates play an important part in dictating their prices and determining whether the coins cross those borders coming or going. When European currencies are weak in relation to the dollar, dealers and collectors from the continent (traditionally the major buyers of foreign and ancient coins) aren't as willing to purchase such material in this country. Their money isn't worth as much when they exchange it for dollars.

Conversely, when the dollar is relatively weak, foreigners' buying power increases, and so does the level of their coin-buying activity. The dollar's strength or weakness is much less of an issue in the U.S. coin market because the overwhelming majority of the buyers and sellers there are Americans.

GRADING AND AUTHENTICITY

Buyers of foreign and ancient coins are far less concerned with superlative condition than their counterparts in the U.S. coin market. High-grade coins command higher premiums than those in lesser condition, to be sure, but the difference in price isn't nearly as dramatic as it is for U.S. coins. As a result, less emphasis is placed on pinpoint accuracy in grading.

Authenticity, by contrast, tends to be more of an issue with foreign and ancient coins. The diversity of material and the relative obscurity of many individual foreign and ancient coins make it easier to produce successful counterfeits. Detection of bogus coins is more difficult in the foreign and ancient market.

Grading with a Foreign Accent

To date, the major grading services have concerned themselves primarily with U.S. coins, and their efforts in that area have reassured many buyers—especially investors with limited knowledge of coins. Some have taken steps to grade foreign coins, as well, but these efforts have been rather tentative for the most part. For one thing, the foreign market's breadth and diversity make it more difficult to quantify and reduce to a simple set of word-and-number grades. The problem is compounded by the fact that foreign coins come from so many different periods of history and methods of manufacture. In addition there has been considerable resistance from the marketplace itself. Collectors outnumber investors by a wide margin, and many have been vocal in asserting their opposition to numerical grades, plastic slabs, and all the other trappings of third-party grading.

The American Numismatic Association Certification Service (ANACS) offers adjectival grading of foreign and ancient coins. But while it recognizes 11 Mint-State grades for U.S. coins, it uses only one ("Uncirculated") for foreign and ancient pieces.

In November 1988, the Professional Coin Grading Service (PCGS) announced plans to certify Canadian coins, complete with the use of plastic slabs, starting in early 1989. PCGS President David Hall said once that program was established, his grading service hoped to expand into British, French, Swiss, and German coins as well. The Numismatic Guaranty Corporation of America (NGC) began grading Canadian coins in August 1989.

The International Numismatic Society Authentication Bureau (INSAB) in Washington, D.C., has been grading foreign and ancient coins for more than a decade. It has done so, however, chiefly as an adjunct to authenticating the coins, according to its director, Charles Hoskins. Like ANACS, INSAB uses only adjectival grades, not numerical ones, for such coins.

SPREADING OF KNOWLEDGE

Although U.S. coins continue to dominate the American marketplace, foreign coins have made substantial gains. In large part this is due to the appearance of major new books on the subject, in particular the *Standard Catalog of World Coins* by Chester L. Krause and Clifford Mishler (Colin R. Bruce II, ed. Iola, WI: Krause Publications).

This large book, first published in 1972 and updated annually since, provides complete details on coins from around the world from 1801 to the present. It has stimulated wide interest in world coins, just as *A Guide Book of United States Coins* (the so-called Red Book) did for U.S. coins in the 1940s and 1950s.

MODERN MINT ISSUES

Some of the less impressive investments in modern world coinage are special "collector" coins and sets sold at premium prices by government mints (see Figure 8-3). As a rule, these are made of gold or silver and issued at prices substantially above the value of the metal they contain. With some exceptions, they soon lose their premium in the secondary market and end up being overpriced "bullion coins"— worth only their metal value and possibly discounted slightly even from that.

In recent years, for instance, the British Royal Mint has been issuing brilliant uncirculated gold coins in a five-pound denomination for $795 apiece. Each of these coins contains just a little more than an ounce of gold—and in early 1989, with gold selling for slightly more than $400 an ounce, a person seeking to resell one of these coins

Figure 8-3. 1988 Korean Olympic Proof set. These are some of the 24 gold and silver coins issued by the Republic of Korea to commemorate and help finance the 1988 Summer Games in Seoul.

Figure 8-4. 1982 Canadian Proof silver dollar, part of an annual series of silver dollars issued by the Royal Canadian Mint for sale to the public at a premium. This example commemorates the centennial of the City of Regina.

probably would have been fortunate to get more than $400. That's barely 50 percent of the issue price.

The "values" are even poorer with coins from many smaller countries that lack the collector base of British coinage. Some countries, in fact, issue so-called coins that are really no more than precious-metal doodads aimed straight at the overstuffed wallets of gullible American buyers. Among them are such dubious dots on the map as the Turks and Caicos Islands, the Cook Islands, the Maldive Islands, and Western Samoa. Typically, the markup on such coins is well over 50 percent above their bullion value; barring a massive rise in the price of precious metal, they'll almost surely never be worth anything close to their issue price at resale (see Figure 8-4). Like some of the Franklin Mint medals of years gone by, they're shiny and pretty, perhaps, but not shimmering investments.

Chapter

9

BULLION-RELATED CHOICES

Liquidity . . . is the greatest single asset of bullion coins. Being well known and accepted, the popular bullion coins are widely available at stock brokerage houses, banks and coin shops. In fact, they can be bought (or sold) in virtually every city of any size in the United States or in just about every country around the world at their current bullion value.

Jeffrey A. Nichols,
The Complete Book of Gold Investing

"Numismatics" is the elegant name for coin collecting, and coins with special value as collectibles are said to be numismatic in nature. "Bullion coins," by contrast, are coins whose market value is based on the value of the metal they contain. These go up or down in price directly according to the rise or fall in value of the metal.

Bullion coins are available in a number of different precious metals. Gold and silver are the ones most widely used, but several major countries recently began producing bullion coins made of platinum.

Supply and demand determine the price of a numismatic coin. Demand is influenced strongly by the quality of a coin: In today's condition-conscious market, coins in an exceptional state of preservation bring exceptional prices.

The price of a bullion coin is determined by taking its bullion value (the value of the metal it contains) and adding a small surcharge to cover the costs of production, distribution, and handling. Normally this surcharge is less than 10 percent of the coin's intrinsic worth.

GOLD BULLION COINS

Gold is the dominant metal in the bullion coin market. Silver bullion coins, being far cheaper, account for the sale of more units. Platinum bullion coins tend to be more expensive. But gold bullion coins set the tone for the overall market, get most of the publicity, figure most prominently in marketing and advertising efforts, and generate the lion's share of the revenue.

A GLOBAL MARKET

The bullion coin market is global in scope. Its three chief components are Europe, the Americas, and the Far East; sales in the United States exceed those in any other country.

At first glance it seems natural that Americans should be the biggest buyers; after all, they reign supreme in most investment markets. In this case, however, their preeminence is truly quite remarkable, considering that until the mid-1970s federal law prohibited them from buying, selling, or owning bullion gold. And until a few years ago, there weren't any U.S. bullion coins for them to buy.

U.S. GOLD COINAGE

For well over a century, gold coins were an integral part of the U.S. monetary system. The act of Congress establishing the U.S. Mint in 1792 authorized three different coins made of gold: an eagle ($10 gold piece), a half eagle ($5 gold piece) and a quarter eagle ($2.50 gold piece).

In time the Mint added new gold coins of other denominations: notably the double eagle ($20 gold piece), whose issue was prompted by the California Gold Rush. Two short-lived denominations—the gold dollar and $3 gold piece—were minted for relatively brief periods in the middle and late nineteenth century.

U.S. gold coinage continued until 1933, and while such coins were never used routinely in everyday commerce, they did circulate freely more often than not.

THE GOLD SURRENDER ORDER

When he became President in March 1933, Franklin D. Roosevelt took a number of steps to jolt the nation out of the Great Depression. One of the most dramatic involved private ownership of gold.

An integral part of FDR's program was devaluation of the dollar, but that required raising the price of gold. Because Roosevelt feared his entire plan would be jeopardized unless the federal government had firm control over gold, he imposed a ban on gold ownership. Less than a week after taking office, Roosevelt clamped an embargo on exports of gold, prohibited banks from paying out gold coins or gold certificates, and ordered individuals holding gold coins or gold certificates to return them to the banking system.

A few weeks later, on April 5, the Treasury issued a formal order requiring the surrender of all gold bullion, gold coins, and gold certificates still in private hands. People who failed to comply were subject to heavy fines and imprisonment for up to 10 years. It was, in effect, a nationalization of gold.

Collector coins and jewelry were exempted from the ban, but many Americans—acting in fear or in ignorance—sold their gold coins to the Treasury anyway. And many who kept gold coins hid them, mistakenly believing their possession was illegal.

In all, the Treasury bought up gold coins with a face value of more than a billion dollars. All of them, rare and common alike, ended up in government melting pots, later to be cast into ingots and stored at federal depositories at Fort Knox, West Point, and elsewhere. It is estimated that 80 percent of the U.S. gold coins then in private hands were turned in.

Four Decades in the Wilderness

Except for jewelry and certain collector coins, gold remained off limits for more than 40 years. But as time went by, agitation to rescind the prohibition grew. Finally, in 1974, Congress passed legislation lifting the long-standing ban. On December 31, 1974, Americans regained the right to buy, sell, and own gold bullion and all gold coins without restriction (see Figure 9-1).

Lingering Suspicion

Removal of the ban didn't exactly stimulate a gold rush. Initially, most Americans seemed to regard gold with a mixture of distrust and

Figure 9-1. 1984 Olympic Proof U.S. Eagle. The first gold coin issued by the United States in more than half a century. One of three coins issued to commemorate and help finance the 1984 Summer Games in Los Angeles.

curiosity—with the emphasis on distrust. Four decades of deprivation had given rise to suspicion about this forbidden fruit. Institutions dealing in traditional investments (brokerage houses and banks, in particular) fed the public's concern with TV commercials and print-media ads warning of the hazards and drawbacks of investing in gold.

Because of this negative climate, the market for gold bullion coins was slow to take root. The fact that it took root at all during the first few years was attributable primarily to a coin that would later be the target of a new ban: South Africa's one-ounce gold Krugerrand.

THE SOUTH AFRICAN KRUGERRAND

Rise of the Krugerrand

From its introduction in the United States in 1975, the Krugerrand was widely unpopular with human-rights activists because of South Africa's racial policy of apartheid. But the free market, like nature, seemed to abhor a vacuum even more than it did the Krugerrand. Critics notwithstanding, the coin quickly vaulted to the top of the bullion-coin sales charts.

Helped by an expensive advertising blitz, the Krugerrand became the dominant coin in the small but expanding United States gold bullion market. It held that position from the mid-1970s through the early

1980s. And in the process it provided American buyers with a basic education in private gold ownership. By the early 1980s, South Africa was selling millions of ounces worth of Krugerrands in the United States every year.

A Tentative American Alternative

The Krugerrand's success, coupled with its tainted image, triggered calls for an American alternative. At first, however, Congress and the Treasury met these demands halfheartedly.

For five years, starting in 1980, the Treasury marketed one-ounce and half-ounce gold pieces known at first as American Arts Gold Medallions and later simply as U.S. Gold. These were bullion gold pieces bearing the portraits of well-known Americans from various creative fields. They were, indeed, an American alternative—but not a very good one. They were medals rather than coins, and they didn't have legal-tender status. For these and other reasons, the public never embraced them.

Fall of the Krugerrand

As time went by, protests against the Krugerrand grew more and more insistent. By 1985, Congress and the White House were compelled to make a meaningful response. In September of that year Congress passed legislation banning importation of any further Krugerrands. Three months later it authorized production of a new gold bullion coin, a coin that would be called the American Eagle.

AMERICAN EAGLES

Family of Eagles

Actually there are four different gold American Eagles: the basic Eagle, which contains one troy ounce of gold, and three subsidiary pieces that contain one-half, one-quarter, and one-tenth of an ounce, respectively (see Figure 9-2). These parallel the sizes of the Krugerrand, which also comes in both the one-ounce size and fractional versions. For that matter, these sizes are standard for most other major gold bullion coins as well—including Canada's Maple Leaf (Figure 9-3), Great Britain's Britannia, and Australia's Nugget.

The obverse (or "heads" side) of each gold American Eagle is patterned after the obverse of the much-admired Saint-Gaudens double eagle, a $20 gold piece designed by renowned sculptor Augustus Saint-

Figure 9-2. The Family of Eagles American gold bullion coins, in face values of $50 (1 oz), $25 (½ oz), $10 (¼ oz), and $5 (⅒ oz). (Photos courtesy Ed Reiter)

Gaudens. The reverse of the new coins portrays a family of eagles—a theme intended to signify the importance of family life in America.

The U.S. Mint also produces a one-ounce silver American Eagle with a $1 face value. Again the design is borrowed in part from a classic U.S. coin of the past: The silver Eagle's obverse duplicates the obverse of the Walking Liberty half dollar, while its reverse depicts a heraldic eagle.

All the American Eagles have legal-tender status, but their face values are considerably less than the value of the bullion they contain.

Figure 9-3. Canadian Maple Leaf platinum bullion coin, containing one ounce of platinum. (Photo courtesy Ed Reiter)

For instance, the one-ounce gold piece carries a face value of $50 and legally can be spent for that amount. But spending the coin would be foolish because $50 is just a fraction of what the coin is worth as gold bullion. The face values of the fractional Eagles are $25 for the half-ounce, $10 for the quarter-ounce, and $5 for the tenth-ounce coins.

Early Success

At first the American Eagles took the market by storm. In less than seven months the U.S. Mint exceeded its first-year sales goal of 2.2 million ounces. But recently the Eagles' wings have been clipped by tough and resourceful competition, especially from the Canadian Maple Leaf. On a worldwide basis the Maple Leaf is the only gold bullion coin that outsells the American Eagle.

From the gold Eagles' first appearance in October 1986 through late 1988, their sales totaled upward of 3.5 million ounces.

Broadening the Base

Contrary to some market analysts' expectations, the American Eagle didn't drive out the competition. In fact it stimulated more new entries by expanding the market's base and making it more attractive to other countries. Both the Britannia and the Nugget were introduced soon after the Eagle made its debut.

THE BULLION COIN MARKET

Dividing a Big Pie

Americans are being bombarded today by glitzy ad campaigns urging them to buy gold bullion coins. Uncle Sam is conducting one of the most aggressive of these campaigns—an interesting commentary on American adaptability, considering that only a few years ago the U.S. government would have treated the very same coins as contraband.

The Gold Institute, a worldwide association of gold producers and sellers, reports that in 1987 usage of gold in coins totaled 6.2 million ounces. Of this, it says, nearly 4 million ounces went into bullion coins and the balance into commemorative coins such as the U.S. $5 gold piece marking the bicentennial of the U.S. Constitution. At this writing, comparable figures are not yet available for 1988.

The bullion-coin statistics translate into a market of close to $2 billion a year. That makes it obvious why so many important nations are getting into the act and scrambling for a slice of this juicy pie (see Figure 9-4).

Seeking a Competitive Edge

A case can be made that one bullion coin is as good as any other; gold is gold, after all, and most of the major bullion coins trade within a very narrow price range. However, each country seeks a competitive edge by stressing the advantages—real or perceived—of its own entry. And in the process, truth doesn't always emerge unscathed.

The U.S. Mint, for instance, touts the American Eagle as a coin of unusual beauty, noting its link to the Saint-Gaudens double eagle. What it fails to mention is that on the bullion coin, Mint technicians modified the artist's original work, enraging purists.

The Royal Canadian Mint proclaims that the gold in the Maple Leaf is .999 fine, making it "purer" than many of its competitors—including the American Eagle, whose fineness is .9167. What it doesn't say is that all contain the same amount of gold. (The ounce of gold in a standard American Eagle is alloyed with silver and copper to make the coin more durable, bringing the total weight to slightly more than an ounce.)

Figure 9-4. 1988 Proof 1-ounce Panda gold bullion coin. Pandas are often viewed as numismatic coins, for they are cute and appealing and in recent years have been a trendy item. The China Mint Company has held down the mintages, despite growing demand.

The British Royal Mint boasts of the Britannia's high face value of 100 pounds, or roughly $175 in U.S. funds. Since the coin is legal tender and spendable, that's the least it will ever be worth. But while it's true that other bullion coins carry lower face values, it's also true that even after a long period of sluggishness, an ounce of gold was still worth more than $400 in early 1989. Thus the $175 "safety net" isn't all that reassuring.

The Sales Chain

For the gold American Eagle, the sales chain begins at the U.S. Mint. Thirty major banks, brokerage houses, and other distributors meet the Mint's criteria for purchasing gold Eagles directly from the government. These firms must order a minimum of 5,000 ounces at a time, although the coins' sizes can be mixed. The Mint charges a premium of 3 percent over bullion value for the one-ounce Eagles, 5 percent for the half-ounce, 7 percent for the quarter-ounce, and 9 percent for the tenth-ounce coins.

The distributors pick up the coins at either the West Point Mint or the San Francisco Mint and must pay for transporting them by armored car to their places of business. Then they sell the coins to dealers or, in some cases, directly to the public.

Typical Surcharges

At each level the surcharge rises by roughly 2 percent. Thus retail customers generally pay a premium of about 7 percent for a one-ounce gold bullion coin, 9 percent for a half-ounce piece, and a progressively higher percentage for smaller coins.

The smaller coins' higher premiums reflect the fact that minting and marketing costs are relatively constant, even when the metal value is less. So while the price is lower than that of a bigger coin, the percentage of that price attributable to fixed costs is higher. Similarly, the premium is likely to be higher on a silver bullion coin than on a gold bullion coin, simply because the base price established by the metal itself is so much smaller.

BULLION ALTERNATIVES

U.S. Silver Coinage

Silver coins jingled routinely in Americans' pockets and purses from the 1790s right through the 1960s. By the mid-1960s, however, the price of silver bullion had risen to the point where silver U.S. coins were starting to be worth more as metal than as money. In 1965 the U.S. Mint started making silverless quarters and dimes (composed of a copper-nickel alloy bonded to a core of pure copper) and reduced the silver content of the Kennedy half dollar from 90 to 40 percent. In 1971 the half dollar lost its remaining silver.

Since then the Mint has issued a number of coins containing silver, but not for use in circulation. All have been made for sale at a premium, either as commemoratives, as bullion coins, or as special collector issues.

Silver Bullion Coins

The one-ounce silver American Eagle was introduced in 1986, around the same time as the gold American Eagle. Typically, retail dealers sell it for a markup of about $1.50 over the "spot" price of silver. Thus with silver bullion at $6 an ounce, a silver Eagle would cost about $7.50. Most dealers offer discounts for bulk purchases.

A $1.50 surcharge on $6 worth of silver represents a premium of 25 percent. As I noted earlier, this is relatively high because the base value of the metal itself is so small. If silver bullion were to double in value to $12 an ounce, the dollar amount of the surcharge might well remain the same; in that case it would be just 12.5 percent of the bullion value.

The Royal Canadian Mint recently unveiled a new one-ounce silver Maple Leaf. This has a face value of $5, which is not much less than its current value as bullion. In effect that becomes the floor: the smallest amount the coin will ever be worth.

Platinum Bullion Coins

Although most bullion coins continue to feature gold or silver, recently platinum has emerged as an increasingly visible—and perhaps even viable—alternative.

In 1988, Australia and Canada both introduced platinum bullion coins: Australia's Koala and Canada's platinum Maple Leaf. These are the first platinum bullion coins to be issued by any major nation on a high-volume basis. In addition, Johnson Matthey, a leading supplier and fabricator of precious metal products, recently introduced a one-ounce platinum medal intended to appeal to the same basic buyers. It's called the Platinum Dragon.

Historically, platinum has been costlier than gold under normal conditions. In December 1988, however, the platinum bullion market was plunged into turmoil when Ford Motor Company announced it had found a way to manufacture catalytic converters without the use of platinum, which formerly had been a critical component of those devices. Overnight the price of platinum plummeted as much as $100 an ounce on some markets.

Platinum value has tended to swing more widely than that of gold, and analysts suggest that this will make platinum bullion coins more appealing to investors who like "action." The gold market's prolonged sluggishness during the last few years has been viewed as a serious drawback for gold bullion coins.

On the negative side, platinum is relatively dull in appearance, less aesthetically pleasing than gold. And, as I noted, normally it is costlier.

Those producing the platinum bullion pieces see them not so much replacing as supplementing gold bullion. "These give investors another convenient option," said Neil Carson, Johnson Matthey's U.S. marketing manager for investment products. "We expect that most will buy platinum in addition to gold, not instead of it."

Ingots, Bars, and Rounds

Privately produced ingots, bars, and rounds (round, coin-shaped pieces) offer investors still another way to obtain precious metal in convenient, portable form. Firms such as Johnson Matthey, Engelhard Industries, and the Sunshine Bullion Company fabricate these items in a variety of precious metals and sizes.

Because of the metals' high intrinsic value, one-ounce bars and rounds are by far the biggest sellers for gold and platinum. One-ounce silver bars and rounds are popular as well, but 10-ounce, 100-ounce, and even 1,000-ounce silver ingots also enjoy brisk sales. With gold at $400 an ounce and silver at $6 (the approximate market levels as of January 1989), a 100-ounce silver ingot would cost only about 50 percent more than a one-ounce gold bar, round, or coin.

Premiums on privately made bullion items vary according to company, metal, and size. As with bullion coins, the percentages are smaller on higher-value pieces. On Sunshine silver items, for example, a buyer might expect to pay premiums over the spot price of silver of 85 cents an ounce for a one-ounce round, 75 cents an ounce for a 10-ounce bar, 55 cents an ounce for a 100-ounce bar, and 29 cents an ounce for a 1,000-ounce bar.

NUMISMATIC AND BULLION COMBINATIONS

"Numismatic" Bullion

Some bullion coins carry higher premiums than others of comparable size. China's gold Panda coins, for instance, retail for about 2 percent more than gold American Eagles or Maple Leafs. Although they are basically bullion coins, the Pandas are perceived by some buyers and sellers as having a numismatic (or "seminumismatic") aspect as well. That's because the China Mint has held down their mintages, even in the face of rising demand.

Proof Bullion Coins

A number of bullion coins are struck in special "proof" editions for sale at heightened premiums to collectors. This is the case, for instance, with the gold and silver American Eagles, the Britannia (Figure 9-5) and the Nugget (Figure 9-6).

A proof is a specimen coin made by taking highly polished planchets, or coin blanks, and striking them two or more times with highly polished dies so that every detail is enhanced. Present-day proofs typically have reflective "mirror" surfaces, and the raised portions of their designs often have an attractive frosted appearance.

Figure 9-5. 1988 Proof 1-ounce British Britannia gold bullion coin. The face value is the highest of the major gold bullion coins (the 100-pound piece is the equivalent of about $175 in U.S. funds).

Figure 9-6. 1988 Proof 1-ounce Australian Nugget gold bullion coin. The design depicts a gold nugget discovered in Australia.

Proof bullion coins are widely viewed as collectibles, and this is reflected in the prices at which they are issued by government mints. The proof one-ounce silver Eagle, for example, has been issued by the U.S. Mint at prices ranging from $21 to $23 apiece. By contrast, the regular silver Eagle could have been purchased for less than half that amount.

I advise against purchasing proof bullion coins directly from the mints at their issue price. The gold American Eagles, in particular, tend to fall significantly below their issue price in the resale market once the official ordering period is over. Thus it makes sense to wait a while and buy them from a coin dealer after the initial excitement dies down. I do recommend buying these proofs if they can be acquired for reasonable premiums—premiums not much higher than those of their ordinary, nonproof counterparts. They're extremely attractive and desirable—at the right price.

Bullion-Related Numismatic Coins

Just as some bullion coins have an overlay of numismatic appeal, certain numismatic coins have bullion-related aspects. Among the most commonly traded of these are Saint-Gaudens double eagles in circulated grades such as very fine (VF), extremely fine (XF) and about uncirculated (AU).

In one sense, these really are bullion coins. Their value fluctuates in direct proportion to the value of the gold they contain (96.75 percent of an ounce). On another level, though, they sometimes have unusual potential as collectibles. At present, you can obtain VF or XF examples of certain scarcer-date double eagles for prices not much higher than bullion levels. In my opinion these are incredible bargains, tremendous opportunities for the knowledgeable buyer.

At this writing, gold is just slightly above $400 an ounce and circulated Saint-Gaudens double eagles can be had for about $450. These are numismatic coins, with all the profit potential of collectibles; yet at the same time they're bullion items.

In cases where the premium is just a bit higher than 15 percent, a buyer gets a bonus: Although the price is still very close to the bullion level, the coin is exempt from Internal Revenue Service reporting requirements.

GOVERNMENT REPORTING REQUIREMENTS

Investors' enthusiasm for bullion coins has been dampened somewhat in recent years by stringent reporting requirements imposed during the early to mid-1980s. Most pervasive of these is the rule requiring coin and bullion dealers to submit reports to the IRS whenever they purchase certain forms of bullion, including bullion coins. This rule is subject to differing interpretations. The reports must be transmitted almost immediately by magnetic media. In some states there are further local regulations governing certain bullion-related transactions. We have even seen proposals that would force buyers and sellers of precious metals to submit a right thumbprint as part of their proof of identification.

While it has hurt bullion sales, this rash of reporting requirements has benefited the rare coin market. It has caused many investors to shift from buying gold and other precious metals to buying numismatic coins instead. These are not subject to the IRS reporting rules and thus provide far greater privacy.

The Industry Council for Tangible Assets, a trade association based in Washington, D.C., has done extensive research on reporting requirements. ICTA has distributed the following policy statement to its members.

Summary and Explanation of the IRS Broker Reporting Regulations as Applied to Bullion and Coins

• *Current Requirements (in effect since July 1, 1983)*

Any purchase by a dealer from a non-corporate customer/seller of a physical commodity is reportable to the IRS on Form 1099B. Sales by a dealer to a customer are not reportable. Any type of property approved by the CFTC for futures contract trading is a commodity subject to the reporting requirement. Gold and silver bullion remain approved by the CFTC and thus fall within the broker reporting requirement. Dealers are required to send copies of the reporting forms for a year to the customer by the end of January following each calendar year, and to the IRS by the end of February following each calendar year. The IRS takes the position that any person or firm regularly engaged in selling coins or bullion to the public is a "dealer" for purposes of these rules.

• *Current Coverage of Specific Kinds of Coins*

Coins are not in terms covered by the existing broker reporting regulation. They become covered only if the CFTC has approved futures contract trading in the coins. In December 1983 the CFTC approved such trading in South African Krugerrands, Canadian Maple Leafs and Mexican one-ounce coins. Therefore, at the present time dealer purchases of these coins are reportable transactions under the regulation. Further, some years ago the CFTC approved futures trading in bags of U.S. silver coins. While such futures contracts are not now approved for trading because more than three years have passed since trades in them occurred, the IRS takes the position that all dealer purchases of U.S. silver coins are reportable. Under the existing regulation transactions in coins (whether or not "numismatic") other than the Krugerrand, Maple Leaf, Mexican one-ounce and U.S. silver coins are not subject to reporting. In a press release dated June 8, 1984, the IRS formally announced its position regarding transactions in particular coins as described above, and stated that the reporting requirement applies to the purchase of any quantity of such coins, including a single coin.

• *IRS Clarification: IRS Private Letter Ruling Issued on October 4, 1984.*

The IRS issued a private letter ruling to a coin dealer (made public on January 30, 1985) in which it ruled that transactions in commodities covered by the outstanding broker reporting regulations are reportable irrespective of the quantity sold, and even if the quantity varies from the quantity approved by the CFTC for futures contract trading. In particular the IRS ruled that purchases of bullion in units less than the amount approved for CFTC trading are reportable.

• *Magnetic Tape Reporting*

Dealers are generally required to make the reports under Section 6045 on magnetic media rather than on Form 1099s. Alternatively, the IRS may permit a dealer to file Form 1099s if the dealer shows "undue hardship" on an application filed with the appropriate IRS Center. No generally prescribed form is used for this purpose, which may be done by letter, nor is there any official guidance as to what constitutes "hardship." Further, the regulation does not state how long a hardship exception will apply once it is granted. The regulation declares that hardship applications by existing dealers were to be filed by September 15, 1983, while a person who thereafter becomes a dealer must file a hardship application by the end of the second month in which he becomes a dealer subject to the reporting rules. Further, the IRS regulation states that if a *timely* hardship request is filed by a dealer, the magnetic media first applies to him for the first reporting period—typically a year—that begins after the hardship request is denied.

• *Proposed IRS Regulations Regarding Coins and Precious Metals Not Yet in Effect*

On January 8, 1984, the IRS published proposed amendments to the broker reporting regulations. These proposals are not yet in effect. The amendments seek to clarify the applicability of the reporting requirement to coins, precious metals and other types of physical property. Under the proposed regulations property that in part is made up of a reportable commodity (such as gold or silver) is reportable if its sales price is no more than 15% greater than the value of the commodity content. For example, a gold coin or gold chain that sells for more than 15% of the value of the gold content is not a commodity covered by the regulations. These proposed regulations remain in proposed form and will not become effective until published by the IRS in final form. However, the existing rules remain fully in effect while these proposals are outstanding.

• *ICTA Arguments*

In connection with the proposed amendments described in item 5 above, ICTA has contended in its submissions to the IRS that:

(i) Retail dealers who only buy for their own inventory cannot be made to report under either the existing or the proposed regulations;

(ii) The regulations cannot fairly be enforced until some accommodation is provided to relieve the burden imposed on small businesses, as required by law;

(iii) An exemption for transactions in amounts less than $10,000 should be provided; and

(iv) Under the existing regulations transactions in quantities less than that approved for CFTC trading are not covered.

ICTA does not know what the outcome of these various arguments will be. It would be unreasonable to expect the IRS to agree with all of them. Each dealer must consult his own advisor in determining what action he should take in light of the information outlined above.

Loopholes

Proof gold American Eagles have been used by investors as a way to avoid the IRS reporting requirements governing bullion-related items. For all their numismatic trappings, these coins retain a strong link with bullion; they fluctuate in price directly in proportion to the market price of gold. Yet, as a rule, they sell for somewhat more than a 15-percent premium; thus, many have interpreted these trades as not being subject to the reporting rules.

When knowledgeable collectors and investors have coins they want to trade and are seeking highly liquid material in return, they frequently choose proof American Eagles and other bullion coins selling for a premium of 15 percent or more. Normal bullion coins would be subject to the 1099-B reporting requirements described elsewhere in this chapter, but these special collector issues often are not. What's more, at current resale-market levels many such coins—including proof American Eagles—have tremendous upside potential and little downside risk.

GOLD'S SUPPLY AND DEMAND

Some market analysts attach great importance to changes on gold's supply side. Newsletter writers who frown on tangible assets argue, for example, that the price of gold is governed strictly by its supply. As more gold is mined and refining techniques improve, demand for gold will lessen, they maintain.

I take strong exception to this view. It's my contention that *demand* for gold, not supply, is the key component of the equation. And all signs point to a sharp growth in demand, what with inflation looming on the horizon and the U.S. economy clearly in trouble. Demand for gold will drive up its price—and no matter how much more gold is mined, it's my belief that we will see the price continue to escalate. In simplest terms, the value of gold really doesn't change at all; what changes is the value of the currencies people use to buy that gold. Gold remains at a constant value; currencies fluctuate.

Demand in the Far East

Demand for gold is strong and growing stronger in the Far East. The Japanese and Taiwanese have tremendous trade surpluses and enormous purchasing power. Japanese businessmen love to buy gold; they view it as a status symbol. Some even sprinkle gold dust on their food or impress their guests by wrapping sushi in thin gold leaf.

According to the December 5, 1988 issue of the *AIC Investment Bulletin* published by the American Institute Counselors, the government of Taiwan recently took an important step to underscore the importance of gold in that nation: In July 1988 it abolished the 5 percent value-added tax on gold bullion and coins. In the eyes of the Taiwanese government, gold is not a consumption item; it's an investment item, and consequently it should not be taxed.

According to the *AIC Investment Bulletin*, Japanese and Taiwanese central banks have been buying large amounts of gold in the United States—partly as an artificial means of improving their trade balance but partly to bolster their reserves, which are being severely depleted by continued depreciation of the dollar. In fact, the bulletin says, U.S. officials have expressed great concern that this action is inappropriate. The *AIC Investment Bulletin* is available by subscription at 7 North Street, Pittsfield, MA 01201. The cost is $48 for 24 issues.

COUNTERFEIT BULLION COINS

People tend to associate counterfeiting more with numismatic coins than with bullion items. But bullion coins, too, have attracted their share of attention from purveyors of the counterfeiting art.

Many bogus bullion coins are of very low quality; they're porous and poorly crafted, and simple common sense should be enough to enable most people to spot them. That's why it's important to inspect all bullion coins (and numismatic coins as well) closely when you buy them. Some phony coins are made from gold-coated lead, in which case specific-gravity tests will tell the investor whether the coins are genuine or fake.

A number of useful tools are available to assist you in detecting counterfeit coins. For example, Fisch Instruments produces a series of gauges with which you can quickly check the weight and dimensions of many of the most popular bullion and numismatic coins. These are available from your local coin dealer or precious metals supplier. Although they aren't foolproof, the gauges can be helpful when you can't find an expert dealer to check your coins. The cruder counterfeits are readily identifiable through the use of these instruments.

Sources of Supply

Counterfeit bullion coins come primarily from Saudi Arabia, Spain, Italy, Syria, India, Kuwait, Yugoslavia, and Morocco. In many cases nationalism serves as a powerful shield behind which the counterfeiters hide. Governments tend to guard their power jealously, refusing to allow police from other governments to cross their borders. Often this enables professional counterfeiters to operate safely in one country while copying the coins of other countries.

It's altogether possible that governments in some of the countries where counterfeiters operate aren't anxious to see them caught, for a nation itself stands to derive substantial economic benefit from the activity. Let's say it costs $20 to make a phony one-ounce bullion gold coin and the coin is then sold for $300. That means there's a $280 profit coming into the nation from which the coin is exported. This money is going to a citizen of that country, and in all likelihood much of it will end up in the nation's economy. In high-volume operations, such profits could even improve the nation's balance of payments.

THE LINK BETWEEN THE COIN AND BULLION MARKETS

Movements in the prices of gold, silver, and platinum clearly have a direct and immediate impact on the prices of bullion coins containing those metals. To some extent they also affect the prices of numismatic coins with high bullion content. Circulated double eagles provide a good example of this. So do rolls and bags of relatively inexpensive silver coins such as Roosevelt dimes and Washington quarters from the late 1950s and early 1960s. Even in mint condition, these sell for not much more than bullion value; so when silver rises or falls by any significant amount, the rolls and bags do likewise.

In theory, fluctuations in gold or silver prices should have little or no bearing on the prices of scarcer and higher-priced coins containing those metals. Their bullion value is negligible, after all, compared to their value as collectibles. But until a few years ago, a clear correlation existed even here. Every time gold and silver would go up, numismatic coins would follow suit within about two months. And every time precious metals would go down, numismatic coins would do likewise, again after a short period of time. What was going on?

Coin dealers, it turned out, held the key. With the dawn of the new age of gold ownership, many coin dealers had expanded their inventories to include bullion and bullion-type coins. Then, when precious-metal prices soared to record heights in 1979 and 1980, and millions of Americans rushed to sell their gold and silver holdings, coin shops became a natural outlet. The coin dealers' increased purchasing power—and their tendency to spend the extra money on rare coins—clearly played a major role in driving the prices of numismatic coins to all-time record highs during that period. When bullion prices began to decline, the dealers slowed the pace of their rare-coin purchases.

Breaking the Pattern

Lately there has been far less correlation between price movements in precious metals and activity in truly rare coins. A psychological link still exists; both belong to the family of tangible assets. But for practical purposes, the two markets now are only distant cousins.

The stringent reporting requirements involving bullion coins were instrumental in severing the bullion market's linkage with rare coins. More and more people moved away from bullion into numismatic coins, and this in turn disrupted the traditional patterns. Nowadays there are occasions when rare coins rise in value at the very same time that bullion market prices are headed the other way.

If anything, the numismatic market should gain even greater independence from precious metals in years to come. Major institutional funds already have entered the market, and more entries are on the horizon. I see $20 million sitting in one place waiting to buy rare coins, $50 million in another place, and $100 million in still another place. With that kind of money poised for investment in rare coins, there wouldn't be much impact on the coin market even if precious metals were to crash.

The rare coin business has become a major industry and a major investment arena. Annual rare coin sales now total $3 billion to $5 billion, and tens of millions of dollars from new sources are being poured into the market every year. A market that substantial is strong enough to weather any foreseeable storm in precious metals.

Capitalizing on Trends

Even though the bullion and rare coin markets have gone their separate ways, savvy investors have hit upon a method to anticipate precious metals trends and then use these insights to purchase numismatic coins advantageously.

Several considerations are involved. One is the theory that any sharp decline in the price of gold will be followed within a short time by a sharp upturn. Another is the fact that historically, when gold has risen sharply in value, the increase has been higher percentagewise for widely traded numismatic gold coins (such as the Saint-Gaudens double eagle) than for gold in bullion form.

During a period when gold is declining in price by a significant amount (say, $30 or $40 an ounce), certain investors and coin dealers will sell off large quantities of their gold bullion holdings—gold American Eagles, Maple Leafs and so on—and reinvest the proceeds in rare U.S. coins, particularly Saint-Gaudens double eagles and other large gold coins. If all goes well, they will reap sizable profits when the gold market heads back up with double eagles leading the surge.

On one occasion there was such a strong flow of investment money out of bullion and into double eagles that the numismatic coins actually rose in value at the very time the bullion market was plunging. Understandably, this caused a great deal of confusion and led to speculation that the numismatic coins were being manipulated; people said it was impossible to sustain such an increase in the face of falling prices for bullion gold. And it *was* sustained, because so many big-money dealers and investors were selling off their gold bullion holdings and buying rare coins instead.

My advice to investors is not to try to capitalize on such trends, because they're unpredictable phenomena. We've seen them happen, but they're far from a sure thing, and it's all too easy to get burned. Volatility can be the investors' best friend, but it also can be their worst enemy. In a volatile, whipsaw marketplace with fast, major changes in valuations, someone who doesn't understand the nuances can lose a great deal of money.

I provide this information not as a blueprint for action, but rather as background knowledge. It's intended as an insight into what may be going on if numismatic gold coins are going up in value at the same time gold bullion is going down.

Chapter

10

RARE COINS AS WORKS OF ART

Every collector should display on the wall a photograph of his favorite coin. We need to get the word out that rare coins are an art form; too many persons just place their coin holdings in a safety deposit box for few to see. Art collectors prominently display their treasures for all to see.

—James L. Halperin,
co-chairman of the board,
Heritage Capital Corporation

In the elegant penthouse of New York City's St. Moritz Hotel, droves of rare coin enthusiasts had gathered to witness the greatest numismatic market event of all time: a single lot—the King of Siam Proof set—hammered down for $2 million or more. The sweeping, panoramic views matched the heightened human expectations at this sale to be conducted by Auctions by Bowers and Merena, Inc.

The television cameras were rolling, and journalist Ed Reiter had just checked in with the news desk at the *New York Times* to assure placement of the story in the following day's edition. There were hushed whispers as Bowers and Merena's auctioneer, William D. Hawfield, Jr., stepped up to the podium to begin the bidding process on the King of Siam set.

"Do I have $2 million?" he asked. There was no response. He asked again. "$2 million anywhere?" Still there were no takers. "Are you sure?" Hawfield asked.

The set, perhaps one of the most important coin offerings of all time, didn't sell that night (see Figure 10-1). Bowers and Merena won accolades throughout the coin market for its treatment of the auction: marketing coins as an art form and issuing catalogs of impeccable quality and superb historic significance.

Figure 10-1. King of Siam U.S. Proof set. This set was presented in the mid-1830s as a gift from the U.S. government to the King of Siam. It resurfaced in 1962 and was offered for sale in 1987 at public auction. The $2.2 million reserve wasn't met. Thus the set did not sell at that sale. It was later sold privately to two dealers for a price reportedly well in excess of $2 million.

What happened?

There was a reserve on the lot that prevented it from selling for under $2.2 million ($2 million plus the 10 percent buyer's fee). Quite possibly the set would have sold for $1.8 million or a little more. Starting the bidding at $500,000 could have accelerated the bidding spirit. But the real reason this set didn't sell is that rare coins have not yet come of age as works of art.

If a painting can sell for $49 million, it shouldn't have made a difference whether the King of Siam set opened at $2 million or $3 million; the set should have sold.

The King of Siam Proof set nonsale for $2.2 million is no reflection on Bowers and Merena; to the contrary, the Bowers firm tried to market the set in a way that could have brought the rare coin field recognition as an art form. It *is* a reflection on the types of buyers who acquire coins, however. The price resistance level, although increasing with the emergence of institutional interest in the field, is around $600,000.

COMPARING RARE COINS WITH WORKS OF ART

Newsletter writer Maurice H. Rosen, in his April/May 1987 *Rosen Numismatic Advisory*, states the following, slightly abridged:

I HOPE YOU'RE SITTING DOWN BECAUSE WHAT I'M GOING TO TELL YOU NEARLY FLOORED ME. Did you know that a chair sold at a Sotheby's New York auction on January 31, 1987, for $2.75 million? A chair! It was a world auction record for furniture. Leigh Keno, a 29-year-old N.Y. dealer was the buyer, saying he was prepared to bid higher, if necessary. The chair didn't even include upholstery.

The chair? A Chippendale carved mahogany hairy-paw-foot wing armchair made for John Cadwalader, a wealthy Philadelphia merchant and Revolutionary War general. The chair was the object of a front page story in Barron's, March 2, 1987, with the title: "Is This Chair Worth $2.75 Million? Or Is The Auction Market Bonkers?" Also mentioned in the article was a pintail drake duck decoy (ca. 1915) which sold earlier for $319,000, top-most fare for a fowl.

While chairs and wooden ducks were bringing outrageous money, truly outstanding, classic American coinage was literally going begging. Forget the Big Black Hole into which things like 1881-S $1s, common Walkers, 1938-D Buffaloes & Proof Franklins were falling, I'm talking Monster Blue-Chip rarities. Let's get a perspective here. I want to show you how far $2.75 million can go in the coin market. Imagine coming into a windfall and going on a wild, numismatic shopping spree. Based on estimated values, here's 2 carts of goodies:

- *Four*, count 'em: 4, complete sets of *Matte Proof Gold* coins, 1908–1915, all in PCGS Proof-65 grade. That's 4 of each date of the $2½, $5, $10 & $20 denominations, *128 Gem Proof-65* pieces in all. Total realistic value: *$2.75 million.*
- You want variety? Don't want all your eggs in one proof gold basket?

1913 Liberty Nickel	$385,000.	1885 Trade Dollar, Proof	$110,000.
1894-S Barber Dime	50,600.	1870-S $3 Gold	687,500.
1876-CC Twenty-Cent Piece	60,000.	1879–1880 $4 Stellas, Set of 4 Proofs	345,000.
1838-O Capped Bust Half	50,000.	1822 $5 Gold	687,500.
1804 Bust Silver Dollar	308,000.		

A super coin library plus some pin money. TOTAL = *$2.75 million.*

Let's look at this sum of $2.75 million in another way—pure & simple financial terms. Here's what that money can produce in income only, without touching the principal:

Type of Account	Yearly	Weekly	Daily	
At 5.7% Money Market	$156,750	$3,014	$430	-All Taxable Income
At 7.5% U.S. Treasury Bonds	206,250	3,966	565	-Federal Taxed Only
At 6.7% Municipal Bonds	184,250	3,543	505	-Non-Taxable Income

Personally, I don't care how rich you are. No chair is worth peeling off 500 simoleons EVERY DAY just to look at! But, what is it about the world of art & antiques that sets it so far apart from the world of coins? Why should a chair (that before it was discovered last year, the owner had no idea of its potential value and stored it above his garage!) be worth more than either of the two mouth-watering coin baskets listed above? To be sure, it boggles the mind, but we are slightly prejudiced here, so here's my guess as to why Rare Coins vis-a-vis Art & Antiques get "No Respect":

- Art & Antiques appeal to Culture, Refinement & Snobbery. They have a heritage of many centuries. They've been commissioned, collected and displayed by Royalty, housed in churches and museums around the world. Whereas coins, in the eyes of some people, are nothing but cute, little playthings without the prestige and accoutrements of social stature and culture. A brutal assessment, but, I feel, on the mark.
- Art & Antiques are often large, beautiful, aesthetic masterpieces, the treasures of history's great creators—why, perhaps even timeless pieces of civilization's soul. Look ye now at coins, which some people view as manufactured products, mere trinkets of older versions of current coinage which jingle in their pockets.
- The aura of the art world connotes a milieu and status far different from that of the coin world. Go to a Sotheby's or Christie's auction. Then go to a coin auction. Go to a Sotheby's or Christie's gallery showing. Then go to a coin show.
- Art & Antiques can be displayed, showed off and made part of people's homes & offices. On the other hand, coins are personal, private items, rarely kept in the home.

Here are some other examples of prices realized for some works of art during the middle to late 1980s:

- Vincent van Gogh's painting, "Sunflowers," was hammered down for $39.9 million at an auction conducted by Christie's.
- A second van Gogh painting, "Irises," realized even more: At a Sotheby's auction it fetched $53.9 million ($49 million plus a 10 percent buyer's fee).
- 1931 Bugatti cars sell for $11 or $12 million, and these are manufactured items, like coins.

In November 1987, as I noted in Chapter 8, two Hindustani gold coins also were not sold when they reached the auction block in Zurich. The coins received big bids—$8 million for the larger piece. In both cases, though, "protective" bids were placed, and the coins went unsold. An 1852/1 Augustus Humbert $20 gold proof sold privately for $1.35 million in 1989, making it the highest price ever paid for a U.S. coin.

THE RARE COIN POTENTIAL

The record of rare coins compared with works of art shows how far the coin field has to go in terms of its appreciation potential. The rare coin marketplace is literally in its infancy. A number of developments that loom on the horizon could help coins to be rediscovered as an art form. For example, Fine Arts Commissioner Diane Wolf has made tremendous congressional and senatorial inroads toward the approval of design changes for all circulating United States coins. If design changes were to become a viable working reality, there would be a resurgence of interest in rare coins as an art form.

HIGH PRICES REALIZED FOR RARE COINS

The following excerpt from *Coin World Almanac* (Beth Deisher, ed.; Pharos Books, 1987) features a list compiled by the editors of *Coin World*. This list includes prices realized for many coins that sold above $150,000 through the year 1987.

The following listing is not strictly a chart of record auction prices, but a listing of every U.S. piece recorded by the *Coin World* staff as having brought very high prices at public auction, both in the United States and abroad. Foreign prices are calculated using a published exchange rate near the time of sale. Some exonumic items appear on the list, including several medals, but no high-priced paper money appears, although many specimens exist. Some specimens may appear more than once, reflecting the rapid turnover some top-level coins bring. In many cases, later sales of the same specimen are for lower prices than earlier sales, indicating the market has lower expectations currently than in 1978–1980. Researchers must be forewarned that different grades may be assigned the same specimen, particularly when it was sold at different times by different dealers.

A consistent style in descriptions has been adopted for U.S. coins appearing in the following chart. The date is followed by denomination, design or type, variety, if any, and condition, which appears in parentheses; pricing information and auction data follow. The dollar coin denomination is preceded by metallic content for clarity. If a date appears within parentheses, it means the date does not appear on the specimen itself, but is generally accepted as the year of issue or production. Coins listed like 1798/7 are overdates, while 5D/50 C. and similar listings represent a punching error in the denomination.

Coins "selling" at auction are not listed if it is known that they went back to the owner or were retained by the auction firm, even if a "selling" price was publicly announced. However, there may be coins listed that did not actually sell to a third party.

The listing is as complete as possible, but the sheer volume of coin sales ensures that some sales may be missing.

The price recorded is the hammer price, and does not include the buyer's fee charged by many firms, taxes or other charges added to hammer prices.

U.S. 1787 Brasher gold doubloon, Eagle's Wing (punch) (MS-63)	$725,000	Bowers & Ruddy-Garrett Nov. 28-29, 1979
U.S. 1787 Brasher gold doubloon, Eagle's Breast (punch) Very Fine	$625,000	Bowers & Ruddy-Garrett Mar. 25-26, 1981
U.S. 1822 $5 Capped Head gold (VF-30)	$625,000	Bowers & Ruddy-Oct. 27-29, 1982
U.S. 1870-S $3 Indian gold (EF-40)	$625,000	Bowers & Ruddy-Oct. 27-29, 1982
U.S. 1851 $50 Augustus Humbert, pioneer gold (Proof)	$500,000	Bowers & Ruddy-Garrett Mar. 26-27, 1980
U.S. 1907 $20 Indian, Roman Numerals, pattern, J-1776 unique (Proof 65)	$475,000	ANA-Bowers & Ruddy, Aug. 1, 1981
U.S. 1787 Brasher gold doubloon (AU-55)	$430,000	Auction '79-Rarcoa July 26-27, 1979

U.S. 1804 silver $1, Class III, Berg specimen (EF-40)	$400,000	Bowers & Ruddy-Garrett Mar. 26-27, 1980
U.S. 1913 Liberty 5-cent (Proof 63)	$350,000	Superior Galleries, Jan. 28-30, 1985
U.S. 1852/1 $20 Augustus Humbert, pioneer gold (Proof)	$325,000	Bowers & Ruddy-Garrett Mar. 26-27, 1980
U.S. 1855 $50 Kellogg & Co., pioneer gold (Proof)	$300,000	Bowers & Ruddy-Garrett Mar. 26-27, 1980
U.S. 1804 silver $1, Class I, Dexter-Bareford (Proof)	$280,000	Stack's-Bareford coll. Oct. 22-23, 1981
U.S. 1804 Bust silver $1 (MS-60+)	$280,000	Superior Galleries, Jan. 28-30, 1985
U.S. 1855 $50 Wass, Molitor & Co., pioneer gold (MS-65)	$275,000	Bowers & Ruddy-Garrett Mar. 26-27, 1980
U.S. 1849 $10 Cincinnati Mining & Trading Co., pioneer gold (EF-40)	$270,000	Bowers & Ruddy-Garrett Mar. 26-27, 1980
U.S. MCMVII (1907) Saint-Gaudens $20 gold Roman Numerals (Proof 65+)	$260,000	Auction '85-Superior, July 26-27, 1985
U.S. 1794 silver $1, Flowing Hair (MS-65)	$240,000	Stack's Jan. 18-21, 1984
U.S. 1854 $50 Kellogg & Co., pioneer gold (Proof)	$230,000	Bowers & Ruddy-Garrett Mar. 26-27, 1980
U.S. 1870-S Seated Liberty half dime, BU	$230,000	Auction '86-Superior, July 26, 1986
U.S. 1907 $20 Saint-Gaudens, Roman Numerals, Extremely High Relief (Proof 69)	$230,000	Auction '80-Paramount Aug. 14-15, 1980
U.S. 1907 $20 Saint-Gaudens, Roman Numerals (Proof 67)	$220,000	Bowers & Ruddy, Oct. 27-29, 1982
U.S. 1873-CC quarter dollar, Seated Liberty, No Arrows (MS-65)	$205,000	NERCA Sale-Apr. 10-12, 1980
U.S. 1830 $5 Templeton Reid, pioneer gold (EF-40)	$200,000	Bowers & Ruddy-Garrett Nov. 28-29, 1979
U.S. 1850 $50 F.D. Kohler, pioneer gold ingot (1,348.9 grains) (EF-40)	$200,000	Bowers & Ruddy-Garrett Mar. 26-27, 1980
U.S. 1792 Birch cent, pattern, J-4 (MS-63)	$200,000	Bowers & Ruddy-Garrett Mar. 25-26, 1981
U.S. 1825/4 $5 Capped Head gold (Proof 60)	$200,000	Bowers & Ruddy Oct. 27-29, 1982
U.S. 1907 $20 gold, Saint-Gaudens Ultra High Relief, Roman Finish (Proof)	$200,000	Stack's, Oct. 22-23, 1985
U.S. 1783 Nova Constellatio Mark, silver (MS-63, prooflike)	$190,000	Bowers & Ruddy-Garrett Nov. 28-29, 1979

U.S. 1804 silver $1, Class III, Berg-Garrett specimen (EF-40)	$190,000	Pullen & Hanks, Inc. Feb. 5-6, 1982
U.S. 1827/3 quarter dollar, Capped Bust, Large Size B-1, original (Proof)	$190,000	Bowers & Ruddy-Garrett, Mar. 26-27, 1980
U.S. 1804 silver $1, Class III, Adams-Carter (EF-40)	$180,000	Stack's Jan. 18-21, 1984
U.S. 1849 $5 Pacific & Co., pioneer gold (VF-30)	$180,000	Bowers & Ruddy-Garrett, Mar. 26-27, 1980
U.S. 1927-D $20 Saint-Gaudens (MS-65)	$180,000	Auction '84-Paramount July 25-26, 1984
U.S. 1879 $4 Coiled Hair Stella, pattern, J-1638 (Proof 65)	$175,000	Auction '80-Superior Aug. 14-15, 1980
U.S. 1907 $20 Saint-Gaudens, Roman Numerals (Proof 65)	$175,000	NERCA-Boston Jubilee July 24-26, 1980
U.S. 1795 Draped Bust $1 (Proof 63)	$170,000	Bowers & Ruddy-Garrett Mar. 26-27, 1980
U.S. 1804 Bust dollar, The Garrett specimen Class III (EF-40)	$170,000	Bowers & Merena, June 23-25, 1986
U.S. 1783 Nova Constellatio Quint, silver (MS-65, prooflike)	$165,000	Bowers & Ruddy-Garrett Nov. 28-29, 1979
U.S. 1829 $5 Capped Head, Large Date, Large Planchet (MS-65, prooflike)	$165,000	Bowers & Ruddy-Garrett Nov. 28-29, 1979
U.S. 1927-D $20 Saint-Gaudens (MS-65)	$160,000	Bowers & Ruddy-Oct. 27-29, 1982

THE NORWEB COLLECTION SALES

Coins of significant rarity and quality can and do realize substantial prices. The collection of R. Henry and Emery May Norweb combined the finest known examples in terms of quality and the rarest known examples in terms of quantity. Auctions by Bowers and Merena, Inc., sold the Norweb collection at three major auctions over a 13-month period during 1987 and 1988.

Famous throughout the world for its successful auctions, Bowers and Merena realized prices that stunned even the most enthusiastic coin market supporters (see Figure 10-2). On the pages that follow are photographs showing 29 of the most significant examples of rare United States coinage from the Norweb collection sales. All photographs are courtesy of Auctions by Bowers and Merena, Inc.

Figure 10-2. William D. Hawfield, Jr., left, recognizes a bid at one of the Norweb collection sales of Auctions by Bowers and Merena, Inc., as Q. David Bowers and Raymond N. Merena look on. (Photo by Ed Reiter)

Figure 10-3. 1861 Philadelphia Mint double eagle, with Paquet reverse. This MS-67 example was captured for $660,000. This is the finer of two known examples. The coin is distinguished by modifications to its reverse by Mint engraver Anthony C. Paquet. (Courtesy Auctions by Bowers and Merena, Inc.)

Figure 10-4. 1792 silver center cent. This MS-60 example was sold for $143,000 at Norweb. (Courtesy Auctions by Bowers and Merena, Inc.)

Figure 10-5. 1792 copper dime grading EF-45. The lucky new owner of this rarity paid $28,600 at Norweb. (Courtesy Auctions by Bowers and Merena, Inc.)

Figure 10-6. 1873-CC Liberty Seated dime, with arrows. This rare Carson City Mint jewel, graded MS-64, was hammered down at $56,000 plus the 10 percent buyer's fee. (Courtesy Auctions by Bowers and Merena, Inc.)

Figure 10-7. 1894-S Barber dime, Proof-65. This highly sought-after coin brought $77,000 when the bidding was over. (Courtesy Auctions by Bowers and Merena, Inc.)

Figure 10-8. 1876-CC Twenty-cent piece, graded MS-65, was captured for $69,300. (Courtesy Auctions by Bowers and Merena, Inc.)

Figure 10-9. 1827 Capped Bust quarter, graded Proof-64 (or finer), was purchased for $61,600. (Courtesy Auctions by Bowers and Merena, Inc.)

Figure 10-10. 1842 Liberty Seated quarter, small date, graded Proof-63 to 64, brought $46,200. (Courtesy Auctions by Bowers and Merena, Inc.)

Figure 10-11. 1873-CC Liberty Seated quarter, without arrows. The Liberty Seated quarter series commands much respect for its artistic significance, and this coin's $88,000 realized price is partial testimony to this importance. It grades MS-63 to 64. (Courtesy Auctions by Bowers and Merena, Inc.)

Figure 10-12. 1797 Draped Bust half dollar, MS-63 to 65, prooflike. It took auctions the magnitude of Bowers and Merena's Norweb sales and $220,000 to own this sensational rarity. (Courtesy Auctions by Bowers and Merena, Inc.)

Figure 10-13. 1822 Capped Bust half dollar, MS-60 to 63. This piece sold for $66,000. (Courtesy Auctions by Bowers and Merena, Inc.)

Figure 10-14. 1838-O Capped Bust half dollar, reeded edge. This phenomenal fifty-cent piece, graded Proof-64 to 65, realized $85,000 plus the 10 percent buyer's fee. (Courtesy Auctions by Bowers and Merena, Inc.)

Figure 10-15. 1794 Flowing hair dollar, MS-60/63. Feverish demand has always persisted for coins of this rarity. The example pictured was captured for $247,500, a price inclusive of the 10 percent buyer's fee. (Courtesy Auctions by Bowers and Merena, Inc.)

Figure 10-16. 1836 Gobrecht dollar restrike, Proof-65. This beaming Proof was hammered down for $75,000 plus the 10 percent buyer's fee. (Courtesy Auctions by Bowers and Merena, Inc.)

Figure 10-17. 1870-S Liberty Seated dollar, AU-50. This rare example was purchased for $126,500 at Norweb. (Courtesy Auctions by Bowers and Merena, Inc.)

Figure 10-18. 1875 gold dollar, graded Proof-63. It took $110,000 to secure this rare and beautiful gold piece. (Courtesy Auctions by Bowers and Merena, Inc.)

Figure 10-19. 1884 Trade dollar. Graded Proof-60 to 63, this lovely specimen was purchased for $57,200. (Courtesy Auctions by Bowers and Merena, Inc.)

Figure 10-20. 1885 Trade dollar. The successful bidder paid $121,000 for this Proof-60/63 example. (Courtesy Auctions by Bowers and Merena, Inc.)

Figure 10-21. 1895 Morgan dollar, Proof-65. This highly desirable rarity realized $33,000. (Courtesy Auctions by Bowers and Merena, Inc.)

Figure 10-22. 1875 Three-dollar gold, Proof-63. This stunning example realized $110,000. (Courtesy Auctions by Bowers and Merena, Inc.)

Figure 10-23. 1804 Capped Bust five-dollar gold. This is a wonderful example of rarity and beauty combined. (Courtesy Auctions by Bowers and Merena, Inc.)

Figure 10-24. 1821 Capped Head five-dollar gold, graded Proof-63 to 64. It took $198,000 to acquire this precious jewel. (Courtesy Auctions by Bowers and Merena, Inc.)

Figure 10-25. 1829 Capped Head five-dollar gold, graded Proof-64 to 65. The successful bidder captured this awesome rarity for $352,000. (Courtesy Auctions by Bowers and Merena, Inc.)

Figure 10-26. 1875 Coronet eagle. This Proof-60 to 63 was sold for $63,800. (Courtesy Auctions by Bowers and Merena, Inc.)

Figure 10-27. 1933 Indian eagle. This glittering MS-64 was hammered down for $87,000, exclusive of the 10 percent buyer's fee. (Courtesy Auctions by Bowers and Merena, Inc.)

Figure 10-28. 1883 Coronet double eagle. This Proof-65 or finer Gem was purchased for $88,000. (Courtesy Auctions by Bowers and Merena, Inc.)

Figure 10-29. 1931 Saint-Gaudens double eagle. This MS-64 example of this important date was captured for $32,000, with a 10 percent buyer's fee added on. (Courtesy Auctions by Bowers and Merena, Inc.)

Figure 10-30. 1932 Saint-Gaudens double eagle. This rare date, graded MS-64 to 65, also sold for $35,200. (Courtesy Auctions by Bowers and Merena, Inc.)

Figure 10-31. 1652 Pine Tree Shilling, graded MS-60. It took $26,400 to buy this rare and sought-after specimen. (Courtesy Auctions by Bowers and Merena, Inc.)

CLASSICAL COIN RARITIES FOR YOU

Type Coins

If the rare coin market experiences a period of rapid expansion, the items that *really* increase may not be the commoditized coins (e.g., Walking Liberty half dollars and Morgan dollars), but the Type coins. Type coins are representative of a major design or coinage type and are not rare dates. Those who collect Type coins are, in a sense, collecting works of art. A Type coin is a representative sample of a series, and Type-coin collectors like a diverse and varied collection symbolizing America's best, most beautiful, and most artistic coins.

The following is an excerpt from *A Mercenary's Guide to the Rare Coin Market*, by David Hall (American Institute for Economic Research, 1987). It features lists of coins that in the opinions of a number of coin dealers (Bruce Amspacher, John Dannreuther, David Hall, Ron Howard, Fred Sweeney, Gordon Wrubel, Jim Halperin, and Joe Flynn) constitute the rarest United States Type coins in gold, silver, nickel, and copper.

. . . the fact is that if you had purchased $1,000 worth of top quality (strictly graded MS65 or better) type coins in 1950, you could now cash out for over $1,000,000!!!

Gem Uncirculated (MS65) and Gem Proof (PR65) type coins have been the number one performers in the rare coin market since 1950, with an average price increase of over 27% per year!!! Since 1970, Gem type has increased by an average of over 40% per year. You could have bought Gem Unc. Bust half dimes for $3 in 1950. You could have bought Gem Unc. Seated quarters for $2.75, Gem Unc. Barber dimes for $2, and Gem Proof Seated dimes for only $3.50. These coins are now worth several thousand dollars each. In fact, $1,000 invested in Gem Unc. and Gem Proof type coins in 1950 would now be worth over $1,000,000!!!

Relative Rarity Lists

The following lists represent six experts' opinions as to the ten rarest coins in MS64 and Proof 64 or better condition.

MINT STATE TYPE

Amspacher

1. Bust 25¢
2. Seated $1—Motto
3. Bust 50¢
4. Bust 10¢
5. Seated 10¢—Stars
6. Seated $1—No Motto
7. Trade $1
8. Bust 5¢
9. Classic Half Cent
10. Twenty Cents

Dannreuther

1. Bust 50¢
2. Bust 25¢
3. Bust 10¢
4. Bust 5¢
5. Seated $1—No Motto
6. Seated $1—Motto
7. Trade $1
8. Seated 10¢—Stars
9. Seated 5¢—Stars
10. Seated 50¢—No Motto

Hall

1. Seated $1—Motto
2. Seated $1—No Motto
3. Bust 25¢
4. Bust 50¢
5. Bust 10¢
6. 3 Cent Silver—Type 2
7. Half Cents
8. Trade $1
9. Seated 10¢—Stars
10. Twenty Cents

Howard

1. Seated $1
2. Bust 25¢
3. Bust 50¢
4. Trade $1
5. Twenty Cents
6. Bust 10¢
7. Seated 50¢—No Motto
8. 3 Cent Silver—Type 2
9. Barber 50¢
10. Seated 50¢—Motto

Sweeney

1. Bust 25¢
2. Bust 10¢
3. Seated $1
4. Twenty Cents
5. Bust 5¢
6. Trade $1
7. Barber 50¢
8. Seated 50¢
9. Flying Eagle 1¢
10. Shield 5¢

Wrubel

1. Bust 25¢
2. Seated $1—Motto
3. Seated $1—No Motto
4. Twenty Cents
5. Bust 10¢
6. 3 Cent Silver—Type 2
7. Trade $1
8. Bust 50¢
9. Seated 10¢—Stars
10. Bust 5¢

Consensus

1. Bust 25¢
2. Seated $1—Motto
3. Seated $1—No Motto
4. Bust 10¢
5. Bust 50¢
6. Trade $1
7. Twenty Cents
8. Bust 5¢
9. Seated 10¢—Stars*
9. 3 Cent Silver—Type 2*

*Tie

PROOF TYPE

Amspacher

1. Seated $1—Motto
2. Seated 10¢—Stars
3. Seated $1—No Motto
4. Twenty Cents
5. Trade $1
6. Morgan $1
7. Barber 50¢
8. Seated 50¢—No Motto
9. Seated 25¢—No Motto
10. Seated 50¢—Motto

Dannreuther

1. 3 Cent Silver—Type 2
2. Twenty Cents
3. Seated 10¢—Stars
4. Seated 5¢—Stars
5. Seated $1—No Motto
6. Seated $1—Motto
7. Seated 5¢—Legend
8. Seated 50¢—No Motto
9. Seated 25¢—No Motto
10. Barber 50¢

Hall

1. 3 Cent Silver—Type 2
2. Flying Eagle 1¢
3. Seated 10¢—Stars
4. Seated 5¢—Stars
5. Twenty Cents
6. Seated $1—No Motto
7. Seated $1—Motto
8. Seated 50¢—No Motto
9. Trade $1
10. Morgan $1

Howard

1. 3 Cent Silver—Type 2
2. Seated $1
3. Seated 10¢—Stars
4. Twenty Cents
5. Trade $1
6. Morgan $1
7. Seated 50¢—No Motto
8. Barber 50¢
9. Seated 50¢—Motto
10. Seated 25¢—No Motto

Sweeney

1. 3 Cent Silver—Type 2
2. Seated $1
3. Twenty Cents
4. Flying Eagle 1¢
5. Seated 10¢—Stars
6. Seated 5¢—Stars
7. Trade $1
8. Seated 50¢
9. Barber 50¢
10. Two Cents (Red)

Wrubel

1. 3 Cent Silver—Type 2
2. Seated 10¢—Stars
3. Seated 5¢—Stars
4. Copper-Nickel 1¢
5. Twenty Cents
6. Two Cents (Red)
7. Seated $1—No Motto
8. Seated $1—Motto
9. Trade $1
10. Barber 50¢

Consensus

1. 3 Cent Silver—Type 2
2. Seated 10¢—Stars
3. Twenty Cents
4. Seated $1—No Motto*
4. Seated $1—Motto*
6. Seated 5¢—Stars
7. Trade $1
8. Flying Eagle 1¢*
8. Seated 50¢—No Motto*
10. Morgan $1

*Tie

Relative Rarity Lists

The following lists represent eight experts' opinions as to the ten rarest coins in MS64 or better condition.

MINT STATE GOLD—12 MAJOR TYPES

Amspacher	*Dannreuther*	*Flynn*
1. Type 2 $1	1. Type 2 $1	1. Type 2 $1
2. Type 1 $1	2. $3	2. $5 Liberty
3. $3	3. $20 Liberty	3. $5 Indian
4. $5 Indian	4. Type 1 $1	4. $3
5. $10 Indian	5. $5 Indian	5. Type 1 $1
6. $10 Liberty	6. $10 Liberty	6. $2½ Indian
7. $2½ Indian	7. $5 Liberty	7. $10 Indian
8. $20 Liberty	8. $2½ Indian	8. $10 Liberty
9. $5 Liberty	9. $2½ Liberty	9. $20 Liberty
10. Type 3 $1	10. Type 3 $1*	10. $2½ Liberty
	10. $10 Indian*	

Hall	*Halperin*	*Howard*
1. Type 2 $1	1. Type 2 $1	1. Type 2 $1
2. $3	2. $5 Indian	2. $3
3. Type 1 $1	3. Type 1 $1	3. $5 Indian
4. $5 Indian	4. $3	4. Type 1 $1
5. $10 Indian	5. $20 Liberty	5. $20 Liberty
6. $10 Liberty	6. $10 Liberty	6. $10 Liberty
7. $5 Liberty	7. $10 Indian	7. $10 Indian
8. $20 Liberty	8. $5 Liberty	8. $5 Liberty
9. $2½ Indian	9. $2½ Indian	9. $2½ Indian
10. Type 3 $1	10. Type 3 $1	10. Type 3 $1

Sweeney	*Wrubel*	*Consensus*
1. Type 2 $1	1. Type 2 $1	1. Type 2 $1
2. Type 1 $1	2. $3	2. $3
3. $3	3. $5 Indian	3. Type 1 $1
4. $5 Indian	4. Type 1 $1	4. $5 Indian
5. $10 Indian	5. $10 Liberty	5. $10 Liberty
6. $2½ Indian	6. $10 Indian	6. $10 Indian
7. $20 Liberty	7. $5 Liberty	7. $20 Liberty
8. $5 Liberty	8. $20 Liberty	8. $5 Liberty
9. $10 Liberty	9. $2½ Indian	9. $2½ Indian
10. Type 3 $1	10. Type 3 $1	10. Type 3 $1

*Tie

Relative Rarity Lists

The following lists represent eight experts' opinions as to the ten rarest coins in Proof 64 or better condition.

PROOF GOLD—TEN MAJOR TYPES

Amspacher	*Dannreuther*	*Flynn*
1. $20 Liberty	1. $20 St. Gaudens	1. $5 Indian
2. $10 Indian	2. $5 Liberty	2. $20 St. Gaudens
3. $3	3. $10 Liberty	3. $10 Indian
4. $10 Liberty	4. $10 Indian	4. $2½ Indian
5. $5 Liberty	5. $5 Indian	5. $3
6. $5 Indian	6. $20 Liberty	6. $20 Liberty
7. $20 St. Gaudens	7. $3	7. $10 Liberty
8. $2½ Indian	8. $2½ Indian	8. $5 Liberty
9. $2½ Liberty	9. Type 3 $1	9. $2½ Liberty
10. Type 3 $1	10. $2½ Liberty	10. Type 3 $1

Hall	*Halperin*	*Howard*
1. $20 Liberty	1. $20 Liberty	1. $20 St. Gaudens
2. $3	2. $3	2. $20 Liberty
3. $10 Liberty	3. $10 Liberty	3. $10 Indian
4. $20 St. Gaudens	4. $20 St. Gaudens	4. $3
5. $10 Indian	5. $10 Indian	5. $5 Indian
6. $5 Liberty	6. $5 Indian	6. $10 Liberty
7. $5 Indian	7. $5 Liberty	7. $5 Liberty
8. Type 3 $1	8. $2½ Indian	8. $2½ Indian
9. $2½ Indian	9. Type 3 $1	9. $2½ Liberty
10. $2½ Liberty	10. $2½ Liberty	10. Type 3 $1

Sweeney	*Wrubel*	*Consensus*
1. $20 Liberty	1. $20 St. Gaudens	1. $20 Liberty
2. $20 St. Gaudens	2. $20 Liberty	2. $20 St. Gaudens
3. $3	3. $10 Indian	3. $10 Indian
4. $10 Indian	4. $5 Indian	4. $3
5. $10 Liberty	5. $3	5. $10 Liberty
6. $5 Indian	6. $10 Liberty	6. $5 Indian
7. $2½ Indian	7. $5 Liberty	7. $5 Liberty
8. $5 Liberty	8. $2½ Indian	8. $2½ Indian
9. $2½ Liberty	9. $2½ Liberty	9. $2½ Liberty
10. Type 3 $1	10. Type 3 $1	10. Type 3 $1

Chapter
11

COMMEMORATIVE COINS

Commemorative coinage constitutes a separate and fascinating branch of U.S. numismatics. Aesthetically, it is the single most interesting segment because it affords a broad diversity of subjects and designs, some of which present magnificent works of coinage art.

Commemorative coins are designed to pay tribute or mark special occasions. Typically, a commemorative is issued for only a short time and in limited quantities. It is offered for sale at a premium, and often the proceeds help finance activities connected with the particular subject that is honored on the coin. Commemoratives have legal-tender status but are treated by both the government and collectors as a separate series, independent of regular-issue coins. Whereas regular coins are made to be spent, commemoratives are made to be saved.

During what is considered the "traditional" period of commemorative coinage in the United States, from 1892 to 1954, the U.S. Mint produced 60 different gold and silver coins, some of which were struck at more than one mint and for more than one year. The series included 48 different types of silver half dollars, one silver dollar, one silver 25-cent piece, six gold dollars, two gold quarter eagles ($2.50 gold pieces) and two $50 gold pieces.

The traditional series was suspended in 1954, and commemorative issues didn't resume until 1982. Since then, Congress has authorized more than a dozen new commemorative coins.

ANTHONY SWIATEK'S TOP TEN COMMEMORATIVES

Anthony Swiatek of Manhasset, New York, is widely regarded as the world's preeminent authority on U.S. commemorative coinage. Specifically for this book, Swiatek has drafted a list of the ten commemoratives he considers most desirable.

Although numbered here from 1 to 10, the coins have no special ranking, Swiatek says. The balance of this chapter is devoted to Swiatek's list. The accompanying comments are his.

1. Panama-Pacific $50 Gold Pieces

In 1915, five coins were issued to commemorate and help finance the Panama-Pacific Exposition in San Francisco. The exposition, in turn, celebrated the completion and official opening of the Panama Canal.

The two largest Pan-Pac coins are $50 gold pieces. These are identical in design, but one is round (see Figure 11-1), whereas the other is octagonal. On the obverse, they feature a portrait of Minerva, the Greek goddess of wisdom; on the reverse, a likeness of an owl. The mintages of both were extremely low: just 483 round and 645 octagonal.

These are beautiful coins—so much so that I even selected their design for my own logo. They also carry beautiful price tags, starting at about $20,000 and rising to the six-figure range. And their large size enhances their aesthetic appeal.

In a sense, these are truffles and caviar. They're big, nice to hold, and exceptionally attractive—and despite their low mintages, they pop up at auction with some regularity. I would put them at the top of the list for both appearance and future appreciation. They're valuable in all grades, but if you're talking about MS-64 and especially MS-65, these coins can take off to the moon because there simply aren't very many around.

The Numismatic Guaranty Corporation (NGC) has assigned a grade of MS-65 to only four round Pan-Pac $50s and one octagonal. It has given grades of MS-64 to four round and two octagonal. Their prices just have to go up. If new demand is created, these coins will be super

Figure 11-1. Panama-Pacific $50 gold piece. (Photo courtesy Anthony Swiatek)

investments in all grades—but I think in MS-64 and higher they're going to enjoy amazing appreciation.

2. Lewis and Clark $1 Gold Pieces

In 1904 and 1905, gold dollars were issued as souvenirs of the Lewis and Clark Centennial Exposition in Portland, Oregon. The show was held to commemorate the trailblazing journey of Meriwether Lewis and William Clark, who from 1804 to 1806 explored the newly acquired Louisiana Territory.

Except for the date, the coins were identical in both years, featuring Lewis's portrait on one side and Clark's on the other. These are the only "double-headed" coins in U.S. history—coins with portraits of coequal subjects on both sides—and that in itself makes them interesting.

The 1905 Lewis and Clark dollar is the rarer and more sought after of the two. As with the Pan-Pac $50s, price appreciation for both dates will be greatest for examples graded MS-64 and higher. To date, NGC has graded only one of these coins—a 1904—as an MS-66.

The mintage for each date was 10,000, which is relatively low, and the coins suffered a great deal of numismatic abuse. To begin with, they didn't get special handling at the Mint. Then they were rolled and shipped to the commission that was handling their sale, and the people who sold them didn't treat them carefully, either. Also, their design is very smooth and open; it does little to conceal any nicks, cuts, and scratches. The 1904 coins received a bit better care, but only marginally so.

These coins are truly rare, and I predict that they will rise in value exponentially. If a nice example comes up, people simply write the check, no questions asked.

3. 1926 Sesquicentennials

In 1926, two coins were issued to commemorate the sesquicentennial (or 250th anniversary) of U.S. independence. One of these was a silver half dollar, the other a quarter eagle (or $2.50 gold piece).

Their designs, while not dazzling, evoke a strong sense of national pride, for they focus on symbols that are quintessentially American.

The half dollar depicts the Liberty Bell on its reverse. Its obverse carries side-by-side portraits of George Washington and Calvin Coolidge, the nation's first president and the man who held the office at the time of the coin's issuance.

Figure 11-2. Sesquicentennial quarter eagle. (Photo courtesy Anthony Swiatek)

The quarter eagle (see Figure 11-2) portrays a draped figure of Liberty on its obverse, holding the torch of freedom in her right hand and the Declaration of Independence in her left. Its reverse features a likeness of Independence Hall in Philadelphia, the national shrine where the Declaration was written.

Unfortunately, both coins typically come with very low relief—probably the lowest of any U.S. commemoratives. Thus sharp detail is lacking on most examples, but this just serves to enhance the desirability of the existing handful of examples with full, sharp strikes. Although the 1926 Sesquicentennials have high mintages, they're extremely scarce and valuable in the highest grades.

Two matte proofs of the quarter eagle were struck. These are coins made by a special process that gives them a softly lustrous surface. Owning one of these may be the ultimate achievement for someone who collects the Sesqui coins. Short of that, a high-grade mint-state piece is the next best thing—and finding one of these is a formidable task, as well.

4. The Hawaii Half Dollar.

In 1928, a half dollar was issued to mark the 150th anniversary of Hawaii's discovery by Captain James Cook, the famed British explorer. This coin has come to be considered the "key" to completing a set of U.S. commemorative half dollars.

Just 10,000 examples were produced, and these were widely dispersed. As a result, the coin is scarce and valuable in every collectible grade, but particularly in pristine mint condition.

Fifty sandblast proofs were struck as presentation pieces for influential people of the time. As the term suggests, the planchets (or coin blanks) used in making these coins were pelted with sand propelled by a jet of compressed air. This gave them a dull but highly appealing surface with exquisitely sharp detail. As you might expect, these are coveted rarities and command enormous premiums.

Even in regular quality, the Hawaii half dollar is a most intriguing coin—one whose design is appropriately romantic, given the exotic setting. The obverse features a portrait of Captain Cook, but also shows eight small volcanoes, which symbolize Hawaii's eight largest volcanic islands. The reverse depicts a native Hawaiian warrior chieftain in full regalia, his hand outstretched in a gesture of welcome. In the background are a coconut tree and a grass hut village.

It's a truly daunting task to try to locate an MS-65 example of this coin. I don't think there are more than 250 pieces in existence in *any* uncirculated grade; all the others have at least a bit of rubbing on the high points, including Captain Cook's cheekbone. Under strict interpretation of grading standards, that reduces these coins to no better than AU (about uncirculated).

5. Matte-Proof Commemoratives

Matte proofs were made of most, if not all, U.S. commemorative coins issued between 1917 and 1946 (see Figure 11-3). This was done in almost every instance at the behest of John Ray Sinnock, who held important posts at the Mint during that period—first as assistant chief sculptor-engraver and then, starting in 1925, as chief.

Sinnock loved the darker background of the matte process, which brought out each nuance of a coin's design. For that reason, he customarily arranged for the striking of small numbers of these proofs whenever a new coin, commemorative or otherwise, was being minted. Normally the number would be fewer than a dozen, but the lowest number I'm aware of is the two examples produced of the Sesquicentennial quarter eagle.

Sinnock retained some of these coins, not as a collector but more as a creator and admirer of fine numismatic material. He also gave some to the coins' designers, as well as to personal friends. Although these coins are worth thousands of dollars today, they had little or no special value at the time. No one dreamed they would be highly prized

Figure 11-3. Matte Proof Connecticut half dollar. (Photo courtesy Anthony Swiatek)

and carry fancy price tags one day. Sinnock and some of the recipients frequently kept them in drawers in their desks, not as valued keepsakes but as casual souvenirs.

Today their value is measured in five-figure prices. And while top condition adds to their appeal, they don't have to be in a state of perfection to bring exceptional prices. Their rarity overwhelms the usual concerns about quality, even for the fussiest collectors.

6. Missouri Half Dollars

In 1921, a half dollar was issued to commemorate the centennial of Missouri's admission to the Union. The authorized mintage was high—250,000 examples—but only about 20,000 actually were struck. Of these, 5,000 were minted with the small number "24" on the obverse, the "2" and the "4" separated by a star. This denoted that Missouri was the 24th state to join the Union. More important from the standpoint of collectors, it split the mintage into two distinct varieties—one with the number and one without.

The coin's design is simple, straightforward, and attractive. Its obverse bears the bust of a stern-faced frontiersman clad in a deerskin coat and buckskin cap. Its reverse features full-length portraits of an Indian and a frontiersman, with 24 stars arrayed in the background.

Both the regular version and the 2-star-4 variety are extremely scarce in grades of MS-65 and above. Despite the disparity in their mintages, both are about equally rare and valuable in the upper uncirculated grades. Both suffered heavy numismatic abuse, first at the Mint and then at the time of their sale at the 1921 Missouri State Fair. And both were highly susceptible to such damage because the high points of their design are relatively exposed and unprotected, being about the same height as the rim.

The 2-star-4 coins were a clever marketing tool. Although they were minted first, the committee handling the coins held them back. Then, when sales of the regular version slowed, they offered the public a chance to purchase one "special" coin for every five regular coins they bought. This, of course, revived the flagging sales.

7. Arkansas Half Dollars

In 1936, Arkansas observed the 100th anniversary of its statehood. From a numismatic standpoint, the celebration was busy and protracted. Two different coins were issued to mark the occasion, and one of them was produced at three different mints for five full years. In fact, it first appeared in 1935, before the celebration even started.

The regular Arkansas half dollar—the one with the five-year run—is a handsome, well-designed coin. Its obverse bears side-by-side portraits of an 1836 Indian chieftain and a modern woman of 1936 wearing the headdress of Liberty. Its reverse shows a spread-winged eagle perched upon a radiant orb. Depicted in the background is a star-studded, diamond-shaped emblem taken from the Arkansas state flag. Around the word ARKANSAS, four stars appear, representing the flags under which the state has been governed (those of Spain, France, the United States and the Confederacy).

There are 15 separate date-and-mint combinations—15 different coins—in a full set of regular Arkansas halves. Of all the components, however, the scarcest and most valuable are the three coins issued in 1939 (one each from the Philadelphia, Denver, and San Francisco mints). Each has a mintage of barely 2,100, and all are extremely elusive in top condition.

Because each is a rare coin in its own right, it would be a real challenge to assemble a matched set of these three coins. But accomplishing this task would surely be a source of tremendous satisfaction, and owning the set would be a thrill.

8. The Grant "With-Star" Half Dollar (Figure 11-4)

In 1922, two coins were issued to honor Ulysses S. Grant on the 100th anniversary of his birth. One was a silver half dollar, the other a gold dollar. And like the Missouri half dollar, both came in two varieties:

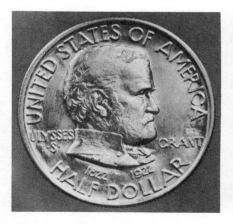

Figure 11-4. Grant "with-star" half dollar. (Photo courtesy Anthony Swiatek)

One had a small star incused (set into the surface) above Grant's name on the obverse; the other was plain.

The two coins' basic designs are identical. Both carry a portrait of the famed soldier-president on the obverse, and both show his Ohio birthplace on the reverse. The coins were designed by Laura Gardin Fraser, a distinguished sculptor-medalist and wife of artist James Earle Fraser, who designed the Buffalo nickel. Her work in this case isn't flashy; the Frasers produced far more stunning designs four years later, when they collaborated on the Oregon Trail commemorative. Still, this is a superior piece of portraiture.

All of the Grant commemoratives are extremely hard to find in top mint condition. But the half dollar *with* the star is a rarity of the first magnitude. Its net mintage of 4,256 is minuscule, even by the more conservative standards used to measure commemoratives. And most of the coins were abused, reducing the number of surviving gem specimens to a veritable handful. This is among the most coveted of all U.S. commemoratives.

9. Columbian Exposition Half Dollars

The very first commemorative coin issued by the U.S. Mint was an 1892 silver half dollar bearing the portrait of Christopher Columbus (or rather, a Mint artist's concept of how Columbus may have looked, since no actual portrait was available for reference).

This coin (see Figure 11-5) was produced in conjunction with the

Figure 11-5. Columbian Exposition half dollar. (Photo courtesy Anthony Swiatek)

World's Columbian Exposition in Chicago—a world's fair tied to the 400th anniversary of Columbus's discovery of America. It was sold at the exposition for $1, or double face, and the proceeds were used to help finance the show. The mintage was enormous by commemorative standards: 950,000 were made in 1892 and another 4 million in 1893. Even after wholesale melting of the 1893 issue, the combined net mintage for both years still totaled more than 2.5 million.

Given the huge mintage, this may seem a somewhat strange selection for a list of the most desirable U.S. commemoratives. What I am recommending, though, are not the regular coins in regular condition but the 100 brilliant proofs that were struck by the Mint in 1892 for presentation to dignitaries. These are truly rare coins, and they are indeed highly desirable—not only for their rarity and beauty, but also for their historic importance: These were our very first proof commemoratives.

Incidentally, I greatly admire the artistry of this coin, even though some critics have belittled it. Some say the portrait of Columbus on the obverse looks more like that of Daniel Webster. Some also criticize the design on the reverse, which shows Columbus's flagship, the Santa Maria, above two hemispheres representing the Old World and the New. I agree that these portraits are somewhat sentimental, but I like them. Artistically, I find them quite endearing.

The Columbian half dollar is unquestionably common and familiar, but only in lower grades. In proof, and even in superior uncirculated condition, it's a coin of surprising rarity and very substantial value.

10. The Lafayette Dollar

In 1900, Paris played host to a World's Fair. As part of the United States' participation in the event, Congress authorized the construction of a statue in the French capital honoring Marquis de Lafayette, the French nobleman who helped American colonists win their freedom from British rule. And to help finance the statue, Congress further authorized the minting of a special silver dollar. This was sold for double face, $2 apiece, by the Lafayette Memorial Commission.

The coin, like the statue, honors Lafayette. Its obverse bears conjoined portraits of the Frenchman and George Washington, the general whom he served in the American Revolution. In a sense what appears on its reverse is a portrait of a portrait: a statue of Lafayette on horseback (although not the identical statue whose construction was partially financed by the coin).

This was the first U.S. coin ever to portray an identifiable real-life American (Washington). Earlier coins had carried the likenesses of models, but they had been depicted as allegorical figures—Miss Liberty, for example—rather than as themselves.

The Lafayette dollar was the only silver dollar issued during the traditional (pre-1982) era of U.S. commemoratives. That enhances its appeal as a "type" coin, since anyone wanting at least one example of every type of U.S. commemorative would have to acquire this coin.

On top of everything else, it's a low-mintage coin, with a net of only 36,000 pieces—and it's all but unobtainable in pristine mint condition. Without the slightest doubt, this coin—like the man it honors—is imbued with nobility. It's part of our numismatic aristocracy.

AUTHOR'S NOTE: Anthony Swiatek is coauthor of *The Encyclopedia of United States Silver & Gold Commemorative Coins 1892–1954* (New York: Arco Publishing Inc., 1981) and author of an award-winning coin newsletter, the *Swiatek Numismatic Report.*

Chapter
12

INVESTING THROUGH COIN DEALERS AND FINANCIAL PLANNERS

Rare coins [if properly selected] provide consistently higher returns and stability when compared to most other investments. Investors looking to maximize their return and diversify their holdings should consider numismatics. Rare coins are wonderful—but some rare coin dealers are *not*. If you buy your coins from a reputable dealer, your investment should outperform other vehicles by a wide margin.

> Leslie W. Agisim, President,
> Trevor, Cole, Reid &
> Monroe, a financial planning
> firm that recommends rare
> coins among other investments

The common-sense precautions that must apply to any investor's coin buying apply with even greater force to financial planners (FPs) faced with the challenging task of providing investment-grade coins for their clients.

The ordinary investor always faces the immediate consequences of heedless buying: the loss of an investment. Financial planners work under the additional requirement of fiduciary responsibility to their clients and the need to demonstrate their exercise of due diligence in the choice not only of the coins themselves but of the suppliers.

The role of the financial planner is a dual one: to determine the investor's suitability for rare coins and the coin dealer's suitability to sell them. With some coin dealers offering double-digit commissions to referring financial planners, it may be convenient to overlook the marginal qualifications of a coin merchant.

CHECKING OUT THE COIN DEALER

In evaluating any dealer, a great deal of intuition is required. But here are some basic questions to which you should know the answers:

- How much commission will the dealer offer? (A dealer who offers too much commission should not be dealt with. *Any commission above 10 percent is excessive.*)
- Does the dealer *only* deal with FPs? (Such a dealer is not exposed to discriminating collectors and may not have to be competitive in pricing.)
- Is the dealer a savvy trader or a retailer who sits in the office all day?
- Does the dealer act like a character out of a gangster movie? (Intuition counts a lot.)
- Is the dealer a convicted felon?
- Does the dealer sell coins that have been independently certified by NGC or PCGS? (A "yes" to this question is *essential.*)

Not long ago I was asked to provide an independent analysis of a client's rare coin investment portfolio. My in-depth examination showed that the portfolio, purchased through a financial planner for $25,000, was actually worth $1,211.

The client's attempts to recover his money soon revealed that neither the financial planner nor the dealer who had provided the coins was still in business. Investigation also revealed that the planner's commission on the coins had been 35 percent.

It was immediately apparent that the financial planner had not examined the coin supplier with sufficient care and had not known enough about the realities of the rare coin market to protect himself and his client adequately.

The coin buyer paid a heavy price for this carelessness. The financial planner would have been better advised to choose a coin dealer who offered a more moderate commission.

COIN MERCHANT RESPONSIBILITY

The far-reaching changes that have taken place in the coin market in recent decades have placed a greater ethical burden on the coin merchant and the financial planner than on the seller of a more uniform commodity. The quaint coin store of yesteryear has been displaced by the multimillion-dollar rare coin investment firm. Many investment-grade coins are no longer bought by the consumer; they are sold by the coin firm through the financial planner to the investor.

Neither the financial planner nor the client may be able to tell the difference between a coin in MS-64 condition and one in MS-65, which is worth thousands of dollars more. Both must depend to a tremendous degree on the honesty of the dealer.

The financial planner's single most important precaution is to know the dealer. FPs can make money for themselves and their clients even if they don't know coins. But they must be absolutely sure that they know the dealers.

DEAL WITH A REPUTABLE DEALER

This used to be a simple caveat for any coin buyer. You could do business with any dealer who held membership in various dealer organizations and be assured of a fair deal. Today, however, far greater sophistication is required in checking out a dealer. A call to the Better Business Bureau (BBB) is not enough.

The Better Business Bureau

The BBB has been a valuable source of reassurance for many years, but developments in the coin industry may have eroded confidence in it by some. A case in point was provided by a client who showed me a portfolio containing thousands of dollars' worth of coins bought from a major firm later charged by the Federal Trade Commission (FTC) with false and misleading practices in trade and commerce.

Before dealing with this firm, the client had written to the BBB, which answered with a most encouraging letter:

"Bureau file reports are confined to the last three years. BBB files show this firm has been cooperative in any matters brought to its attention and has maintained a satisfactory business performance record according to our files.

"The Bureau has no reason to deter anyone from doing business with this firm. [This coin firm] is a member of the BBB and has demonstrated its support of BBB goals of private business promoting the public interest through self-regulation."

The coins my client had bought were worth a mere fraction of the purchase price. The firm spoken of so reassuringly by the local BBB went out of business soon after, signing a consent order with the FTC and placing its remaining assets in a consumer redress fund.

It certainly would not hurt to get a BBB "business referral" (the

Bureau's own words for the text quoted above) for the dealer with whom you intend to work. You would be far better off, however, making inquiries of the attorney general of your state and the state in which the dealer's firm is based.

Other Sources of Information

Some government agencies can be approached with hopes for meaningful results. An inquiry to the FTC can be useful, but this agency is prohibited by federal law from revealing information about a pending investigation—or even confirming that there *is* a pending investigation—unless the firm has actually been charged with false or deceptive practices in trade or commerce.

An inquiry to the American Numismatic Association (P.O. Box 2366, Colorado Springs CO 80901-2366) will reveal whether any complaints are on file against the firm.

Felons as Coin Dealers

Avoid any dealer who has been convicted of a felony or found guilty of racketeering by a civil court. Membership in leading dealer organizations is no assurance of this, however. I know of one such organization that heavily publicizes its "no felons allowed" policy, but has at least one convicted felon who is a member.

Dealer Accreditation

Your most valuable contact may be the Industry Council for Tangible Assets (ICTA, 25 E Street, Washington DC 20001). ICTA has created the Coin and Bullion Dealer Accreditation Program (CABDAP), a self-regulatory body for coin and precious metals dealers.

CABDAP has adopted a Code of Ethics, violation of which may be deemed just cause for disciplinary action: expulsion, suspension, or censure. ICTA president Howard Segermark has pointed out that some questionable firms will refund money to the occasional customer who raises a serious protest.

CABDAP views refunding of money as insufficient. It believes that the actual offense lies in the initial violation of its Code of Ethics and judges all such proven violations accordingly.

Before accreditation, each dealer applicant must submit to screening by Pinkerton's to confirm that he has no criminal record whatsoever. At press time, CABDAP has certified fewer than 100 dealers and expelled at least three.

CABDAP member-dealers are required to provide the following risk disclosure information to their clients.

CONSUMER RISK DISCLOSURE

Retail purchases of rare coins for investment should be acquired on a long-term basis. The purchaser should anticipate holding such items for a period of years. When rare coins are sold, dealers generally make offers at wholesale prices. Offers at wholesale may vary from dealer to dealer.

It should also be understood that grading is subjective. Different grading standards vary and are subject to interpretations which could change over time. Because of this, opinions on grading as well as value can and often do differ among experts. Therefore the ability to sell a coin at a price commensurate with listed quotations may depend on the willingness and financial capabilities of the original selling dealer to repurchase the coin based on the listed grades.

When purchasing from a CABDAP accredited dealer, all established business policies concerning grading, valuation, referrals, buybacks, returns, terms of delivery, shipping and storage shall be furnished each customer in writing at the time of sale or delivery of goods.

The need for dealer credibility is certain to significantly expand CABDAP membership in the near future. Verification of dealer membership may be made by calling CABDAP in Washington, D.C. The number is (202) 783-3500.

Another popular disclosure document is a booklet provided by Heritage Capital Corporation. In disclosing the risks of coins as investments, the Heritage document offers the following statement.

During the past decade or so, the value of rare coins has soared, and provided substantial profits for those who have invested wisely. Stories abound of collectors who, after years of prudent buying, have liquidated their holdings for ten to fifty times the amount of their original investment. The U.S. gold collection of Harold Bareford realized $1,207,215 in 1978, after having been assembled during the early fifties at a cost of $13,832. If sold today, it would probably bring over $3 million.

While these examples are true, the fact of the matter is that an investment in rare coins may not be ideal for everyone. Two important prerequisites are long-term funds which you can commit for a number of years, and the ability to meet ordinary living expenses from other sources. Rare coins are a non-income producing asset. While certainly capable of strong capital gains, they should not be viewed as a "savings account" which earns 25 percent per year with any certainty. They can serve as an excellent vehicle for capital preservation, as well as a hedge against inflation and other forces which erode the value of more traditional paper assets. Rare coins have demonstrated a pattern of growth spanning many years, and for those who have held them over extended periods, profits have been the rule rather than the exception.

But to view rare coins in their proper perspective, a few words concerning the risk/return tradeoff are needed. Perhaps no concept is more basic, or essential, in the field of investment planning than an understanding of the inherent tradeoff between risk and return. Simply stated, as the return one is seeking on a particular investment rises, the risk of loss associated with that investment tends to rise. In the area of finance and investment, this is a law. The chart below contains some everyday examples which illustrates this relationship:

Risk: 0   Expected Return: 0
Wall safe or safety deposit box to keep cash.

Risk: Negligible   Expected Return: 4–8%/yr.
Passbook savings account, U.S. Government bonds.

Risk: Very Low   Expected Return: 8–12%/yr.
Money Market certificates, corporate bonds, blue chip stocks.

Risk: Low   Expected Return: 12–18%/yr.
Mortgage bonds, Mid-size NYSE company stocks.

Risk: Moderate   Expected Return: 18–30%/yr.
Most hard assets such as coins, stamps, art, oil, certain precious metals, and moderately leveraged real estate.

Risk: High   Expected Return: 30–100%
OTC or penny stocks, commodities, futures, venture capital, colored gemstones, and stock options.

Risk: Very High   Expected Return: 100% +
State lotteries, longshot horses, and commodity options.

As can be seen by the above, rare coins fall into the moderate risk area. While they possess their own unique characteristics as collector-based tangibles, they can be compared with the other investments in their class with regard to market volatility and movement.

The traditional advantages of rare coins, such as liquidity, portability, anonymity and high historical rates of return remain undiminished in today's market. The corollary benefits, of the enjoyment of a hobby, also hold as true today as they ever have. What has changed, however, has been the increased sophistication of the market under which coins are traded, and the need for an understanding of the dynamics at work behind the scenes.

Postal Inspector

Another source of information should be your United States Postal Inspector. In states such as New York and Florida, many telemarketers and mail-order firms have been charged with defrauding customers. It should be no surprise that New York has one of the most active postal inspectors in the country, who can be contacted at U.S. Postal Inspector's Office, 1 Old Country Road, Room 295, Carle Place, NY 11514.

A Case of Changing Names

In the Fall of 1986, Florida's Comptroller Gerald Lewis subpoenaed the records of 33 suspected boiler rooms in his state's crackdown against fraudulent telephone solicitors. Most of the 33 firms allegedly sold overgraded and overpriced coins through high-pressure telephone sales.

The comptroller's action gave a forceful reminder to any financial planner: Always be sure that the firm you are considering has operated under the same corporate name for a number of years. The question that must be asked is not how many years the dealer has been in business, but how many years he or she has operated under the same corporate name.

The Florida probe uncovered an example of the same principals operating under a series of ever-changing corporate names. Randy and Larry Webman of Miami were convicted on multiple mail- and wire-fraud charges stemming from telemarketing coin sales under a variety of names.

Many of the 33 firms named by the comptroller either went out of business or moved to other states. Unless they were specifically asked how long they had been in business under the same corporate name, many of these companies' principals could have told inquiring financial planners and their clients with complete accuracy that they had been "in the coin business for many years."

The Bankruptcy Issue

Another aspect of coin dealership is the issue of bankruptcy. In all fairness, it would be unreasonable for this writer to advise you never to deal with a dealer who has ever declared bankruptcy.

Many of the nation's leading dealers have done it more than once, and a recent declaration of bankruptcy might even have a positive aspect. It would mean that the dealer could not do it again in the near future.

A Final Word on Dealer Evaluation

There are some truly expert coin dealers who would not qualify to be your coin dealer if you were to follow *all* the steps suggested here. Few investors or financial planners will ever know the inner workings of some firms of yesteryear until these become public knowledge through the courts.

SELLING COINS THROUGH FINANCIAL PLANNERS— 1980 STYLE

Abuses by rare coin investment firms selling coins "raw" (that is, without certification) took place primarily in the early 1980s, before the self-regulatory mechanism of independent grading services became widely available and depended on.

Through the eyes of a former employee comes our chance to examine one such firm, which looked quite respectable from the outside but may have systematically overcharged its customers and been guilty of grossly negligent management of its clients' (as well as its own) finances, if the allegations against it have basis in fact.

The former employee of this firm, whose identity is shielded here, provides the following account of his experiences there.

Occupying leadership positions were staff members who possessed no professional qualifications but who enjoyed varied levels of intimacy with [a firm principal]. Unique in numismatic annals was . . . a female officer bringing research materials to [a male principal who was making use of the company's restroom].

Its salespeople combined telephone solicitation and selling trips through assigned territories to bring the message of rare coin investment to financial planners all over the United States. The cost of all this expensive preparatory work was handed on to the final customer through markups starting at 30 percent on coins neither strictly graded nor priced remotely near their actual grade.

Without disclosure of actual costs of the coins offered [or independent certification], it was impossible for financial planners to form an accurate idea of the real market values of pieces they were expected to hand on to their clients at vastly inflated prices. The firm's lack of strict internal accountancy was further confused by spur-of-the moment "just for you" rebates and kickbacks that fatally confused the profit and loss picture.

While the firm projected the image of financial stability, bills were routinely stalled for 30 to 90 days while substantial checks written for purchase of coins were maneuvered through the bank by the heroic efforts of the firm treasurers.

Coherent inventory control, an accurate mailing list, and client histories were essentially nonexistent. A jerry-rigged homemade computer took the place of a modern system. Loss [of coins sent in by clients] was continuous. There was neither a system for acknowledging receipt of [coins sent in] nor an orderly storage system for company or [client] properties.

The firm vault boasted swaybacked wooden shelves that spilled their contents over the back and sides, losing coins bearing no indication of ownership on their holders in spaces under the lowest shelves. Coins of high value were sometimes found discarded along with unwanted holders in an unsecured basement storage area.

A particularly vivid experience was the loss for more than three weeks of [a coin of very high value]. This coin eventually was found in a cardboard box, jumbled among completely unrelated junk coins owned by the firm itself.

During one office relocation, a steel desk being removed by a second-hand furniture dealer was found to contain thousands of dollars in negotiable antique currency in a supposedly empty drawer. The packet was returned only because the movers thought it worthless or counterfeit.

This firm was also active in leveraged buying, which involved a close relationship with [a bank]. Loans were obtained for clients based on artificially high "independent" appraisals, ultimately traced back to [affiliated parties] posing as third-party appraisers.

Managed portfolios that could be buried in a bank vault accessible only to the company often contained coins and currency chosen only because the firm happened to purchase hundreds of pieces. Many of these were low-priced foreign coins and bank notes. . . .

Fortunately, few such cuckoo's nests exist in the world of professional numismatics anymore.

HOW TO INFORM YOURSELF

Today's adage is this: *Buy the book or videocassette before you buy the coin.* Financial planners should educate themselves in the ways of the coin marketplace. This does not mean that planners or their clients are expected to be able to tell the difference between a high-end MS-65 and an MS-66. It does mean you should learn basic grading skills and become familiar with how the market works.

A number of books will be helpful in your quest for knowledge, including two of my own, *The Coin Collector's Survival Manual, Second Edition* (Prentice-Hall Press/Simon & Schuster, Inc., 1988) and *Rare Coin Investment Strategy* (Prentice-Hall Press/Simon & Schuster, Inc., 1986). The best annual pricing guide is *The Coin World Guide to United States Coins, Prices and Value Trends*, trends values by Keith M. Zaner, text by William T. Gibbs, edited by Beth Deisher (Signet/New American Library, yearly).

A Guide Book of United States Coins, by R.S. Yeoman, edited by Kenneth E. Bressett (Whitman/Western Publishing, Inc.) is one of the most widely available and helpful additions to any coin library. But be wary of coin merchants who hold it out as the *only* book you'll ever need in grading or pricing coins.

Today many people are more comfortable gaining information through the electronic media. Two excellent coin-related videotapes have been produced by Educational Video Inc. (31800 Plymouth Road, Livonia, MI 48150): *Collecting and Grading U.S. Coins* and *Coins: Genuine, Counterfeit and Altered.* Both videotapes are available in Beta and VHS formats.

Your fiduciary responsibilities oblige you to arm yourself with basic knowledge before investing thousands of your clients' dollars. Surely it makes sense to equip yourself with the basics of grading by buying a videotape that costs less than $100.

INDEPENDENTLY GRADED COINS FOR THE PLANNER

Every financial planner who has approached the rare coin field in recent years has heard of the problem of coin grading. I examined independent grading services in depth in Chapter 4 and have affirmed my endorsement of the two established services throughout this book. Planners can eliminate most grading difficulties by directing their clients to coins graded by Numismatic Guaranty Corporation of America (NGC) and the Professional Coin Grading Service (PCGS).

The encapsulated or slabbed coins that have been processed by these services and the nationwide sight-unseen trading network serving them have made investment grade coins a viable financial product.

THE COINS-AS-SECURITIES QUESTION

While relief from grading anxieties is one result of independent certification, financial planners should take precautions to ensure that neither they nor the coin dealers are selling unregistered securities. If the planner and dealer intend to use the coins as securities, they must file the required disclosure statements with the Securities and Exchange Commission (SEC).

The landmark case of *SEC v. W.J. Howey and Co.* (328 U.S. 293, 1946) decided what constitutes an "investment contract" for SEC purposes. The Howey firm had offered investors Florida orange-grove land, divided into strips one-quarter mile long by five feet wide.

Although it claimed it was only selling land, the firm offered a contract to harvest the oranges growing on these otherwise useless strips. The U.S. Supreme Court decided that Howey was actually selling a contract to harvest oranges, crudely disguised as a land sale. In other words, an investment contract had been formed.

The Court held that three things were necessary to establish such a contract:

- the existence of an actual investment of money,
- the existence of a common enterprise involving investors, and
- investment profits derived from the efforts of others.

SEC associate general counsel Phillip D. Parker said in January 1989 that "securities" are rather broadly defined today. According to Parker, "Rare coin and other collectible investments become investment contracts as defined in the Howey case if the seller-promoter says to give him the money and let him buy the coins, insure and store them, then buy them or find you a buyer when the time comes to sell them."

"What he's really saying," the SEC counsel pointed out, "is that the buyer should invest in his skill and industry in the management of his money."

Legal writer Carl Schneider explored this matter in an article, "The Elusive Definition of a Security" (*Standard and Poor's Review of Securities Regulations* 124: 2, January 23, 1981).

Schneider wrote that an investment becomes a "personal security" if the seller-promoter offers his or her skill in selecting items to purchase; manages the asset after the investor purchases it; assists when the asset is sold; undertakes to buy the asset or to find a buyer for it; or if the buyer has an undivided interest with others in a pool of assets.

Thus far, most coin investments have not been deemed securities by the SEC. To prevent crossing the line into this dangerous area, care should be used to avoid guaranteeing profits from rare coin investments, making exuberant predictions of future market growth, and borrowing terms wholesale from the securities industry.

PCGS has offered the following legal compliance guidelines to its dealers.

---

1. Each PCGS Dealer must determine by itself the bid and ask prices it will offer. You *cannot* confer or discuss these decisions with other PCGS dealers.
2. PCGS Dealers can *only* confer with each other regarding bid and ask prices for the purpose of pursuing a *bona fide* purchase/sale transaction between them.
3. PCGS dealers who accept coins from others for grading by PCGS are required by PCGS to accept suitable coins for grading from *anyone*— including other dealers, collectors, and fiduciaries.
4. If PCGS, due to grading volume, restricts the volume of coins you can accept, you should allocate that available volume among customers with grading requests pending and maintain a wait-list for the balance and for subsequent requests.
5. You must charge all customers the PCGS grading fee and remit the fee to PCGS with the coins to be graded. Grading is PCGS's service, *not yours*, and PCGS reserves all rights to set its fees for its services.
6. In its promotional materials and in its statements or representations to existing or potential customers relating to the PCGS program, Dealer shall make it clear that the PCGS program involves only a grading service and does not constitute an investment program, and that the undertaking of PCGS dealers to accept PCGS coin grades, sight-unseen, does not imply that the customer will make a profit upon resale of such coins.
7. With respect to any PCGS coins purchased from Dealer, Dealer will deliver such coins or ship them via registered mail within fifteen (15) days of Dealer's receipt of payment in full from customer.
8. With respect to coins submitted by a customer to Dealer for grading by PCGS, Dealer shall send a copy of its PCGS submission form to customer

at the time such coins are sent to PCGS, and shall return graded coins to customer promptly upon Dealer's receipt of same from PCGS.

9. Dealer will not enter into any of the following types of agreements with customers in connection with their purchase of PCGS coins:

(a) A repurchase agreement pursuant to which the Dealer agrees to repurchase a coin sold to a customer at some future date at a fixed dollar amount.

(b) A guaranty agreement pursuant to which a Dealer guarantees a certain value or increase in value for any PCGS coin.

(c) Any margin or financing agreement pursuant to which the Dealer extends credit to its customer for any portion of the purchase price of a PCGS coin. This does not apply to any bank financing arrangement pursuant to which a customer borrows money from a bank or other financial institution to finance his purchase of PCGS coins, or to any "layaway" program providing for installment payments (without interest or storage fees) by a customer purchasing PCGS coins so long as the payment period does not exceed one hundred eighty (180) days.

(d) Any option contract pursuant to which a customer or dealer has the right, but not the obligation, either to buy from Dealer (a "call" option) or sell to the Dealer (a "put" option) any PCGS coin within a specified time at a specified price.

(e) Any leverage contract pursuant to which a customer buys PCGS coins from Dealer, paying only a portion of the purchase price and paying storage costs, carrying costs and/or interest charges for the period of time until full payment is made and delivery taken.

10. Dealer will refrain from making any statements or representations to customers regarding the specific profit potential or specific profits or gains to be derived from the purchase of PCGS coins.

For example, the following statements are acceptable:

(a) PCGS represents a standardized system for grading coins consistently and accurately by a number of the top grading experts in the United States.

(b) The PCGS system provides liquidity through its network of authorized dealers, many of whom will buy PCGS coins "sight-unseen" at their current bid prices for the particular coin at the grade indicated.

(c) PCGS guarantees the authenticity of each coin and the accuracy of grading in accordance with PCGS standards.

Other factual statements regarding the number of graders, the volume of coins graded, the number of authorized dealers, and similar matters are acceptable.

Examples of statements which are *not* acceptable are the following:

   (i) PCGS coins will increase in value.

  (ii) PCGS coins will increase in value faster than other coins.

 (iii) PCGS coins are or will be more valuable than coins given the same grade by other grading services.

 (iv) Authorized dealers will buy back any PCGS coin sight-unseen at their current bid prices for that coin (this is true only of certain authorized dealers as to the PCGS coins in which they make a market).

  (v) PCGS coins provide "instant liquidity" or "100 percent liquidity" (see item 9(b) above).

11. In its advertising and promotion, whether written or oral, Dealer will promote the positive aspects of the PCGS system and refrain from any form of "negative advertising" or other statements or communications which make disparaging comments about other dealers, other grading systems or the PCGS system.

SELECT HIGH-QUALITY COINS FOR PLANNER CLIENTS

Always buy high-quality coins that are scarce or rare. Scarce coins can become scarcer or rare; coins that are already rare can only become rarer. Coins that are common today will probably remain common in the near future.

Historically, U.S. coins in high levels of preservation have been the top performers. Coins touted by mass marketers as having "potential to increase 500 percent in six months" may not increase 5 percent in six years.

Mass marketers often need large quantities of a coin to fill anticipated orders. A mass marketer couldn't possibly promote a Proof Liberty Seated quarter with a mintage of 800 pieces if it anticipated 2,000 orders. Thus such dealers promote less popular modern-issue foreign coins and hype lower-grade, but very available, U.S. coins.

Don't Avoid Some Common Coins that Can Be Promoted

Some coins have universal appeal to investors. Morgan dollars and Saint-Gaudens double eagles are two examples. These coins are scarce enough to be considered investment items, but are common enough to be hyped and promoted.

If you buy these coins in MS-65 at the market low, you can make a lot of money in a short period of time. But if you buy them at a high (as too many people do), you can lose a small fortune in just as short a period of time. It is important to know a reputable dealer who knows market trends and advises regularly on when to sell these coin types.

Grading of Morgan dollars and Saint-Gaudens double eagles is so treacherous that it is my personal advice to both financial planner and investor to buy only those coins that have had both grade and authenticity confirmed by an independent certification organization.

WHY YOU SHOULD EXAMINE THE COINS

Whether you are buying the coins yourself or are passing them along to your client, use your common sense and carefully examine each coin. If it looks like you had it taped to the bottom of your shoe and did a tap dance on it, it isn't an MS-65—no matter how many certificates say it is.

Check each coin against your invoice, as you might have received someone else's order by accident. And by all means open the box. I know one investor who never bothered to open his box of coins until it was too late: The box proved to be empty and the dealer had gone out of business.

BUY THE COIN, NOT THE SLAB

Although the certified coin is a marvelous investment medium, remember that you're buying a coin, not just its slab. As we have seen, MS-65s from different grading services will not be the same. Make sure you are personally satisfied with the coin.

Recalling the heyday of the ANA Certification Service, former ANACS authenticator-grader Michael R. Fuljenz says that unlike fine wines, which increase in value as time progresses, ANACS certified coins turn to vinegar. ANACS tried to halt this perception by removing the date from its certificates, but the industry's massive shift to PCGS and NGC left the ANA service far behind.

SAVE RECEIPTS AND PROOFS OF PURCHASE

Saving all original holders, invoices, receipts, canceled checks, and other proofs of purchase is a practical necessity. Such papers prove that you bought the coins when you say you did, and they identify the supplier from whom you bought them.

Although the entry of the slab has reduced the problems, some dealers may still offer "raw" coins in unsealed holders without any method of linking photographs to the coins. Confusion can arise if you bring a complaint, and an occasional dealer will accuse the buyer of switching coins. Always record the certification number of each coin on your invoice.

MAINTAIN YOUR COINS IN THE GRADE THEY CAME IN

Make every effort to assure that you and your clients keep coins in the same grade in which they were purchased. Many a classic nineteenth-century rarity existing today was ruined by improper handling.

One unfortunate risk is that if you buy a $5,000 coin and drop it on the way home, its value may plummet to $1,000. Careless handling, storage, and preservation of Uncirculated or Proof coins can be as harmful financially as an overpriced or overgraded coin in your portfolio.

Coins should be neutralized in trichlorotrifluorethane before long-term storage if they have not been encapsulated by a grading service. Grading services will not grade coins that have polyvinylchloride damage (plastic from a coin holder) on them. Nevertheless, slabs should be examined at least once every six months for signs of deterioration of the coins.

A vapor-phase inhibitor such as Metal Safe (E & T Kointainer Co., P.O. Box 103, Sidney, OH 45365) should be used to prevent deterioration. Vapor-phase inhibitors change the molecular composition of the air so that coins do not deteriorate. These capsules will *not* permeate a slab and need not be used with coins that have been encapsulated.

In a very real sense, each owner of a high-quality coin is actually a trustee, responsible for the well-being of a fragile asset. Unless we take the greatest care with our rare coins, we can reduce the number of high-quality survivors for future investors.

Chapter

13

THE NEW RARE COIN INVESTMENT PLAN

Third-party grading appears to have brought a "comfort level" and investors are now treating rare coins as commodities. This means that there is an increasing amount of investment money entering the coin market via limited partnerships and mutual funds.

Keith M. Zaner, *Coin World*
"Trends," February 8, 1989

Until a few years ago, the primary marketplace risk in purchasing coins was misrepresentation in the form of overgrading. Unwary collectors and investors would buy a coin represented to be in one level of preservation, only to learn later that it actually was of a different, lower grade.

Since then, the so-called grading problem has been resolved. Today's consumers no longer have to worry that their coins are overgraded, so long as they buy only those that have been independently graded by the Professional Coin Grading Service or the Numismatic Guaranty Corporation.

In this respect the coin industry's self-regulatory mechanism has worked beautifully. But while overgrading is no longer a major concern, another nagging problem persists: the problem of overpricing.

Unscrupulous telemarketers haven't disappeared. They're simply using a different kind of pitch. It goes something like this: "I've got a wonderful deal for you. I have this fantastic coin, an 1879-S Morgan dollar, that's been independently graded by the Professional Coin Grading Service. Everyone knows that PCGS is a great grading service, and PCGS has graded this coin Mint State-65. I'll tell you what: I'll give you a great deal on this coin. If you buy it right now and give me your credit card number before you hang up the phone, you can have this coin for $7,000. And that's a terrific deal."

Of course, the coin is worth a mere fraction of that amount. So although coin grading is not a risk today, pricing is.

This comes as no surprise to sophisticated investors who have monitored this marketplace over the years. They've been saying all along that no matter what grade is assigned to a coin, what really matters is its price; overgrading becomes a major problem only to the extent that it leads to overpricing.

THE NEW DIRECTION OF LIMITED PARTNERSHIPS

Investors can avoid the pricing risk today by purchasing shares in limited partnerships formed to acquire independently certified coins. These partnerships provide full disclosure of their acquisition plans and entrust the selection of coins to experts who are intimately familiar with the marketplace.

Much as professional third-party grading services have all but eliminated the grading problem, limited partnerships are neutralizing the pricing problem. And they offer far more than just passive protection: They're making it possible at last for coins to be traded with the kind of liquidity and fluidity they deserve.

To a very great degree these partnerships also will eliminate the disclosure problem we've seen in the coin market during recent years. In its prospectus, each limited partnership describes in detail how much money will be used to purchase coins and how much of the profit the general partners will get for running the partnership. And there's very little doubt that people will be watching the managers closely: With millions of dollars involved, they'll certainly be subject to close public scrutiny.

RARE COINS ALLOWED IN MANAGED RETIREMENT PLANS

The Economic Recovery Tax Act of 1981 prohibited the inclusion of rare coins and other collectibles in self-directed retirement plans, thereby repealing advantages enjoyed previously by many coin collectors and investors. However, there may be cases where rare coins still can be used in certain pension plans and other retirement funds.

According to Dr. D. Larry Crumbley, Shelton Taxation Professor at Texas A&M University and author of many books and articles on collectibles and taxes, rare coins and other hard assets "can be used in

corporate pension plans and Keogh plans for self-employed people."
Crumbley says they may *not* be used in *self-directed* plans, but may
be used in some *managed* plans.

I caution you that this is a subjective area requiring professional
advice. Do not place coins in any retirement plan without consulting
your tax advisor and lawyer. However, you can ask them to consider
Dr. Crumbley's analysis.

I cited this analysis in my book, *The Coin Collector's Survival
Manual*, quoting from his paper entitled "Yes, Virginia, Rare Coins
Can Be Used as Pension Plan Investments." Here's part of what Dr.
Crumbley said in that paper:

Rare coins as well as American Eagles [U.S. gold bullion coins] may be
placed into many corporate and self-employment retirement plans. . . . A
defined *benefit* pension plan [corporate or Keogh plan] may purchase rare
coins because they do not provide for individual accounts. But a defined
contribution plan [i.e., money purchase pension plan or profit-sharing plan]
may be "individually directed." . . . These individually directed plans are
rare, however.

Sometimes, the participant may also be the trustee. Here, the person
wears two hats, and he must be careful. But a self-trusteed plan is not the
same as an individually directed account. The trustee-employee must direct
the investments into rare coins as a trustee of the plan and *not as a participant.*
When the "collectibles prohibition" was passed in 1981, the Joint Committee on Taxation indicated that "a participant's account in a qualified
defined contribution plan is not individually directed" merely because "the
participant, acting as a fiduciary with respect to the plan, directs or otherwise
participates in the investment of plan assets." Be very careful here, however,
and consult your tax advisor.

WHY COINS NEED NOT BE DISCLOSED
AS COMPONENTS OF NET WORTH

People who have collected coins or invested in them for years
often have collections of very substantial value. It's not uncommon
for these to be worth several hundred thousand dollars.

Despite their high value, these collections sometimes can be excluded in reports requiring disclosure of net worth. Rare coins are the

most private of the investment vehicles, and this is good news for the many people who prefer not to reveal their assets.

A case in point would be the forms that students' parents are required to submit in connection with applications for scholarships or other college assistance. These forms almost always require disclosure of the parents' net worth. Several law firms pooled their resources to research this subject for a well-known Midwestern coin dealer. Following considerable study, they concluded that under applicable laws, rare coins need not be listed as part of one's net worth when filling out these scholarship application forms. The basis for this conclusion is that rare coins aren't securities; they're collectibles.

THE TAX IMPLICATIONS OF COIN TRADING

You can gain substantial tax advantages through long-term trading of rare coins. The benefits derive from using coins in what are known as like-kind or like-for-like exchanges. A number of people employ this technique, and their cumulative tax savings often amount to many thousands of dollars.

Suppose you buy a gold coin for $1,000, and over a period of time its value increases to $5,000. You can take that coin and trade it for another gold coin that's also worth $5,000, and that trade will be deemed a like-kind or like-for-like exchange. If the second coin goes up from $5,000 to $10,000, you then can trade that for another gold coin, or group of gold coins, worth $10,000.

This process can be repeated at progressively higher levels, and you won't have to pay any taxes on your gains until you actually sell the coins for money.

Be sure to consult your tax advisor to confirm that each transaction is in fact a like-kind exchange. You may encounter problems if a coin for which you trade is of a different metal or varies otherwise in some important way. If any given trade isn't deemed like-for-like, you may not be able to defer payment of taxes on your gains.

Like-kind or like-for-like exchanges are extremely popular and widely recommended by many accountants and other tax professionals.

People who use this technique tend to start with coins worth a few thousand dollars, trading up on a like-for-like basis until they accumulate a rather substantial coin portfolio. When they reach retirement age, they sell off the coins on a systematic basis year after year. At that point they're in a lower tax bracket, so they pay lower taxes on the gains. And because they sell the coins year by year rather than in one lump sum, they defer their income tremendously and derive a significant tax benefit in the process.

PAYING FOR YOUR CHILDREN'S EDUCATION
WITH TANGIBLE ASSETS

A number of coin dealers have encouraged people to purchase rare coins systematically, build a nest egg, and then use these coins to pay for their children's education. I take exception to this. And I sternly warn you not to believe that this can be done.

True, it's a possibility; many rare coins have gone up in value at an awe-inspiring rate. However, as I stated in Chapter 1, rare coins should be viewed only as a supplement to traditional modes of investment, not as the primary vehicle. And under no circumstances should coins ever comprise your entire nest egg or bread basket. Never put all your eggs in one basket.

It's all right to take 10 or 15 percent of the funds you've earmarked for college and invest them in prudently purchased rare coins. It's *not* all right to invest 100 percent of those college funds in coins.

Appendix A

COIN PERIODICALS

COINage Magazine. Miller Magazines, Inc., 2660 East Main Street, Ventura, CA 93003. One-year subscription (12 monthly issues) $18; two-year subscription $30. Add $6 per year for all foreign countries, including Canada.

Coins Magazine. Krause Publications, Inc., Iola, WI 54990. One-year subscription (12 monthly issues) $17.50; two-year subscription $31. For other countries, including Canada and Mexico: one year $27, two years $50.

Coin World. Amos Press, Inc., P.O. Box 150, Sidney, OH 45365. One-year subscription (52 weekly issues) $26; two-year subscription $46. Outside U.S., add $40 per year. Air mail subscriptions available; write for rates.

Legacy. Ivy Press, Inc., 311 Market Street, Third Floor, Dallas, TX 75202-9990. One-year subscription (six bimonthly issues) $30.

Numismatic News. Krause Publications, Inc., Iola, WI 54990. Six-month subscription (26 weekly issues) $12.95 U.S., $33.70 foreign, including Canada and Mexico. One-year subscription $24.95 U.S., $66.45 foreign. Two-year subscription $46.50 U.S., $129.50 foreign. Special subscriptions are available, including first- and second-class plain-wrapper delivery, regular delivery by United Parcel Service, and standard air delivery by Federal Express. Write for rates.

The Numismatist. American Numismatic Association, 818 North Cascade Avenue, Colorado Springs, CO 80903-3279. Published monthly and mailed to all members of the ANA without cost other than annual dues.

Rare Coin Review. Bowers and Merena Galleries, Inc., Publications Department, Box 1224, Wolfeboro, NH 03894-1224. Issued six times a year; $5 per copy. Special subscriptions available in conjunction with other publications, including the company's auction catalogs. Write for rates.

World Coin News. Krause Publications, Inc., Iola, WI 54990. Six-month subscription (26 weekly issues) $12.95 U.S., $29.95 foreign, including Canada and Mexico. One-year subscription $24.95 U.S., $58.95 foreign. Two-year subscription $46.50 U.S., $114.50 foreign. Special subscriptions available, including first- and second-class plain-wrapper delivery, regular delivery by United Parcel Service, and standard air delivery by Federal Express. Write for rates.

Appendix B

A TELEMARKETER'S USE OF NCI GRADING

In July 1989, the Federal Trade Commission accused a Florida coin dealership, Certified Rare Coin Galleries (CRCG) of Miami, of using Numismatic Certification Institute (NCI) grading as a vehicle to overcharge consumers.

NCI is a widely recognized grading service which, by its own admission, grades coins less conservatively than the Professional Coin Grading Service (PCGS) and the Numismatic Guaranty Corporation of America (NGC). However, a number of telemarketers reportedly are selling the less strictly graded NCI-certified coins at prices commensurate with their more strictly graded PCGS and NGC counterparts with the same numerical grade. This practice clearly is not encouraged by NCI's parent company, Heritage Capital Corporation of Dallas.

The practice came under scrutiny by the Federal Trade Commission, in 1989, and the FTC alleged that Heritage had provided "substantial assistance" to Certified Rare Coin Galleries in the form of a business loan.

Heritage agreed to pay $1.2 million into a consumer redress fund for customers of CRCG. However, Heritage and its principals, Steve Ivy and James Halperin, did not admit having done anything wrong and vigorously defended their position. In fact, they were supported by a former FTC commissioner; and FTC chairman, Daniel Oliver, voted against Heritage and its principals being charged with anything.

In conjunction with the CRCG case, the FTC announced that it had obtained a consent decree from Heritage and NCI, prohibiting them from "disseminating grading certificates likely to mislead consumers . . ."

The FTC contended that through failures to disclose pertinent information, consumers were misled regarding the market value of NCI-certified coins.

"In fact," the complaint stated, "the grading standards used by NCI are less strict than those reflected in the Coin Dealer Newsletter . . . Thus, consumers who invest in NCI-certified coins by paying at or near the prices quoted in the CDN for coins of the stated grade do not receive fair value on their coin investments . . ."

Under the terms of the settlement reached by the FTC, Heritage agreed to "prominently disclose on all grading certificates" issued by NCI the following statement:

"The grading standards used by NCI generally result in a coin receiving a higher grade than the 'consensus' grade that would be assigned by most dealers.

"The grading standards reflected in the Coin Dealer Newsletter are stricter than NCI's and, accordingly, CDN prices in general significantly overstate the wholesale value of NCI-graded coins.

"The Certified Coin Dealer Newsletter ('CCDN'), Box 11099, Torrance, CA 90510, is a better wholesale reference for NCI-certified coins than CDN."

The consent decree and permanent injunction were approved by the U.S. District Court for the Southern District of Florida.

The agreement was signed by Ivy, Halperin and their counsel, Bennett Rushkoff. In announcing it, however, the FTC pointed out that a consent judgment does not constitute admission of the violation of any law.

Ivy said he and Halperin had decided to accept the settlement, rather than fight the case further, because the legal costs of pursuing the matter in court would have been prohibitive.

Ivy said Heritage never sold NCI-graded coins to CRCG. It sold only "raw," or uncertified, coins to the Florida firm, he maintained.

"It was Certified Rare Coin Galleries who alleged that their coins would meet NCI standards, neither Heritage nor NCI," he said.

George W. Douglas, a member of the FTC from 1982 to 1985, came to the defense of Heritage and its principals. Douglas contended that in its complaint against Heritage, the FTC had embarked upon a "radical and ultimately untenable expansion" of the law, which would not hold up if tested in court.

"If the FTC's new standard is embraced in the courts [which I am confident will not be the case]," Douglas wrote in a prepared statement, "it would unduly burden legitimate wholesale business suppliers. In effect, it would force them to police their downstream dealer customers for fear that they might be charged with liability in the future for their customers' business conduct."

Douglas said NCI had recognized the potential for problems and taken several steps to mitigate any such abuses. He noted, for example, that the company had placed a clear, concise disclosure on its certificates; persuaded the CDN to publish the fact that values differed, sometimes by "vast" amounts, for coins graded by different services; written its own customers to advise them of the differences; and implored retailers not to misrepresent the value of NCI coins.

INDEX